The Kogod Library of Judaic Studies
2

Judaism and the Challenges of Modern Life

EDITED BY

Moshe Halbertal and Donniel Hartman

מכון שלום הרטמן
SHALOM HARTMAN INSTITUTE

continuum

Published by Continuum

The Tower Building, 11 York Road, London SE1 7NX

80 Maiden Lane, Suite 704, New York, NY 10038

www.continuumbooks.com

First published 2007

Reprinted 2009

British Library Cataloguing-in-Publication Data

A catalogue record for this book is available from the British Library

Typeset by Data Standards Ltd, Frome, Somerset, UK.

Printed on acid-free paper in Great Britain by the MPG Books Group, Bodmin and King's Lynn

ISBN-13: 978 0 82649 668 3 (paperback)

Contents

For Bob Kogod

Introduction

Modernity does not merely signify one particular period in world history. Beginning towards the end of the eighteenth century, this era has fundamentally transformed how we think and live, and especially how we understand and relate to religious traditions. With modernity, as Peter Berger argues, some measure of heresy, from a traditional perspective, has penetrated into our lives. It is this heretical imperative more than anything else that places at our doorstep the challenges of choice. As the ghetto walls have fallen, both empirically and metaphorically, Judaism has had to learn to compete in an open marketplace of ideas. Jews can no longer count on an assumedly necessary Jewish identity or commitment, nor on the rallying force of anti-Semitism to ensure our individual and collective sense of belonging. Rather, if they are to continue to serve as building blocks for contemporary Jewish life, the books and ideas which constitute our moral, spiritual and intellectual history must be read with new eyes and challenged to address modernity's proliferating array of questions and realities.

In this context, tradition has two choices: fight modernity or embrace it. Within Judaism, there are those who choose the former, such as the Hatam Sofer, founder of ultra-Orthodoxy in the early nineteenth century, whose response to modernity was 'everything new is forbidden according to the laws of the Torah'. Yet this work is written by and for those who make the second choice. Despite its heresies and dangers, Jews who make this choice do not view modernity as a problem but rather as an opportunity and a challenge. The pertinent questions we face are how to embrace modernity as Jews, and what such an embrace means for the meaning and future of Jewish life.

This collection of essays, authored by scholars of the Shalom Hartman Institute, addresses three aspects of Judaism and the challenges posed by modernity: the challenge of ideas, the challenge of diversity, and the challenge of statehood.

Part One

The challenge of ideas refers to the most basic of modernity's challenges, whereby it offers alternative and competing truths to those found in traditional teachings. While religious law and ideology, grounded in a particular time and context, invariably confront the need to assimilate new ideas and practices, the challenge posed by modernity in this context is unique. Both the scope and nature of the changes being called for are unprecedented. Assimilation, not in a practical sense but first and foremost in an intellectual and spiritual sense, defines the reality of modern Jewish life. We live in multiple, parallel contexts, each posing its own notions of value, meaning and truth. To live within these parallel conversations, modern Judaism must refine old approaches as well as develop new approaches to the questions of what tradition means, what loyalty to tradition entails, whether and how traditions can change, and what the sources of authority are for moral, legal and intellectual issues.

This section includes seven articles. Menachem Fisch's 'Judaism and the Challenges of Science' explores the ways in which the Jewish tradition can engage and assimilate modern scientific notions of rationality. Zvi Zohar's 'Tradition and Legal Change' reflects on the ability of the Jewish legal tradition to change and assimilate new ideas and rulings into its legal corpus. Vered Noam's 'Tradition: Continuity or Change' presents a model of Jewish tradition's understanding of the tension between the need to see itself as continuous and unchanging, and the need to recognize the reality and inevitability of legal change and development. Donniel Hartman's 'Revelation and Ethics' explores the question of the source of moral authority within the Jewish tradition, and its implications for Judaism's ability to respond to and function within the changing moral sensibilities of modernity.

Two critical expressions of modern moral sensibilities pertain to the status of women and sexual orientation. Chana Safrai's 'Traditional Judaism and the Feminist Challenge', written from an Orthodox perspective, outlines the ways in which feminism challenges traditional Judaism and calls for a reassessment of specific areas within the tradition. Rachel Sabath Beit-Halachmi's 'The Changing Status of Women in Liberal Judaism: A Reflective Critique' examines the steps that liberal Judaism has taken to promote gender equality, and argues for the need to take a further step beyond the issues of rights and legal status. Jonathan Malino and Tamar Malino's 'Judaism, Feminism and Homosexuality' offers an analysis of the grounds for the Jewish tradition's classification of homosexuality as a moral abomination, and argues for the need to morally reclassify homosexuality.

Part Two

The second section of this book deals with the challenge of diversity. Jewish life in the modern era is bifurcated. Instead of serving as a uniting force around which the community is formed, Judaism has become a source of division. Prior to the modern era, Jewish life was by and large shaped by a shared notion of tradition and clear boundaries distinguishing insider from outsider, 'us' from 'them'. However, with modernity there is a sense that the Jewish people have entered a new phase of existence. Elements of Judaism and Jewish life that previously informed our boundaries have been challenged, reinterpreted and even set aside. The traditional characteristics of Jewish cultural space have been exposed to attack by individuals as well as by strains of thought that preach change, integration, secularization and a new interpretation of Jewish tradition appropriate to the spirit of modernity. Beliefs and customs that in the past would have been beyond the pale of consensus now permeate communal life.

As a consequence of such sweeping changes, new and diverse notions of Jewish identity have led to denominationalism and factionalism unprecedented in Jewish history. The advent and growth of the Reform movement, the formation of Orthodoxy as a distinct denomination, the rise of Zionist nationalist and secular approaches to Judaism, and the subsequent development of the Conservative and Reconstructionist movements – these are only the most prominent expressions of this pervasive trend. Within two centuries, the Jewish people have transformed from a more or less cohesive, traditional communal unit into what Jakob Katz refers to as 'A House Divided'. To survive as a people, we need to develop new approaches for accommodating diversity and comprehending Jewish identity and people-hood.

This section of the book includes four articles. David Hartman's 'The Religious Significance of Religious Pluralism' establishes theological foundations for religious pluralism, along with a reading of biblical theology that rejects the notion that religious faith and passion must be accompanied by exclusivist and triumphalist claims. Moshe Halbertal's 'Monotheism and Violence' argues against the idea that monotheism is inherently intolerant and leads to violence, and offers an understanding of the monotheistic impulse that privileges transcendence over exclusivity. Focusing on the challenge that Jewish diversity poses to Jewish collective identity, Donniel Hartman's 'Who is a Jew? Membership and Admission Policies in the Jewish Community' explores the ways that membership has been allocated and how Jewish denominationalism is undermining a shared membership policy. Michael Walzer's 'The Anomalies of Jewish Political Identity' analyses the unique way that national and religious identity are interwoven within Jewish communal identity and the implications of this for the complex, anomalous identity that Jewish life entails.

Part Three

The final section of this book addresses the challenge of statehood. As an outgrowth of our modern condition, the Jewish people have realized the centuries-old aspiration for political and national independence. Yet the rebirth of the State of Israel does not merely expand the location where Jews live, nor is it simply a haven against anti-Semitism. Rather, its most central function in the modern context is to redefine the issues which Judaism and the Jewish people must confront. As long as Jews were stateless, we did not have the responsibility to develop or review, for example, our notions of morality of war, power and the rights of minorities. Living in states where Jewish culture was itself a minority culture, Jews endorsed the separation of state from religion out of self-interest, if not self-preservation. But with the gift of self-determination, Jews became responsible for the duties such a gift engenders. How we understand the meaning of statehood and deal with the moral and political challenges of self-government as well as the government of others will significantly impact on the role that Judaism plays in the modern context of Jewish life.

This section includes four articles. David Hartman's 'The Significance of Israel for the Future of Judaism' re-conceptualizes the meaning of the rebirth of Israel, not merely for Israelis but for a thesis as to Judaism in the modern world. Menachem Lorberbaum's 'Religion and State in Israel' explores the various models of separation of state and religion, and presents the optimal relationship between the two in the modern state of Israel. Noam Zohar's 'War and Peace' discusses how Jewish tradition relates to the moral legitimacy of war and argues that the Jewish state must adopt a narrow notion of just war. Finally, Moshe Halbertal's 'Human Rights and Membership Rights in the Jewish Tradition' addresses the moral, spiritual, legal and political status of non-members within Jewish law, and offers foundations for rethinking and reconstituting the relationship between members and non-members.

The Shalom Hartman Institute, located in Jerusalem, is a multi-denominational and pluralistic centre for Jewish research and education. The aim of the Institute is the aim of this book: to explore and develop ways in which Jewish tradition can enrich life in the modern world. As a multi-denominational institution that passionately promotes pluralistic approaches to Judaism, the Institute does not create policy or extend legal rulings. Its task is to expand the horizons of Jewish thought, and to advocate a wide range of opinions with the belief that such plurality is both a core feature of Jewish tradition and a vital tool in creating a Judaism that can accommodate variety in backgrounds and ideologies.

Honouring this spirit, this collection of articles does not present any single position endorsed by the Institute. Rather, it reflects the range of thinking of some of the Institute's scholars on a number of central questions facing contemporary Jewish life. Furthermore, and in the spirit of the Institute's work, wherever possible opinions are presented in a way that preserves and even expands the complexity and debate inherent within Jewish tradition.

D. H.

Part I: The Challenge of Ideas

ONE Judaism and the Challenges of Science

Menachem Fisch

From the advent of the scientific revolution in the mid-sixteenth century onwards, the ethos and mindset of modernity and those of modern science have evolved hand in hand, bringing in their wake a mounting secularism, and with it the now familiar tensions between science and religion. By the mid-nineteenth century, the strained relations between science and religion had acquired the dimensions of a full-blown crisis. Many tend to ascribe it to the marked discrepancies between what scientists were willing to say about the world and what devout Christians thought their religion required them to believe. What developed, however, was far more than mere mistrust, or even condemnation of science by pious Christians. In fact, the late Enlightenment witnessed far less religious suspicion of science than scientifically motivated exasperation with religion. And it is this latter tendency, culminating in the open contempt toward religion and religiosity in general expressed by such thinkers as Ludwig Feuerbach and Friedrich Nietzsche, which strongly suggests that much more was at stake than a conflict between truth claims.

Modernity's scornful dismissal of all forms of religion and religiosity – Judaism included – along with the reciprocal reaction to which it gave rise, especially in the Christian world, runs much deeper, I believe, than any prosaic disagreement as to, say, the validity of geological dating can reasonably account for. The tension resides less in what science and religion have to say about the world than in the conflicting conceptions of human rationality that they have come to premise.

Inspired by religion, and taking their cue from science, early Enlightenment visions of human rationality measured it in terms of epistemic trustworthiness. To act rationally, on such a showing, is to act in accord with and on the basis of trustworthy knowledge. Science was upheld as a paradigm of rational endeavour precisely because of the way it succeeded in accumulating great bodies of truth by applying valid, trustworthy methods of reasoning and 'reading' to valid, trustworthy data gleaned from 'the book of nature'. The same was said of religious truth. Here too, Christians of all early denominations believed, they were in possession of great bodies of religious truth arrived at by applying valid, trustworthy methods of reasoning and 'reading' to the 'book of Scripture'.

However, during the nineteenth century it gradually became apparent that, as far as science was concerned, this notion of rationality was a conceit.

The acquisition of scientific knowledge, it was realized, involved much more than applying foolproof rules of inference and computation to reliable data. The creation of scientific theories, argued philosophers like William Whewell, and later Karl Popper, required imaginative speculation and bold hypotheses that could be rigorously tested though never proven true. Science continued to be hailed a paradigm of rationality, but the very notion of rational endeavour had changed.

Rationality, philosophers had come to realize, was not so much a matter of proven confidence in what one believes, as a matter of humble, self-doubting, yet constructive awareness of one's liability to err. Science came to be thought of as far less an inferential, computational or purely observational enterprise than it was (and still is!) thought to be. It is first and foremost a wisely *interpretative* enterprise, and a highly imaginative one at that, advancing by relentless trial and error, rather than by carefully accumulating validated findings. Human rationality thus became associated with the healthy wariness exhibited by science, with its robust and perpetual self-criticism, rather than with its seeming ability to vouch for the truth of its findings.

While Protestants and Catholics continued to lay claim to vast bodies of religious truth, science, by contrast, gradually ceased to be identified with the systems of knowledge it erected, and came to be thought of primarily as an activity in the course of which, quite unlike religion, its tentative claims to truth are persistently put to the test. The divide between science and religion was thus rendered complete: if science is what human rationality can amount to, then religion is not merely different, but downright irrational!

Viewed thus, modernity's great challenge to religion has, therefore, far less to do with questions concerning the age of the universe, or squaring neo-Darwinism with Scripture, than with the accusation that in submitting to their faith's demand for epistemic commitment, religious individuals were surrendering something central and constitutive to their very humanity: the healthy, humble and reflective self-questioning which, thanks to science, we deem to be the epitome of rationality.

How does Judaism fare with this challenge? Is it possible to remain true to the Jewish tradition and yet be rational in the scientific sense of the word? Are the commitments to scientific rationality and religiosity ever compared or contrasted from a Jewish perspective?

In the early 1860s, Rabbi Naftali Tzvi Yehuda Berlin, legendary head of the great Yeshivah of Volozhin, better known as the Natziv, explains why he undertook the composition of a commentary on the Pentateuch:

Just as it is not possible for the wise student of nature ever to boast knowledge of all of nature's secrets ... and just as there is no guarantee that what his investigations do accomplish will not be invalidated in this generation or the next, by colleagues who elect to study the same things differently, so it is not possible for the student of Torah ever to claim that he has attended to each and every point that claims attention, and even that which he does explain - there is never proof that he has ascertained the truth of the Torah![1]

Students of Torah, Rabbi Berlin argues, resemble students of nature not in the confidence they feel about their findings, but, on the contrary, in their persistent distrust of the fruits of their efforts. Both science and the study of Torah, he clearly implies, lack the means for determining either conclusiveness or truth!

Humbly aware of their own limitations, scientists and students of the Torah become likewise aware of those of their predecessors. Because they can never vouch for the truth of their findings, all they can do is to criticize former efforts in the hope of proposing better alternatives of their own, which in turn their students will treat with similar wariness. Science and Torah study, according to Rabbi Berlin, are both ongoing, open-ended exercises in epistemic humility; both consisting of creative yet humbly self-doubting cycles of relentless trial and imaginative error. Rabbi Berlin's vision of religious learning and knowledge thus dovetails intriguingly with latter-day conceptions of scientific rationality.

But to what extent is Rabbi Berlin's position representative of the Jewish tradition? To many readers it must surely sound deliciously anarchic - coming, as it does, from so very orthodox an Eastern European rabbi - and wholly untypical. But in truth, it is far less surprising than it might seem. As far as rabbinical attitudes to biblical interpretation go, Rabbi Berlin's description rings not only true, but entirely commonplace.

The idea of there being a single, true and humanly discernible reading of the biblical text is quite foreign to the Jewish exegetical tradition. The rabbinical exegetical canon presents a clamorous, jarring and unresolved polyphony of conflicting voices to which each generation of learners is invited to add its own - and most often does. Students of the Torah strive to perfect their readings by critically engaging others. They argue and reason and make every effort to convince, but it is the din of the study-hall rather than any one victorious voice that the canon ends up preserving.

Here and there the Talmudic literature hints that this interpretative plurality is a result of the very nature of the enterprise. Two conflicting interpretations are often granted equal status - both are the words of the living God! Nowhere does the Talmudic literature seem ill at ease with the interpretative under-determination of Scripture. On the contrary, it appears to rejoice in the spirited, creative free-for-all that it perpetuates.

Scripture seems to function for Jews less as a source of religious truth and values than as a divine invitation or challenge to try and work these out for ourselves. Most importantly, with regard to biblical exegesis, the Jewish tradition is unique in not even presupposing a single point of interpretative convergence. It solemnly recognizes the binding sanctity of the Written Torah but does not recognize any particular reading of it as sacred or binding! In fact, one gets the impression that the Bible's very sanctity is attested to by the lavish abundance of *conflicting* readings to which it gives rise. Just as God's image resides in the infinite variety of human dissimilarity, so, it seems, the omnisignificance of his word resides in the rich plurality of its different possible readings.

The story of Noah's ark, recorded briefly in BT, Sanhedrin 108b and more fully in Genesis Rabbah, offers a good example of the type of exegetical pluralism of which I speak. In Genesis 6.18 we read: 'and thou shalt come into the ark, thou, and thy sons, and thy wife, and thy son's wives with thee'. Sensitive to the slightest textual irregularity, the Midrash takes note of the rather artificial separation of husbands and wives in the phrasing of God's instructions to Noah, concluding that, apart from everything else, they included a prohibition on cohabitation: 'whence Noah entered the ark copulation was forbidden, hence, "thou and thy sons" to themselves, "and thy wife and thy son's wives" to themselves'. Read along these lines, Genesis 7.5–7 is taken to imply that Noah did as he was told: 'So Noah did according to all that God commanded him . . . And Noah went in, and his sons, and his wife, and his sons' wives with him into the ark'. In keeping with this reading, upon leaving the ark a year or so later, it seems that family life was allowed to return to normal, for God's instructions no longer implied the same separation of the sexes: 'Go out of the ark, thou, and thy wife, and thy sons, and thy son's wives with thee' (Gen. 8.16). This time, though, Noah appears to have decided not to comply, choosing, seemingly on his own initiative, in the words of the Midrash, 'to extend the commandment'. 'And Noah went out, and his sons, and his wife, and his sons' wives with him' (Gen. 8.18).

It is at this point that the following debate between Rabbi Yehuda and Rabbi Nehemiah is recorded apropos of Gen. 9.8–9: 'And God spoke to Noah, and to his sons with him, saying, And behold, I establish my covenant with you etc . . .'. The former is of the opinion that since Noah 'transgressed the commandment' he was disgraced, and is no longer addressed personally by God. The latter disagrees, concluding that 'since Noah extended the commandment and elected to conduct himself in holiness, he and his sons were rewarded by God's word'.

The controversy is fundamental. Does the Torah teach us, as Rabbi Nehemiah would have it, that one achieves sanctification by suppressing the flesh, or rather, as Rabbi Yehuda opined, by appropriately acknowledging and fulfiling one's bodily needs? Are human beings considered by the Torah to be immutable souls seeking to suppress and transcend their bodily needs, constraints and confinements, or well-balanced, mutually dependent, constructive combinations of body and spirit? The two profoundly conflicting anthropologies and subsequent readings of Scripture are sharply stated, and played off against each other, but no attempt whatsoever is made, here or elsewhere, to decide the issue.

And yet, it is not as if anything goes in the study of the Torah. The rabbis treat the Scripture with the utmost seriousness, paying close attention to every single word, and every unusual or seemingly redundant turn of phrase. Nonetheless, much leeway remains, and among the multitude of possible readings, none are deemed obligatory. Rabbi Berlin's fascinating description of Torah study as a constructively sceptical and self-doubting, critical engagement with tradition, intriguingly akin to modern science, is far less a radical battle cry than an apt and commonplace observation. The Bible's narratives, its portrayals of God, humankind, Israel and the nations; its accounts of creation, the end of days and the world to come; its poetics, prophecy and philosophy, are all energetically discussed, heatedly disputed, yet nowhere adjudicated and never decided.

But Judaism involves more than an effort to interpret Scripture. It is primarily a form of life governed by a set of practices, a religion of meticulously regulated works, not merely one of words. And with regard to Judaism's performative elements, does one still find the same happy disputative polyphony? Does Rabbi Berlin's acute portrayal of the Jewish interpretative tradition extend to the normative and the legal? Rabbi Berlin himself did not think so. A very different consensus, he and most observant Jews believe, grounds and regiments the realm of religious law and divine commandment, rendering it, very differently from Biblical exegesis, profoundly uncritical and monolithic. And if that is so, then despite the exegetical sceptical pluralism that marks the Jewish tradition's attitude to the Bible, Judaism's uncritical legal compliance would easily fall prey to the critique of modernity of which we have spoken.

Unlike biblical exegesis, religious law, like any system of law, is indeed binding. It derives its normative mandate from three main sources of religious authority: the halakhic tradition (the existing body of Jewish law), the halakhic authorities (the courts and sages whose job it is to make and state the law), and the Almighty himself. In the realm of religious performance, many maintain that religious Judaism is inextricably bound to devout and uncritical submission to authority. The covenant of Sinai, many insist, is primarily a halakhic covenant of solemn obedience that is summarized forcefully by the phrase from Exodus 24, '*na'ase ve-nishma*' – first we undertake to do, and then, only then, reflect and assess.

I do not deny that such a view exists within rabbinical Judaism. It is, as we shall see immediately, an authentic voice of the tradition. But I would strongly oppose the claim that it is this tradition's only voice. Contrary to the consensus surrounding the freedom and development prevalent in biblical exegesis, no such consensus exists with respect to halakhah. On the question of obedience and submission to the three sources of religious authority, the Jewish tradition is sorely and intriguingly divided – certainly at the formative level of the Talmudic literature of late antiquity. At this most fundamental level, the Jewish sources are in profound disagreement as to the very meaning of religiosity itself. Judaism, one could say, is a religion constituted by a foundational dispute about what a religion should be.

Take, for example, the two very different ways in which Deuteronomy 17.11 is understood. The verse states that once a matter has been brought before the halakhic authorities, and the Jerusalem Court issues a ruling, 'Thou shalt not deviate from the sentence which they shall tell thee, to the right hand or to the left'. Horrified by the thought of a society whose governing body was not granted absolute authority, Nahmanides, the great thirteenth-century halakhist and exegete, commenting on the verse, gives vigorous expression to the voice of religious submission. The Sifre, the Tannaitic commentary to Deuteronomy, reads the verse as a demand for absolute compliance with the Court's decisions: 'Even if they tell you that right is left and left right, you are to obey them!' Nahmanides follows suit, and citing the Sifre declares:

> Even if you think in your heart that [the court is] mistaken, and even if the matter is as obvious to you as the difference you discern between your right and left, you are to follow their command![2]

It is hard to imagine a clearer and more vigorous statement of religious obedient surrender to the institutions of halakhah.

However, Nahmanides knew well that in citing the Sifre and adopting its position he was not stating the obvious, but making a choice between the Sifre's submissive rendition of the verse and the very different rendition of it found in the Palestinian Talmud (the *Yerushalmi*), with which he was well acquainted.

> Can it be the case that if [the court] tells you that right is left and left is right, one should obey them?! Scripture therefore teaches us: 'to the right or to the left' (Deut. 17.11): that [is to say, that

only if] they say to you, right is right and left is left, [should you obey].[3]

According to the *Yerushalmi*, if one prudently believes the court to have ruled mistakenly, one's religious obligation is not to comply. A clearer or more vigorous expression of a critical, non-submissive religious attitude towards the institutions of halakhah is hard to find.

The disagreement between the Sifre and the *Yerushalmi* clearly illustrates how this dispute plays itself out with regard to the halakhic institutions. Let us now see how it manifests itself with regard to the ultimate source of religious authority, God himself. To this end let us look briefly at two very different midrashic renditions of the same rather surprising moment in the Bible. In the course of his long farewell speech, recorded in Deuteronomy, Moses recalls how, upon nearing the Holy Land, God had instructed him:

> Saying: 'Rise, take your journey, and pass over the brook Arnon; behold, I have given into your hand Sihon the Amorite, king of Heshbon, and his land; begin to possess it, and provoke war with him. For this day will I begin to put the dread of you and the fear of you upon the nations that are under the whole heaven, who shall hear the report of you, and shall tremble, and be in anguish because of you.' [But] I sent messengers out of the wilderness of Kedemoth to Sihon king of Heshbon with words of peace, saying: 'Let me pass through your land; I will go along by the high way, I will neither turn to the right hand nor to the left ...' (Deut. 2.24–28)

Moses, it seems, chose knowingly to disobey God's explicit command, deciding on his own accord to seek peace with the Amorites rather than provoke war. The midrashic commentary Deuteronomy Rabbah explains his insubordination thus:

> Although the Holy One, blessed-be-He, instructed Moses 'Begin to possess', he did not so do, but rather 'sent messengers'; Although He told him 'Make war', he sought peace! [He did so, however,] because it is written in the Torah: 'When thou comest near to a city to fight against it, then proclaim peace unto it' (Deut. 20.10), that is why he sent words of peace to Sihon, for it is written 'out of the wilderness of Kedemoth', on account of words of the Torah that come before those of the Almighty. Therefore it says 'words of peace'.[4]

This, I believe, is about as submissive a reading as the verses in Deuteronomy can be given without doing them real violence. Moses is described as apologizing piously for not heeding the Lord's instruction to provoke war, arguing that he is not at liberty to defy the Torah's very commandment (in Deuteronomy 20.10) to always propose peace before attacking. In case of contradiction, he explains, the words of the Torah are to 'come before' those of God. Even within a thoroughly submissive religious framework, questions will always arise regarding possible or actual conflicts between its various sources of authority. According to this midrashic reading, the question Moses faced and answered was to which of the conflicting sources of authority he should properly submit, the Torah or the Almighty. He opts for the former, but questions neither.

Bamidbar Rabbah to Numbers 19.20, however, tells a different story entirely:

> This is one of [the] things said by Moses to the Holy One, blessed-be-He, to which the latter replied: 'You have taught Me something!' ... when the Holy One, blessed-be-He, said to him: 'Make war with Sihon. Even though he does not seek to interfere with you, you must provoke war with him' ... Moses did not do so, but, as it is written further down, 'sent messengers'. The Holy One, blessed-be-He, said to him 'By your life! You have spoken well! You have taught Me something! And I shall thereby cancel My words and adopt yours'; and hence it is written: 'When thou comest near to a city to fight against it, then proclaim peace unto it.'[5]

Unlike the submissive Moses of Deuteronomy Rabbah, in a bind over deciding between the conflicting instructions of the Torah and its author, Moses is here forcefully portrayed as having challenged God's decree by refusing to attack on moral grounds. God, in response, is said not only not to have demanded obedience, but to have heeded to Moses' objection and to have introduced the required changes in the Written Torah! According to the first Midrash, Moses disobeyed God's explicit command because the Torah instructs differently. In the second Midrash, the Torah ends up instructing differently because of Moses' critique. God is astonishingly described as having produced a morally deficient early draft of the Torah, Moses is portrayed as refusing to comply and challenging it on moral grounds, and the Written Torah, the very Word of God, is subsequently described as having been revised by virtue of God acknowledging and accepting Moses' superior moral judgment!

The theology at work here, especially the notion of religiously appropriate conduct implied by these passages, differs radically from the kind of submissive dogmatism one normally associates with religion, and against which Feuerbach and Nietzsche lashed out so vehemently. The God portrayed here is not the all-powerful, all-knowing and perfectly moral deity to whom we have become so accustomed in virtually all religious discourse. The God of this Midrash and others is a covenanting God, but the covenant his human partners are invited to enter is not one of religious obedience and surrender but rather a covenant of constructive confrontation, a sacred partnership dedicated to the betterment of the world, the Torah and the self. God's need for the critical input of his human partners is as real as theirs should be for his. It is, therefore, a partnership of mutual learning. God makes known his imperfection by initiating real engagement, by learning and by admitting his mistakes. And in doing so he urges humans, by example, to openly confront each other and acknowledge their mistakes. Confronting the Almighty can be terrifying, of course, and taking moral responsibility is never easy. The temptation of pious surrender is ever-present.

The opening chapter of the Mekhilta – the Tannaitic midrashic commentary to Exodus – offers another powerful example of this approach. There are three classes of prophets, states the Mekhilta: those who will plead both the cause of the father against the son and that of the son against the father, and those who will only plead one or the other, but not both. The perfect prophet is described as a Janus-faced critic who chastises the people in the name of God, but also challenges God's judgement on behalf of the people. Jeremiah is approvingly depicted as just such a prophet. 'We have transgressed and have rebelled', he rebukes the people, and 'Thou hast not pardoned' (Lam. 3.42), he complains against God. Elijah, on the other hand, is portrayed as having avidly reproached the people for their idolatrous ways (citing the spectacular scene on Mount Carmel), but never questioning God's judgments or actions. Elijah's replacement by Elisha is described dramatically as an act of impatient divine dismissal owing to God's reluctance to employ prophets who refrain from speaking back! 'We have no use for your prophecy', God is said to have stormed, 'go anoint Elisha in thy stead!'[6] This rabbinical voice has little patience with religious yes-men.

Two objections might be raised at this point. First, one might object to the attempt to infer a general perception of religiosity from depictions such as these that clearly concern God's dealings with, and expectations from, such saintly figures as Moses, Jeremiah and Elijah, who obviously enjoyed privileged status. Second, even if such an inference were justified, it could still be claimed that in halakhah one nonetheless finds the truly submissive element of the Jewish faith. Although the tradition contains brave dramatic moments of confrontation with the divine, the law, many argue, always remains the law. When it comes to halakhah proper, one might object, even this kind of dramatic conflict with the Almighty gives way to full compliance.

But, as we will see with the following texts, the voice of religious submission speaks clearly, but it does not speak alone. In its commentary to Genesis 30, the Tanhuma, the late eighth-century Palestinian midrashic compilation, confronts both the Mishnah's ruling and theology head-on. It does so vis-à-vis the story of the birth of Leah's daughter, Dina, and in the most forceful terms. The Tanhuma openly questions the Mishnah's ruling on the religious inappropriateness of prayers of anguish:

> 'And afterwards she [Leah] bore a daughter' (Gen. 30.21). May our Rabbi teach us: If a man's wife is with child is one allowed to pray 'May it be Thy will that my wife bears a male child' – for so teaches [the Mishnah]: 'If a man's wife is with child and he prays: "May it be Thy will [O God] to grant that my wife bears a male child" is this a prayer in vain?'

> R. Huna in the name of R. Yossi says, despite the fact that [the Mishna] teaches that '. . . this is a prayer in vain', [the law] is not so. Rather, one may pray for a son even as she is giving birth, because it is not beyond God's power to change females to males and males to females.[7]

It is very rare indeed to find a later, essentially exegetical source such as this explicitly contest a Tannaitic ruling. The Tanhuma is not suggesting that the Mishnah has been misunderstood, but boldly asserts that it is wrong! And it does so not by piously appealing to a higher halakhic authority, but by contesting the Mishnah's theological basis. The question, the Tanhuma dramatically implies, is not a technical one, but pertains to the very foundations of the religion. The Tanhuma continues with a quotation from Jeremiah:

> 'Then I went down to a potter's house, and, behold, he was at work on the wheels. And the vessel that he was making of clay was spoiled in the hand of the potter: so he made it again into another vessel, as it seemed good to the potter to make it. Then the word of the Lord came to me, saying, O house of Israel, cannot I do with you as this potter? said the Lord. Behold, as the clay in the potter's hand, so are you in My hand, O house of Israel.' (Jer. 18.3-6). Says the Almighty to Jeremiah: 'if a potter can break a cruse after he has made it and make it into something else, can I not do likewise to you O House of Israel!?'[8]

The Tanhuma reads the Jeremiah verses as claiming that not every state of affairs for which God is responsible comes out well. They liken him to the imperfect potter whose handiwork is not always up to par. But by citing these verses in the course of discussing prayers of anguish, the Tanhuma lends them an additional and radical twist. Jeremiah's potter is self-sufficient. He may be imperfect, but he is an effective self-critic who can tell when a vessel comes out right or wrong. Jeremiah's divine potter is his own best critic, as it were. But in drawing on the potter analogy in support of the appropriateness of prayers of anguish and complaint, the Tanhuma implies that God is not self-sufficient in this respect, that not only is his handiwork occasionally flawed, but that if the flaws are not pointed out to him, he is liable not to notice them. This, as the subsequent passage makes clear, lies at the heart of the Tanhuma's radically different approach to prayer and to the religious covenantal relation in general:

> And similarly in the case of Leah, who after bearing [Yaakov] six sons, saw prophetically that twelve tribes were to emerge from Yaakov. Having born six already, and pregnant for the seventh time, and with the two sons born to each of the two maidservants, ten had already been born. Therefore, Leah stood, angrily confronting the Almighty, saying: 'Lord of the Universe, twelve tribes are to emerge from Yaakov, of which I have six, and am pregnant with a seventh, and by means of the maidservants two and two, hence there are ten. If this (unborn) child (I am carrying) is also a son, then my sister Rachel's share will not (even) be that of the maidservants!'[9]

At this point the Midrash could have easily described God as having scolded Leah in the way he scolded the laughing Sarah when she doubted his promise of a child (Gen. 18.14). 'Do I not know that this would not be fair to Rachel?! Of course you are carrying a girl!', the Midrash could have had God respond. But the Tanhuma opts for the far more radical option. God is depicted as having erred in giving Leah a seventh male child. Realizing his mistake, 'The Almighty immediately responded to her prayer and the boy in her womb was rendered a girl ... and why did she name her (daughter) Dina? Because Leah in her righteousness called the Almighty to task.'

As in the stories about Moses mentioned above, God is here too astonishingly described as being corrected on moral grounds, admitting his mistake, and righting the morally flawed situation for which he was responsible. But unlike the Moses encounters, the Tanhuma text conveys two important additional points that render the previously mentioned objections groundless.

First, the dramatic story of Leah's confrontational prayer is cited explicitly to prove a halakhic point of law applicable to each and every person, namely that everyone should thus pray if he or she suspects that they may not have been dealt with fairly. Unlike the Moses encounters, Leah's confrontation is cited as a model of religious conduct. According to the Tanhuma, one should not suppress prayers of anguish, or accept the dreadful as the work of a perfect judge. On the contrary, God, the Tanhuma all but states openly, is simply *not* the perfect judge and should not be treated as such by anyone! To act in supreme religious righteousness is to act like Leah, and call the Almighty to task whenever one suspects he was wrong.

Second, the Tanhuma's entire move is first and foremost an open, self-conscious, anti-traditionalist challenge to the halakhic tradition as it finds it – it openly confronts the Mishnah's ruling. In defying the Mishnah's ruling as it does, the Tanhuma seems clearly to apply to the realm of halakhah exactly the same confrontational attitude that over a millennium later will be so vividly applied to biblical exegesis by R. Berlin. The Tanhuma does not attempt to offer a new reading of the Mishnah, but openly challenges and subsequently overturns what it takes the Mishnah to be saying.

If there is any truth to my readings of these texts, then there are two foundational theologies, rather than one, hard at work at the heart of the formative canon of the Jewish tradition, each generating a very different notion of religious commitment. One insistently advocates a religious culture of uncritical halakhic compliance, based on faith in a perfect system of law sanctioned by a perfect, intervening God; the other, equally insistently, advocates one of constant moral rethinking based on consider-ations of epistemic and moral humility that it attributes to all involved, including to the system's very sources of authority. This latter voice, as we have seen, extends to all aspects of Jewish religiosity the open-ended, constructive scepticism with which Rabbi Berlin introduces his great exegetical undertaking. As such, it is an exceptionally timely voice. It is a voice that not only avoids the dismissive critique of modernity regarding religion, but lends modernity's vision of humanity an intriguing religious grounding.

Judaism's formative canon is divided, one could say, with regard to its very meaning and mission. And yet, intriguingly, its two voices somehow remain fully accommodated within a single religious framework. How is that possible, with so vast and fundamental differences? How can such conflicting accounts of religiosity, pertaining to such different theologies, remain authentic expressions of one and the same religious culture? What do they share? What common ground binds them?

The answer, I believe, lies in Judaism's unique and undisputed approach to the very notion of a religious canon – the approach expressed so vividly by Rabbi Berlin. Unlike other forms of religion, Judaism makes clear and undisputed distinctions between its holy texts, the religious obligation to study and make sense of them, and the resulting plethora of readings thereby produced. Its unique feature is that while the texts themselves are deemed to be solemnly sacred and their study deemed the very highest of religious works, none of the readings and understandings thereby produced are collectively treated as final. Judaism in its Talmudic constructions succeeds in forming a single and coherent religious entity by becoming a 'people of the book' – a people constituted by its books and not by the ways they are read, or by any one of the various readings they are given.

As we have seen, Judaism's foundational project of religious self-understanding produces not one, but two radically different self-readings. The submissive version of Jewish religiosity, we have seen, is an authentic voice of Judaism, whose presence in Talmudic culture is beyond dispute. But by being but one of *two* such voices, it is incapable, in principle, of viably accounting reflectively for the very second-order dispute of religiosity to which it is party. And it is here, with respect to the question of religiosity itself, that the confrontational voice rules supreme, despite its resolute opposition to all manner of final religious ruling. It is here that the Jewish tradition can boast solid and authentic resources for a religiosity that is grounded in a vision of human rationality and human agency intriguingly akin to that of the modern era; a vision grounded in a religious yet humble epistemology that stands in Janus-faced opposition to the two highly worrying forms of latter-day irrationality. In a world caught between uncritical dogmatism on the one hand and equally uncritical radical relativism on the other, the critical voice of Judaism's confrontational theology is a voice much needed both within the Jewish community and without.

Notes

1 N. T. Y. Berlin, *Chumash Ha'ameq Davar* (Jerusalem, El Hamekoroth, 1984), Introduction # 5; emphasis added.
2 Sifre Deuteronomy 154.
3 *Yerushalmi* Horayot 45d.
4 S. Leibermann (ed.), *Midrash Debarim Rabbah* (Jerusalem, Wahrmann, 1964), pp. 29–30.
5 Bamidbar Rabbah Vilna 19.33.
6 Mekhilta deRabi Yishmael, *Bo* 1.
7 Midrash Tanhuma, Genesis, Vayetze 8.
8 *Ibid.*
9 *Ibid.*

TWO

Tradition and Legal Change

Zvi Zohar

'There is nothing so flexible as the flexibility of halakhah,' wrote Rabbi Hayyim David HaLevi, chief rabbi of Tel Aviv, in 1989. Most other rabbis, upon coming across this statement published in the *Yearbook* of Israel's Chief Rabbinate, probably thought it quite strange. Seriously devoted to the vision of an eternal and unchanging Judaism, they suspected that beyond simply 'getting it wrong', Rabbi HaLevi was undermining the bastion of religious commitment by such talk of 'flexibility'.

On the other hand, 'dynamic', 'development' and 'progress' have become such accepted values in the modern world that it can be difficult to appreciate why anyone would oppose the application of such wonderful, self-evident ideas to the realm of halakhah. In this chapter I will explore the religious rationale for what is called the fundamentalist approach to halakhah and then, using the case of marriage and divorce as an example, argue for a different approach, one which recognizes halakhah's dynamic nature.

A fundamentalist position begins with a commitment to the service of God. Here is how a deeply religious Jewish fundamentalist might present the rationale of his position: God is eternal and transcendent; He does not change; and He is above the vicissitudes of this transient, shifting world. God is the source of the true and the good. God is worthy of worship, and human beings ought to seek to lead their lives in tune with His will. Jews know how to worship God, and what actions and behaviours are favourable in His eyes, because God has revealed to us His Torah. If we allow our lives to be guided by Torah, we will be living as God wills. By following this eternal, God-given way, we can raise our lives above the transient, mundane and arbitrary aspects of human existence, and imbue them with the truth, good and holiness that derive from closeness to God.

It is thus clear why change, progress and development are regarded by fundamentalist Jews as antithetical to Torah Judaism, for when the initial state of affairs is flawed and lacking, movement towards a better condition is good; but when the initial state of affairs is perfect, any movement is a movement away from that condition. Since Torah is perfect, any change can only be for the worse. What is appropriate, then, is not change in Torah, but rather change in our imperfect, all-too-human lives: Jews can (and should) involve themselves in spiritual-religious endeavours that bring about positive change, progress and development in their fulfilment of the perfect, eternal Torah. But to speak of Torah as 'progressing' is an oxymoron.

From a fundamentalist perspective, the above is true for all times and cultural contexts, but is all the more crucial in our modern, Western world. In contemporary Western culture, the new, the innovative and the iconoclastic are seen as expressions of rationality and human autonomy. Betterment of the human condition is said to require rejection of the past; social and moral problems can be overcome by discarding old values and behaviours in favour of new ones. In this cultural atmosphere, a call for change in Torah Judaism is seen by fundamentalists as not merely a misunderstanding of what Torah is all about, but also as a call for displacement of authentic internal Jewish values by the antithetical alien values of secular modernist society. Thus, from this perspective, it is especially imperative today to advocate a totally non-dynamic view, and to unequivocally espouse adherence to the holy ways of life that characterized Jewish existence in the past.

Following the argument above, it is easier to understand the appeal of such a fundamentalist presentation of Torah and of halakhah's unchanging, stable nature. However, such a position is not consonant with what actually happened in the past. Any examination of the actual practice of Torah reveals that dramatic changes in halakhah took place over the course of Jewish history. To illustrate this, let us examine the various changes and alterations that actually occurred in one of the most basic elements of Jewish life: marriage and divorce.

What human framework is more basic than marriage? Undoubtedly, Torah is in favour of marriage. But what *kind* of marriage does Torah advocate? Abraham had only one wife – but several concubines. Isaac had one wife and no concubines. Jacob had two wives, and two concubines. King David had eighteen wives, and Solomon had a thousand. According to rabbinic law, as interpreted by Maimonides in twelfth-century Egypt, a Jewish man may have several wives – but no concubines. At that time in northern Europe, however, Jews were forbidden by the 'Edict of Rabbenu Gershom' to have more than one wife. In eighteenth-century Germany, Rabbi Jacob Emden wrote a passionately argued halakhic treatise advocating non-marital sexual partnerships for unmarried Jewish men and women, and extra-marital sexual partnerships for Jewish married men only, explaining that this was simply a revival of the biblical institution of concubinage. Quoting many source-texts, he explained that this was perfectly fine according to Torah, and that any children born out of such relationships would be of absolutely kosher halakhic status. By way of contrast, Reform Judaism holds that Judaism sanctifies sexual relations only within monogamous marriages.

This concise example suffices to illustrate that whatever certain ideologues may claim today, change in very basic Jewish norms is an innate feature of Jewish law. The rabbis who themselves instituted or justified these changes did not see themselves as operating against or outside of Torah. Rather, they thought that such changes expressed authentic commitment to Torah.

The flexibility of halakhah is grounded in three different internal sources: interpretation, legislation and custom. Each in their own way creates a dynamic dialogue between the eternal Torah and the way it is implemented and lived. To illustrate the various models and thought processes utilized by the rabbis in their treatment of halakhah, I turn now to the example of divorce law. Each source of halakhic innovation, i.e. interpretation, legislation and custom, will be explored independently.

Changes through Interpretation

The Torah (see Deut. 24.1) describes a divorce occurring through a 'writ of [marriage] termination' (*sefer kritut*) given by the husband. The Talmud explains that such a document is valid only if given in free will. Thus, there seems to be no way in which a woman can receive a divorce if her husband is recalcitrant.

Maimonides rules, however, that a woman cannot be forced to remain in a relationship in which she feels her husband to be sexually repulsive: 'she is not a captive of war, who must have sex with a man she despises'.[2] Therefore, the court 'immediately forces him to divorce her'. But is not such compulsion contrary to the requirement that a divorce be given willingly? Since Maimonides not only recognized Torah as eternal, but also included belief in the eternality of Torah as one of his 'Thirteen Principles of Faith', how could he validate a divorce to which the husband was coerced?

Maimonides himself raised this question and provided the answer:

Since he was compelled, why is this divorce not invalid? ...
because a person who was overcome by his evil inclination to desist from performing a positive *mitzvah* or to commit a transgression, and who was then beaten [by the authorities] until he did what he ought to do or desisted from what he was forbidden to do, is not considered to be acting under compulsion ... with regard to this man who refused to divorce [his wife]: since he does want to be a Jew, he *ipso facto* wants to fulfil the commandments and to refrain from sin, but his evil inclination overcame him. When he was beaten, his evil inclination

weakened, and so when he says 'I want [to divorce]' – the divorce is in accordance with his will.[3]

Maimonides' move is an interpretive one: he changes the law by interpreting 'will' to mean not a subjective feeling but an objective mental position, which is assessed according to the overall context of a person's life choices. A person who consents to be a Jew thereby consents to what is entailed by being a Jew, and the court is merely enabling him to overcome a powerful urge that conflicts with his own deeper and more serious will.

The important point for us is that acknowledging Torah as eternal does not mean acknowledging our understanding of Torah as eternal. Our understanding of Torah can change, and when that happens, we will begin to permit actions our ancestors thought that Torah forbade, or we will begin to forbid what they thought Torah permitted. And we will be right in doing so; for we can do no more (and no less) than follow the best interpretation of Torah that we have. Sincere commitment to Torah does not always lead, then, to 'adherence to the holy ways of life that characterized Jewish existence in the past'.

In re-interpreting the notion of 'will' and thus changing the law, Maimonides uses three distinct assumptions. The first relates to human psychology: Maimonides has a theory of human personality that recognizes several 'levels' of will that can be in simultaneous conflict. While he did not arrive at this view by studying Torah, he is nevertheless confident that since the theory is correct, Torah must be in consonance with it. In other words, he assumes that Torah is a rational document, and his reading of Torah is informed by his general understanding of reality. If so, it seems plausible that if his understanding of rationality or of reality were to change, his understanding of Torah would change, too.

Maimonides' second and third assumptions are not about reality, but about values. He holds that the status of a married woman is not like that of a captive, and that she is under no obligation to submit to the sexual advances of a man she finds repulsive – even if that man is her lawful husband. He also clearly assumes that sex is an essential component of marriage, that a woman cannot be expected to be bound in a sexless marriage, and that divorce is therefore an absolute necessity in such situations. Now, Torah never expressly states either of these things about marriage. While some biblical passages might seem to support such views of marriage, others might be cited against them, as in Psalm 45.11 where the bride is enjoined 'he is thy lord, and do homage to him'. In any case, Maimonides' decision that Torah here requires an immediate, forced divorce is dependent upon his value-laden understanding of what marriage is all about – an understanding that informs his reading of Torah no less than it derives from such reading.

At the very same time that Maimonides was composing these passages, his contemporary, Rabbi Jacob ben Meir (known as Rabbenu Jacob Tam), was teaching a radically different doctrine. The grandson of Rashi and considered the greatest rabbi in twelfth-century France, Rabbenu Tam held that if a man could be forced to divorce his wife when she declared that he repelled her, any married woman who was attracted to another man would claim her husband disgusted her, receive a forced writ of divorce, and go off to her new sexual partner against her husband's will!

It seemed self-evident to Rabbenu Tam that this was deeply antithetical to Torah values, and he therefore argued that the possibility of forced divorce in such cases simply could not and did not exist in Torah law. But, if the husband is not forced to divorce her, and she remains married to him against her will – what of Maimonides' value-judgment that a woman may not be compelled to have sex with a man repulsive to her?

Rabbi Asher ben Yehiel (Ashkenaz and Spain, thirteenth–fourteenth centuries) responded:

> Is this a reason to force a husband to divorce, and thereby permit a married woman [to other men]? Let her not have sex with him, and remain a straw widow to the end of her days! In any case, a woman is not commanded to have children. Can it be, that because she wants to follow her headstrong desires, and has fastened her eyes on another man and desires him more than the champion of her youth, that we should fulfil her lust and force the man, who still loves the woman of his youth, to divorce her?! God forbid that any rabbi should rule thus! ... In this generation, the daughters of Israel are impudent and if a wife will be able to extricate herself from under her husband by saying 'he repulses me', not a single daughter of Abraham will remain with her husband, [rather] they will fasten their eyes on another and rebel against their husbands![4]

According to this view, women are not interested in marital stability but in following their lust and desire. Indeed, if given the choice, *not a single woman would remain married to her present husband*! One might argue that if that is truly what women want, perhaps they should be freed from their current unwanted state? But this is not the view of Rabbi Asher. His analysis is grounded in a deeply held understanding of the purpose of marriage. Marriage is a bulwark against socio-sexual chaos. Such chaos will occur if women are able to follow their desire for men other than their husbands by forcing their husbands to divorce against their will. Therefore, it is only by absolutely closing such options that social stability can be ensured.

This does not mean that Rabbi Asher is in favour of forced sex. If a wife claims that her husband disgusts her sexually, she need not have sex with him. But that does not entitle her to a divorce. Better that she remain without sex for the rest of her life, he argues, than that her husband be forced to capitulate and give her up, against his will! Unlike Maimonides, who holds that a sexless marriage is a moral oxymoron and must be terminated by divorce, Rabbi Asher holds that if such a divorce will enable a woman to seek sexual satisfaction with another man, it is absolutely preferable *morally* that she remain married against her will – and if she will not have sex with her husband, let her not have sex at all.

It is apparent that a deep difference of values and worldviews informs this sharp debate between Maimonides and Rabbi Asher. However much a contemporary reader may be turned off by the latter's view, it is very important to note that this is not a formal-authoritative presentation of halakhah, but rather, Rabbi Asher clearly bases his position on what he holds to be central Torah values: the sanctity and stability of marriage, the suppression of social chaos, the preference for marriage without female sexuality over an alternative of lust and licentiousness.

Changes by Legislation

Since the values he set forth are seemingly eternal, why did Rabbi Asher explicitly contextualize his ruling by noting that: '*in this generation* the daughters of Israel are impudent'? The answer is that he himself was aware of a very different legal tradition, one that had prevailed in Jewish law for many centuries. This tradition began in the year 650/651 CE, when a dramatic legal enactment was instituted by the halakhic leaders of Babylonian Jewry, immediately following the Muslim conquest of that area in 637–650:

> When our masters in the times of the Sevora'im saw that Jewish women were going to the Gentiles and with their assistance were obtaining forced divorces from their husbands, and the husbands were writing bills of divorce under compulsion and these were illegally forced divorces – and this resulted in disaster – they enacted, with regard to a woman who rebels against her husband and demands a divorce, that ... we compel her husband to divorce her immediately.[5]

In contrast to the policy of the Sassanid Persian kingdom that had previously ruled in Babylonia, Muslim legal authorities provided succour to Jewish women seeking divorce, and forced their husbands to acquiesce and issue a writ of divorce. However if a husband is unlawfully forced to write a bill of divorce, it is invalid. Therefore, the Muslim coercion resulted in divorces that were halakhically invalid but at the same time made it impossible for the rabbis to prevent the women from re-marrying, because doing so would enrage the Muslim authorities who had validated the procedure. The result was a disaster, because according to halakhah, the women's second marriages were adulterous, and children born from such unions were *mamzerim* who would never be able to marry other Jews. Since the rabbis could not change the political-legal reality of Muslim rule, they decided to institute a change in halakhah. From then on, any Jewish woman demanding a divorce (not only on the grounds of sexual repulsiveness) would get it immediately – no questions asked – from a Jewish court! And since a writ of divorce lawfully imposed upon the husband by a Jewish court was valid, any subsequent marriage and children would be fully 'kosher' according to halakhah.

Here, we have a change in halakhah that is not interpretive, but legislative. The rabbis in the year 650 did not claim that they had reached a new understanding of what Torah had always meant. They clearly stated that Torah strictly limited the cases in which husbands could be forced to issue a divorce. But they held that within the realm of values recognized by Torah, it was possible for rational human beings to recognize a hierarchy. Torah upheld the husband's prerogative not to grant a divorce against his will, but it also regarded the prevention of adultery as a major value – and it was crystal-clear to the rabbis at that time that if historical conditions prevented the realization of both values, then prevention of adultery should be given preference over retaining the husbands' unilateral prerogative. They canonized this recognition by legislation and for hundreds of years (from 650 until *c.* 1100, and in certain localities until after 1400), this change in law was recognized as valid and binding.

Legislative change in halakhah does not see itself as undermining the eternality of Torah. But while Torah is eternal and perfect, human beings are imperfect, and historical reality is fickle. It is therefore possible that under certain conditions, implementation of (what we understand to be) the eternal norms of Torah will entail results that are destructive to (what we understand are) the eternal values of Torah. In some cases, such as the one above, this calls for abrogation of certain norms of Torah. In other cases, it calls for adding on limits or stringencies not required by Torah. However, all legislation under the aegis of Torah is by definition focused on the alleviation of such contextual conflicts, and is therefore – in principle – limited in duration: when the context changes, the enactment may no longer be valid.

Changes by Custom

A third source of change recognized within halakhah is custom. If we return once again from divorce to marriage, we see that a lot of what happens in the course of a Jewish wedding is grounded in custom: the melodies, the dances and the breaking of the cup, for example. But most people are unaware of how much more of the ceremony is merely customary: the *chuppah* is a custom; the participation and role of the rabbi is a custom; even the wedding ring is a custom, not required by halakhah. When we think of custom, we usually think of it as preservation of the past, not as innovation. But when did today's customs begin? If people living in Western countries consider the melodies they use at weddings, they will recognize them to be European in character, which means that they cannot be from rabbinic times, because the Talmudic rabbis were Middle Eastern. And for each custom that we follow, mediaeval texts report customs that were then in vogue, which have since fallen into disuse. In other words: the things we know as customs began, in some historical context that we usually don't think about, as innovation. And in other cases, what was once custom is now no longer followed even by the most religious among us. In other words: custom reflects change.

What gives custom power and authority? There are two schools of thought within halakhah that answer this question. One holds that since what is now customary began as innovation, it must have been validated originally by the rabbis of that time. The authority of customs we follow today derives, then, from past rabbinic decisions. The other view holds that custom – as opposed to textual study and interpretation – begins not with rabbis, but with the people. The Jewish people, the Jewish community, possess creative powers that do not derive from texts, but from life and culture, and halakhah recognizes and validates these powers.

These two schools of thought differ most of all with regard to what should be done if custom and halakhah seem to conflict. The first view argues that if a custom conflicts with halakhah, that must mean that the custom was not originally validated by rabbis. Therefore, the custom should be changed so as to conform with our understanding of halakhah. According to the second view, since the custom was created by the people, rabbis should try to reinterpret or reformulate their understanding of Torah, so as to provide halakhic justification for the custom. A more general formulation of this principle is that rabbis should cultivate an orientation which seeks to view the actual religious praxis of the Jewish people in the most positive possible light, rather than an orientation that tends to focus on where the community is 'getting it wrong'.

Interpretation, Legislation, Custom – and the Eternality of Torah

Our brief survey of laws and customs relating to marriage and divorce reveals that there were many *different* 'holy ways of life' that Jews followed in the past, and that these ways of life were themselves characterized by a dynamic of change. The adoption of a non-dynamic view of Torah is therefore itself contrary to the reality of Torah. This, however, only becomes evident through the study of Torah, which frees us from the chains of anti-dynamic rhetoric and empowers us to realize that Torah changed not because Jews got tired of Torah, but because they were enamoured of Torah and deeply committed to halakhah. This love motivated them to interpret Torah in the best possible light, as understood by the most outstanding moral and religious minds of their time.

Halakhah changed because Jews wanted to celebrate Torah with the most beautiful and moving melodies, dances and ritual objects they were aware of or that they could create; and it changed because of shifts in the wider world of which Jews were a part. At the same time, though, change is not the most central value of Torah. Living a Jewish life characterized by a sincere sense of organic continuity with the ways Jews lived in the past and with the ways they understood God and Torah is arguably more important and spiritually satisfying than incessantly seeking to re-create Judaism in consonance with current trends and mores.

A religious life in the spirit of Torah should grant the *presumption* of authenticity and validity to the living traditions and interpretations we have received from our great cultural and religious past, but never allow that presumption to override our critical commitment to interpret, to legislate and to live Torah in the light of our own sincere rational, moral and religious recognitions. It is by achieving the best possible balance between a deep commitment to organic Jewish continuity and a no less deep commitment to a critical vision of what Judaism can and should become that we will really be in step with the rhythm of Torah itself.

Notes

1 H. D. HaLevi, *Yearbook of Israel's Chief Rabbinate* (Shana b' Shana, 1989), pp. 185–6.
2 Maimonides, *Laws of Relationships* 14.8.
3 Maimonides, *Laws of Divorce* 2.20.
4 R. Asher ben Yehiel, *Responsa* 43.8.
5 R. Sherira Gaon, *Responsum 478*, in *Otsar HaGeonim to Tractate Ketubot*.

THREE Tradition: Continuity or Change – Two
Religious Options

Vered Noam

With the onset of the Enlightenment, Western thought has reflected
frequently on the gap between a traditional religious outlook and the
modern sense of reality. One manifestation of this abyss pertains to the place,
and recognition, of change and development within religious traditions,
which I will refer to as a 'perspective of continuity' versus an 'acknowledgement of change'. The classical *posek* (adjudicator) and commentator,
who operate within the defined boundaries of tradition and see themselves
as a link in its chain, attempt to present all of tradition over the ages as one
continuous unified body whose teachings exhibit maximum uniformity.
This perspective seeks to maintain the authority and origins of tradition
from time immemorial. But the contemporary observer criticizes this
process for being either naïve, or lacking in intellectual integrity, or both.
The latter seeks to separate the various historical levels of tradition and
sources with the scalpel of exegesis, to reveal their essence and development.
This act of unravelling the colourful carpet of tradition into its various
threads intentionally sets aside the 'religious' values of authority, precedence,
continuity and harmony in favour of two aspects of 'the truth': the historical
truth as it relates to the evolution of tradition in general, and the exegetical
truth of each separate text. The encounter between the sceptical, reflective
consciousness of modern times, which reads tradition as developmental and
breaks things down into their separate elements, and the tendency of more
traditional rabbis and teachers to seek continuity and harmony often
produces uneasiness (either covert or blatant) or outright distress.

The question I seek to explore is whether this dissonance is necessary.
Is it possible to maintain a commitment to religious tradition while at the
same time recognizing the developmental dimension within tradition's
discourse? This question, while more acute in the modern context, is not
new. Over the ages, Jewish tradition has had to continuously reflect on the
way it perceives these developments. Are they viewed as innovations or are
they understood as interpretive unfoldings of the inner meaning of
traditional texts? Consequently, in exploring this question I propose to
investigate the model set by the Talmudic sages, and particularly the
Tannaim, who shaped a new religious-halakhic world for their generation
and the following ones. In so doing, I will focus on the reflection and

treatment of the gap between the Bible and halakhah in the consciousness of the sages. When a sage deals with rabbinic halakhah and what is supposed to be its biblical source, he has two basic approaches open to him. The first is to present continuity – that is, chart a path leading from the verse to the halakhah. This approach subordinates the verse to the halakhah in question and removes the biblical verse from its plain meaning. At the same time, however, it also regards halakhah as a product of interpretation and not as an outcome of independent innovation or separate transmission. The second approach is to acknowledge change – that is, present halakhah itself as an innovation of the sages or as an independent tradition transmitted across the ages, though not on the strength of biblical interpretation. In the case of this second approach, the biblical source is interpreted independently and with a view to its simple meaning.

'Continuity' and 'Change' in Rabbinic Literature

We tend to automatically identify the rabbinic world, starting with the Talmudic sages, with the first approach, which I call the 'perspective of continuity', and to ascribe every modern observation to the second approach, which I term 'acknowledgement of change'. Furthermore, it is common to describe the 'perspective of continuity' as a conservative and frozen approach that discourages or even precludes creative and innovative human impulses, and to ascribe to the 'modern' outlook of 'acknowledgement of change' the dynamic optimism of an enlightened era. The discussion below seeks to shed some light on this crossroads within the world of the sages. To what extent do our sages appear to have been aware of the gap between what they created and the biblical foundation upon which they declared they stood? To what extent were they willing to recognize their own creative independence? Did they pay tribute to this independence or did they seek to downplay it? Did they see themselves as committed to simple meanings on a biblical level, on the one hand, and to the independence of the later halakhah, on the other? Or were they perhaps seeking to subordinate one to the other, and even both to the consciousness of continuity and uniformity which they wanted to impart to students and future generations?

This investigation yields several surprises. It turns out that both approaches, the 'conservative' and the 'critical' – the latter being the ostensible product of modern reflection – are patently alive in the sages' world, as is a realization of the aims and obstacles of each. It thus becomes clear that the foregoing dichotomic description – distinguishing between the rigid and conservative 'perspective of continuity' and the historic, conscious and realistic outlook of 'acknowledgement of change' – does a disservice to both approaches by stripping them of their complexity.

'All was Revealed to Moses at Sinai' – Continuity

The enormous body of literature known as the oral law, which sets down the basic foundations of Jewish life, philosophy and intellectual discourse for generations, has been presented by our sages, as well as by Jewish educators throughout the ages, as commentary and a direct continuation of the written law. This claim contains two highly significant axioms: (1) the oral law is merely a simplification and explanation of the written law; it is part and parcel of the written law and contained in its words; and (2) the oral law stems from the same source as the written law and was given to Israel at the same time and at the same place; it too was revealed by God at Sinai at the same time that the Torah was revealed. 'These are the laws, rules, and instructions (*torot*) that the Lord established, through Moses on Mount Sinai, between himself and the Israelite people' (Lev. 26.46); '. . . and the use of the plural *torot* teaches us that both *torot* were given to Israel, one written and the other oral' (Sifra Be-Hukkotai 2.8). This idea is pointedly expressed in the following Midrash, which plants the roots of the entire range of oral law compositions, as well as any future halakhic innovations, in the Sinaitic revelation:

> 'And the Lord gave me the two tablets of stone inscribed by the finger of God, with the exact words that the Lord had addressed to you out of the fire on the day of the Assembly' (Deut. 9.10). Rabbi Joshua ben Levi said: *aleyhem* (on them) – *ve-aleyhem* (and on them); *kol* (all) – *ke-chol* (as all); *devarim* (words) – *ha-devarim* (the words); *mitzvah* (commandment) – *kol mitzvah* (all commandment[s]). ['You shall faithfully observe all the Instruction that I enjoin upon you today, that you may thrive and increase and be able to possess the land the Lord promised on oath to your fathers' (Deut. 8.1)]. *The Bible, the Mishnah, the Talmud, the Tosefta, Aggada, and even what a veteran student would say in front of his teacher in the future, all was said to Moses at Sinai*: because it has been stated: 'Sometimes there is a phenomenon of which they say "Look, this one is new!" – it occurred long since, in ages that went by before us.' (Eccl. 1.10)[1]

The verse that opens the Midrash deals with the tablets of law given at Sinai. On the level of its simple meaning, the verse teaches us that all the *devarim* (words) that God spoke at Sinai were written on the tablets. However, Rabbi Joshua ben Levi infers that at the time the Torah was given, the

Mishnah, Talmud, Tosefta, and Aggada were also given. Not only were these works given to Moses at Sinai, but the debate renewed every day in the bet midrash on the opinions of the sages and their students also originated with the revelation of the Torah. The verse selected to conclude the homily comes from Ecclesiastes and teaches that even what seems to be new 'occurred long since, in ages that went by before us'; in other words: what appears to the observer in the bet midrash to be an ongoing process of inventive human creation is in reality ancient tradition – fixed, rigid, and complete – of divine origin.

This position is a sort of general, fundamental declaration on the authority and origins of the oral law; however, it clearly cannot exist in a literal sense in the everyday world of the Talmudic sages. This world, familiar to us from the rabbinic halakhah and Aggada, is based entirely on vital human discourse, dialectical and renewing, and not on sacred and rigid tradition. The words of the sages are not portrayed as an anonymous monolith of divine origin. On the contrary, the Mishnaic and Talmudic sages are human beings, distinguished by name, whose identity is drawn from known circumstances of time and place. The oral culture of the sages takes pains to convey statements in the name of the person who says them. It attributes halakhic opinions and religious philosophy to those who propound them and not to an ancient tradition, making sure to differentiate between what is said by a sage himself and what he transmits in the name of his teacher.

The Talmudic sages do not deny innovation and change in the oral law. It is clear to the various speakers that they are creating a multi-layered, dynamic edifice, and they openly acknowledge the effects of circumstances of time and place on halakhah. Expressions such as 'at first', 'the first elders', 'it was said', 'it was actually said', indicate an earlier halakhic level that changed as the result of determinations made by later sages. *Takkanot* (ordinances), *gezeirot* (edicts), and determinations are ascribed to the various generations and institutions that created them, often in disagreement with prior rulings. The Talmudic sages distinguish between the halakhic practices of Palestine and those of Babylonia ('this is for us and this is for them'); between 'before the legislation of Ezra' and thereafter, between 'the days of the Temple' and 'contemporary times', between the halakhot of 'the first' and those of 'the last'. The law that emerges from the various Babylonian Talmudic academies is influenced by the collective attributes that characterize the sages of a particular place.[2]

And of course, the particular nature of the oral law also derives from its most obvious characteristic: debate. The many opinions and variety of voices cannot easily exist side by side with a belief in divine, uniform and eternal halakhah that is not subject to change. Indeed, Tannaitic literature contains precepts that consider the historical moment of the birth of controversy, the inauguration of Bet Hillel and Bet Shammai, a moment of breakdown and deviation from the process of the oral law as it ideally should be: 'Rabbi Jose said that in the beginning there was no debate in Israel ... but when the students of Shammai and Hillel argued who did not serve to the fullest, controversy increased in Israel and two laws were made'[3]. Nevertheless, nobody would consider returning the bet midrash to the utopian era prior to debate, just as it is impossible to turn the pages of human history back to the Garden of Eden prior to sin. Hence a monolithic halakhic world will not exist in the future until the advent of the Messiah.

> At first there was no debate in Israel ... After the students of Bet Shammai and Bet Hillel fought and did not serve their rabbis to the fullest, and debate in Israel increased and was divided into two classes, one defiles and the other purifies and is no longer expected to return to its original state until the son of David arrives.[4]

In contrast to this approach that sees debate as a necessary evil resulting from the reality of human existence in the world, there are also those who believe that argument is the result of the primaeval nature of the divine law, and that it would be impossible to study and abide by such a body of law had it not been given to human hands with the understanding that it is open to interpretation:

> Rabbi Yanni said if the Torah had been given 'incontrovertibly' it would not have had a leg to stand on. What does this mean? 'And God said to Moses.' (Moses) said to Him: 'God, tell me what is the halakhah'; he said to him, 'Rule in accordance with the majority. If those who exonerate are in the majority, exonerate. If those who ascribe guilt are in the majority, ascribe guilt. The Torah was given such that it could be interpreted with 49 arguments (lit. faces) to find something impure and 49 arguments to find it pure.'[5]

In this story, God refuses to reveal the Torah 'incontrovertibly', that is, with one explicit and unequivocal interpretation. Its interpretation is given over to sages who make determinations by majority rule, and from the outset it is intended to be understood in contradictory directions: '49 impure faces and 49 pure faces'.

The Torah unto Itself and the Sages to Themselves – The Gap

The general religious understanding of the continuum and connection between biblical and Talmudic literature appears to further break down when examined in light of the gulf between biblical law and its halakhic interpretation in Tannaitic and Amoraic works of the Tannaim and Amoraim. How great is the gap between the nature, spirit, and even concise and decisive wording of biblical law, and the highly detailed, dialectical, and long-winded halakhic discourse conducted in the everyday language spoken by the sages (and even adopted vernacular when discussing the Talmuds – Galilean Aramaic in Palestine and Babylonian in Babylonia)? Moreover, it appears that the sages intentionally strive to emphasize the external gap between the language of the Bible and their form of expression. They resolutely refrain from writing down their theories in order to preserve the hierarchical differentiation between the written law and the human law, which is only conveyed orally. It would seem that from the outset they attempt to formulate their laws in ordinary, spoken language. This aspect becomes even more obvious through comparison to the halakhot of the Qumran sect, which are composed in biblical language, written down, and integrated with the biblical verses to the point of being indistinguishable from them. Furthermore, the halakhic commentary of the sages is clearly differentiated from the words of the verse they seek to interpret, not only by means of employing a different register and writing nothing down, but also through an extensive system of terminology that mediates between the written word and the Tannaitic exegesis ('why was this stated', 'could be', 'I hear', 'I have nothing but', 'to show that', etc.). The external linguistic contrast between biblical and rabbinic language embodies the profound differences of nuance between the supremacy of the Bible and the human, earthbound rabbinic experience. This linguistic differentiation is not denied by the sages, and is even openly articulated by them: 'The language of the Torah is distinct and so is the language of the sages.'[6]

The linguistic plane is but one facet of the centuries-old cultural and historical distinction which lies between the biblical and rabbinic creation. Added to it is the fact that the world of the Bible is historic, vital and colourful. It outlines the way of life and chronicles the history of an independent, mainly agricultural nation that lives in the land of Israel, while its religious life revolves in concentric circles around the Temple and its ritual. Biblical law addresses the individual Israelite farmer as well as biblical society and its institutions: judges and police, kings, prophets and priests. The heroes of the biblical narrative are doers – forefathers, leaders and prophets – who operate in the national arena (or, in Genesis, on the familial-tribal plane); they shape a national reality out of a direct dialogue with God, who commands, supervises, rewards and punishes. In contrast, the Talmudic sages operate in the closed world of the bet midrash and halakhah, whose heroes are religiously observant people whose only activity is the study and teaching of Torah. The sages see their role as one of shaping the details of the daily religious life of a closed and introspective Jewish community whose focal point is the synagogue and bet midrash, a community ruled by a more or less hostile foreign power. Their literature has no national connection; it is devoid of heroic narratives, and almost blind to historical reality and the panorama of its surroundings. It operates in an abstract spiritual, 'virtual' world. In this literature, the worship of God takes place within the sphere of human activity, not through channels of miraculous revelation.

The sages are well aware of the halakhically closed nature of their world. The following statement in Tractate Berakhot seems to be worded as a protest against the question that arises in regard to the limitations of the religious discourse that they develop: 'Since the day that the Temple was destroyed, the Holy One, blessed-be-He, has nothing in this world but the four cubits of halakhah alone.'[7] Indeed, the sages do not ignore the differences between the biblical atmosphere and that of the rabbinic bet midrash, nor the contrast between the model of exemplary religious life in the Bible and that of their world. Many Aggadic Midrashim attempt to bridge this gap by 'rabbinizing' the biblical heroes. In other words, Talmudic Aggada superimposes the shadow of the Jewish sage of Roman Palestine or Sassanid Babylonia on the biblical character, and the biblical scenery is replaced with that of the bet midrash.

> For so said R. Aha ben Bizana in the name of R. Simeon the Pious: A harp was hanging above David's bed. As soon as midnight arrived, a North wind came and blew upon it and it played of itself. He arose immediately and studied the Torah till the break of dawn. After the break of dawn the wise men of Israel came in to see him ... Levi and R. Isaac: The one says ... The other one says: Thus spoke David before the Holy One, Blessed-be-He: 'Master of the world, am I not pious? All the kings of the East and the West sit with all their pomp among their company, whereas my hands are soiled with the blood [of menstruation], with the foetus and the placenta, in order to declare a woman clean for her husband. And what is more, in all that I do I consult my teacher, Mephibosheth, and I say to him: "My teacher Mephibosheth, is my decision right? Did I correctly convict, correctly acquit, correctly declare clean, correctly declare unclean? And I am not ashamed [to ask]?" '[8]

When confronting the subject of halakhah, the gap between the two constitutive foundations of the Jewish heritage – the Bible and rabbinic literature – is both much more difficult and more dangerous to obfuscate. Aside from the vast differences with regard to internal focus, linguistic and cultural characteristics, as well as historic circumstances in these two disparate literatures, their vast differences of halakhic content and scope are immediately and patently obvious. The enormous expansion of certain halakhic matters in relation to their circumscribed origins in the Bible, and the total invention of halakhot with no biblical source whatsoever bother the early sages in the last centuries of the Second Temple era, the period in which the following Mishnah was apparently composed:

> The laws about the dissolving of vows hang in the air, and have no basis (in the Bible). The halakhot concerning Sabbath, feast-offerings, and trespasses are as mountains suspended by a hair, because the verses of the Bible concerning this are very few, and the halakhot are very many. The jurisprudence, the Temple services, and the purification, and uncleanness, and the cases of illegal unions, have a basis in the Bible, and they are the essential parts of the Law.[9]

In light of the deep chasm that separates the Bible and the literature of the sages, let us return to the question we started with: How do the sages define their enterprise in relation to the Bible? Do they attempt to present it as deriving from the Bible or as a separate and independent creation? Do they seek to camouflage the gaps, or acknowledge and define them, and what are the spiritual-cultural ramifications of their choice?

The Sources for Halakhah: Midrash and Transmission, Continuity and Change

As is well known, Tannaitic law is presented in two main genres: (1) the Mishnah and the Tosefta, worded as clear-cut halakhah, presented according to topical order, and completely detached from the biblical level; and (2) halakhic midrashim, which construct halakhot from the words of biblical verses and are organized according to biblical order. In some cases the very same laws are presented in different compositions within Tannaitic literature both as clear-cut determinations and as the outcome of the exegetical process of the written law. Yet, it is clear that these two genres, halakhah and Midrash, do not express world views that are divided with regard to the source from which halakhah is derived. Nevertheless, the very duplication of the Tannaitic literary system shows that the bodies of halakhah in general are perceived simultaneously as both an organized and independent collection that no longer needs its biblical roots, and detailed and dialectical interpretation that still clings to its lover, the Bible. In fact, in rabbinic literature the matter of which direction to choose is debated. Some see the primacy of continuity, and others believe that change must be recognized and admitted.

The main explanation voiced in support of the 'continuity position', that is, in favour of an interpretative process that sets forth, even artificially, a biblical verse as the source for a later halakhah, is authority. The early Mishnah refers to all areas of halakhah that do not have a source in the written law as laws that are 'hanging in the air'. Halakhot whose scope is very broad in relation to their biblical source are given the colourful metaphor of 'mountains suspended by a hair'. In the first metaphor, the biblical basis is presented as the grounding for the halakhah, whereas in the second metaphor, it is a hook on which halakhah is suspended. These descriptions plainly express the position that independent halakhot cannot exist on their own. Their *raison d'être* stems from the biblical foundation, which supports the full force of their weight. Or, in other words, *awareness of continuity is the key to the existence of a post-biblical halakhah and to its acceptance.* Several generations later, in the days of Rabbi Akiva's primacy, the connection to the written law is still perceived as the means for defending halakhah from being discarded or forgotten.

Thus we find the following discussion. R. Johanan ben Zakkai is concerned that a certain law pertaining to the transmission of impurity from one item to the next may be removed from the legal code because it lacks a biblical foundation. As a result, R. Akiva, his student, identifies such a foundation:

> On that day, R. Akiva expounded: 'And if any of those falls into an earthen vessel, everything inside it shall be unclean and [the vessel] itself you shall break' (Lev. 11.33; that is a vessel into which a dead insect (*sheretz*) has fallen, becomes unclean and makes whatever food is in it unclean.) It does not state '*tameh*' [is unclean] but '*yitma*', i.e. to make others unclean. (In other words, the fact that the word '*yitma*' and not '*tameh*' is written leads Rabbi Akiva to interpret the word '*yitma*' as if it is vowelized '*yitameh*' i.e. the food in the unclean vessel not only becomes unclean itself, but can also make other non-sacred foods unclean.) ... R. Joshua said: Who will remove the dust from thine eyes, R. Johanan ben Zakkai, since thou sayest that another generation is destined to pronounce clean a loaf which is unclean on the ground that there is no text in the Torah according to which it is unclean!? Is not R. Akiva thy pupil? He adduces a text in the Torah according to which it is unclean, viz. 'whatsoever is in it shall be unclean'.[10]

Rabbi Joshua is amazed at Rabbi Akiva's skill in anchoring the halakhah in the Bible. Even though he finds Rabbi Akiva's biblical basis far removed from the simple meaning of the text, Rabbi Joshua sees this homiletic creativity as a guarantee for the future existence of the halakhah. Now, the validity of Rabbi Akiva's move to create, seemingly out of thin air, biblical foundations for halakhic tradition is contested by R. Tarfon in a debate which took place dozens of years after the destruction of the Temple. The two argue about the suitability of priests with deformities to blow the trumpet while sacrifices are being made in the Temple. According to Rabbi Tarfon, a priest with a deformity, who is disqualified from performing the sacrifice itself, is nonetheless fit to sound the trumpet. In Rabbi Akiva's opinion, what holds true for sounding the trumpet holds true for performing the sacrifice, and a priest with a deformity is disqualified from playing the trumpet, just as he is from performing the sacrifice. Rabbi Akiva brings as proof a *gzerah shava* (analogy), a homiletic interpretation that he makes between one verse that deals with burnt offerings and another that deals with the sounding of trumpets. Rabbi Tarfon, in contrast, cites solid, factual proof. He remembers that in his childhood, when the Temple was still standing, he actually saw his uncle, a priest with blemishes, sound the trumpet. Here a homiletic interpretation of the verse is pitted against contradictory evidence about a halakhah that was actually practised in the Temple.

> Rabbi Tarfon said to R. Akiva: How long will Akiva continue to bring a confusion of words? I cannot tolerate it. I swear by my son that I saw Simon the brother of my mother who would tie something to his leg who would stand and sound trumpets! Akiva said to Tarfon: Rabbi, perchance it was in a *hakhel* that you so saw for those with blemishes are fit for *hakhel* and on Yom Kippur and at the Jubilee. Tarfon said to Akiva: Worship, which you did not fabricate! Happy are you, Akiva, since you are the issue of our forefather Abraham! Tarfon said and forgot, Akiva interpreted on the basis of his own thought and agrees to the halakhah! Anyone who separates himself from you it is as if he separates himself from his own life.[11]

Mincing no words, Rabbi Tarfon argues the preference for proof and tradition over homiletic interpretation. He swears on the lives of his children that his memory is reliable, and sees Rabbi Akiva's homiletic interpretations as a groundless and tiresome heap of arguments. In the end however, it becomes clear that human memory is fallible, and it is halakhic exegesis that shows the way to the truth of the Torah. Anyone who separates himself from Rabbi Akiva, the great originator of such homiletic exegesis, 'separates himself from his own life'.

In both of the foregoing narratives, Rabbi Akiva is lavishly praised for his homiletic interpretations which formulate halakhah from the Bible. In the first example, homiletic interpretation helps save a halakhah from being discarded or forgotten, and in the second instance it reveals the original, correct halakhah. Nonetheless, a careful reading shows that couched in the words of praise is a criticism of the method of halakhic Midrash. Initially, Rabbi Tarfon's statements express genuine fear regarding the independence of homiletic interpretation, which is liable to get in the way of tradition. Only when this fear is removed and it becomes clear that Rabbi Akiva's halakhic Midrash reveals or confirms an existing tradition can it be accepted and admired: 'R. Akiva interpreted the basis of his own thought and agrees with halakhah.' That is to say, according to both sources, what makes the art of creating a connection between the Bible and halakhah significant is precisely its ability to reinforce an ancient halakhah! The message conveyed by these and similar narratives is this: At first we are concerned about the highly imaginative and bold homiletical interpretations that Rabbi Akiva originates (*doresh mi-atzmo*), which could undermine halakhic tradition. However, thanks to his greatness, and possible divine inspiration as well, it repeatedly turns out that Rabbi Akiva's independent halakhic Midrashim coincide with the previously handed-down halakhic truth, confirming it and aiding in its preservation.

It is interesting to note, however, that the tension reflected in these two narratives overturns the dichotomy presented above. It is precisely the supposedly conservative attempt to ascribe halakhah to an earlier source – the Bible – thus endowing it with continuity, importance and authority, presented here as an independent, creative process ('interpreting on the basis of his own thought'), that could jeopardize tradition. In reality, it is the opposing outlook, which does not rely on biblical verses and in this way purportedly declares the independence and differentiation of halakhah, that represents conservatism and adherence to ancient tradition, which it is forbidden to change. If we return to the contemporary confrontation between the traditional 'perspective of continuity' and the modern 'acknowledgement of change', we see that the 'modern' value of freedom and creative independence is actually found in the world of the traditional 'continuity position', in the system of halakhic Midrash. This system, though obligated to show that it is grounded in the Bible, grants a tremendously broad exegetical space for the homiletic interpreter, and the external dependence is, in reality, what gives it internal freedom.

Recognition of the creative force of halakhic Midrash which lies behind the continuity position engenders, for some, a lowering of its status.

The halakhah was not known to the children of Bathera; for it once happened that the 14th (Nisan) occurred on a Sabbath, and they did not know whether the Passover sacrifices superseded the due observance of the Sabbath or not. They said: There is a man here that came from Babylonia called Hillel who had learned under the two greatest men of that generation, namely, Shemaiah and Abtalion; he would probably know if the Passover sacrifices supersede the Sabbath or not. He could be of use to us. They sent for him and asked him: Have you heard whether the Passover sacrifice supersedes the Sabbath? And he answered: Have we only one Passover sacrifice that supersedes the Sabbath every year? Are there not several sacrifices that supersede the Sabbath every year? (i.e. the continual daily offerings, which are offered twice on the Sabbath and the additional two sacrifices which are brought especially on the Sabbath) ... They responded: Indeed, we have already stated that you will be of use to us. And he (Hillel) then began to interpret for them using analogy, *a fortiori* reasoning, and analogous deduction ... But they said to him: Indeed, we have already questioned whether this Babylonian will be useful. The analogy that you pronounced may be refuted ... the *a fortiori* you said, may be refuted ... the analogous deduction you pro-nounced, a person can not make up an analogous deduction on his own ... Even though he would sit and interpret for them all day, they did not accept what he said, until he said to them: This is the tradition which I have received from my masters Shemaiah and Abtalion. When they heard this, they immediately placed him at their head and made him a prince. He (Hillel) then proceeded to criticize them saying: Who made you have recourse to this Babylonian? Was it not that you did not appropriately serve the two great masters Shemaiah and Abtalion, who dwelled among you?[12]

The people of Bathera turn to Hillel because he is the student of Shemaiah and Abtalion rather than on his own merits, as is obvious from their denigration of 'this Babylonian' 'who may be of use to us'. This is why they ask him if he has 'heard' about the halakhah in regard to the Passover sacrifices on the Sabbath, that is, if he has received a halakhah from his teachers Shemaiah and Abtalion about this tradition. Hillel does not answer this question but instead responds with homiletic interpretations of his own: analogy, *a fortiori* reasoning and analogous deduction. But the people of Bathera reject his halakhic Midrashim, since they believe that homily, unlike tradition, is subject to deliberation and can be disproved just as easily as proved. From their perspective, Hillel is only qualified to ascend to leadership when he conveys the halakhah via tradition in the name of his masters.

One of the most strongly worded criticisms of the use of Midrash to establish halakhah and make a determination is found in the words that Rabbi Ishmael uses to malign his colleague Rabbi Akiva, the classic representative of the midrashic method that ventures far afield from the *peshat* (simple meaning) of the verse. The two argue with regard to the form of death penalty to be used against the married daughter of a priest defiles herself through harlotry. At issue is whether the more stringent death penalty by fire is to be applied, similar to the law with regard to a betrothed daughter, or whether death by stoning is to be used. R. Ishmael argues that there is only an explicit obligation to resort to death by fire in the case of a betrothed woman, not a married one. Rabbi Akiva, in contrast, cites a midrashic reading of the biblical verse which supports expanding the ruling.

> R. Akiva replied: My brother, I interpret 'daughter' and 'and the daughter' etc. [Rabbi Akiva interprets the word '*u-bat*' in the above passage (Lev. 21.9) that deals with the daughter of a priest. Since it is written '*u-bat*' and not '*bat*', he infers, in keeping with his homiletical interpretive method, that the additional '*vav*' means that the law must be broadened to apply to a married daughter of a priest as well.] R. Ishmael said to him: Since you interpret 'daughter' and 'and the daughter' shall we except this woman [i.e. married women] and impose [the severer penalty of] death by fire?[13]

Here Rabbi Ishmael's question is a moral one. Should a person's fate by means of a harsher form of capital punishment hinge on the mere presence of an additional *vav*? The interpretative freedom embedded in Midrash requires, according to Rabbi Ishmael, the adoption of greater care and limitations, as the consequences may be severe.

Rabbi Ishmael rejects overly creative homiletic interpretations for fundamental-theoretical reasons and not just on practical halakhic grounds. The case of *sara'at* (mold disease of fabrics) in the Torah begins with the verse: 'When mold disease occurs in a fabric, either a wool or linen fabric' (Lev. 13.47). Rabbi Eliezer infers from the addition of the '*vav*' and the '*heh*' in the word '*ve-ha-beged*' (and the clothing) a whole series of halakhic extensions about the types of clothing to which the rule of *sara'at* of fabric applies, until Rabbi Ishmael's patience gives out: 'Rabbi Ishmael said to Rabbi Eliezer: You say to Scriptures: "Silence until I create a halakhic Midrash!" Rabbi Eliezer said to him: 'Ishmael, you are a 'mountain palm!'[14] Rabbi Ishmael's argument is a general one against all types of daring halakhic

Midrash. The attempt to tie the verse to the relevant halakhah deviates from the original intention of the written text. The *darshan* (homiletic interpreter) professes to be a commentator whose task it is to serve the needs of the written law; but in point of fact he forcibly silences the original biblical dictum and subordinates it to his own needs. No modern scholar, I believe, would be able to word more vehemently the attack against the traditional bet midrash's search for unification and harmony: 'You say to Scriptures: Silence until I create a halakhic Midrash!'

Rabbi Eliezer, however, does not take this lying down. If we equate Rabbi Ishmael's position with the modern point of view, Rabbi Eliezer's response may be considered in keeping with the postmodern spirit. He calls Rabbi Ishmael a 'mountain palm' – a palm tree that does not bear fruit. Rabbi Eliezer accuses Rabbi Ishmael of not 'bearing fruit'; in other words, the latter's refusal to compose more unrestrained midrashic interpretations makes him intellectually unproductive. The obvious tension emerging from this amusing discussion between the sages stems from the conflict between two fundamental and opposing principles: being faithful to the written text which is being interpreted, and being responsive to the internal creative force of the homiletic interpreter. Rabbi Eliezer openly prefers creativity to commitment. He may also firmly believe that such commitment does not exist: the halakhic *darshan* does not silence the primary voice of the written text, since it has no voice anyway! The verses are open and amenable to creative homiletic interpretation by the sages, and the *darshan* is under no obligation to be faithful to any voice other than his own and to the halakhah at hand.

In view of this insight, the sages' words with which we introduced this discussion, consigning all of the oral law to the handing down of the Torah at Mount Sinai, should perhaps be understood in the same light. They do not mean to imply that everything new conceived over time was already said at Mount Sinai, or that it constitutes the original interpretation given to the written law. On the contrary: the written law given at Mount Sinai is to be interpreted by succeeding generations, and from the outset its inherent meaning is subordinate to human creativity. In this sense, the authority of later interpretation derives from Sinai and, therefore, can be said to help shape the new simple meaning of the text, which is constantly being recreated over the generations.

Even though Rabbi Ishmael founds a midrashic school of his own, which utilizes creative techniques to support existing halakhah on the basis of biblical verses and distances itself from the simple meaning of the text, in these and similar stories he is presented as someone who prefers accepting the simple meaning of the Bible. In any case, this recognition demands acknowledgement of the separation of halakhah from the Bible or, in other words, awareness of the fact of change. Hence, it is not surprising that Rabbi Ishmael himself declares explicitly that in several matters, 'halakhah bypasses the Bible'.

> '[and his master shall pierce his ear] with an awl' (Exod. 21.6). I have but an awl [i.e. it is ostensibly permitted to pierce the ear of a slave who wishes to remain a slave, but only with an awl]. Wherefore even with a *sol* (=a sharpened piece of wood), or even a thorn, or a piece of glass? This teaches us: '*ve-ratza*' (and he pierced) [i.e. the additional '*vav*' makes it possible that other types of tools could have been used to pierce the ear], this is the opinion of Rabbi Akiva. Rabbi Ishmael said: In three places [halakhah] bypasses the Bible. The Torah states 'with an awl' and the halakhah states 'even with a *sol*, even with a thorn, or glass'.[15]

Both rabbis agree that the halakhah allows the use of other instruments besides an awl. Whereas Rabbi Akiva finds a way to interpret the halakhah expanding the variety of tools that can be used on the basis of the verse, thereby anchoring the halakhah in the Bible, Rabbi Ishmael chooses to separate between homiletic interpretation faithful to the original written text, on the one hand, and halakhic details absent of any biblical foundation, on the other.

Summary: Between Creator and Curator

It is common to attribute to the traditional religious world a tendency to harmonize between different and varying sources and thereby blur differences. The philosophical and scholarly research of the last two hundred years regard such a tendency as a naïve denial of the existence of the dynamics of renewal and change within Judaism's 3000-year-old religious–cultural heritage. The modern critical outlook seeks to unravel the bonds between the levels of tradition, interpret their essential meaning and reveal how they came into being. In essence, this dismantling effort seeks to undermine the religious aspiration toward union and fusion. Thus, when the modern religious person stands face to face with his spiritual heritage, he finds himself in an unavoidable conflict between satisfying his religious and intellectual drives. But this conflict is not new. The enterprise of the sages of the Mishnah and Talmud is drawn entirely from the empty spaces that developed over the ages between different layers of religious heritage: between the Bible and the Tannaitic world; between Tannaitic halakhot and halakhic interpretations of the Amoraim; between the words of the early Amoraim and the interpretations of those who followed them.

The present chapter, which focuses on the gap between the two formative building blocks of Jewish heritage – the Bible and the Tannaitic halakhah – attempts to reveal the presence of a similar tension between preserving continuity and acknowledging change in the religious consciousness of the Tannaim themselves. Aside from the very existence of these two types of Tannaitic literature, one which closely adheres to the Bible and another which distinguishes itself from it, we can look to the candid statements made by various sages regarding the attitude that should be taken toward the chasm between the world of the Bible and their own world. It is clear that the two approaches of unifying and separating exist side by side in the work of the sages. Oddly enough, the supposedly conservative approach, that seeks to camouflage what is being renewed and changed in the Tannaitic *oeuvre*, turns out to be the one that is, manifestly, the agent of creativity and change.

It seems that the choice faced by the sages of Israel during the first centuries CE is not so very far removed from the challenge facing contemporary Jews in confronting the heritage of our forebears. Two paths to our ancient inheritance with its multiple generations and levels are open to us, and neither is perfect. One is the traditional stance, which may be called, metaphorically, 'the path of halakhic Midrash'. Its appeal lies in the attempt to create one flowing and coherent meaning unifying the separate links through the participation and commitment of the student-homiletic interpreter. It is surprising that this seemingly conservative outlook, which is firmly planted within the boundaries of tradition and sees itself as a link in its chain, is the one that empowers human creativity and that enables ever-renewable senses of relevance, vitality and poetry. Nonetheless, this path has a price: the blurring of the distinctions between various phenomena and levels of creation, and the subordination of their original content to the most recent layers of tradition, or worse, to the emotional needs of the *darshan*. Those who tread this path declare to the sacred texts, day after day, subconsciously: 'Silence, until I have made my homiletic interpretation'. The other path is that of acknowledging change. It dismantles the structure and examines the essence of each source, every composition and every phenomenon. This is the ostensibly 'modern' academic outlook, which is surprisingly committed to the preservation of the primordial meaning of the sources, that is, to a type of conservatism. It turns out that, in contrast to expectations, it is precisely this outlook that is characterized by caution and stagnation. Through its ideological detachment and academic quality of preservation and restoration, it renounces its share in the creative process. It becomes a 'mountain palm tree', planted unwillingly among the well-preserved ruins of the bastion it has dismantled. In the struggle between the options of continuity and change we may be destined to choose between a vitality that contains a certain amount of academic distortion and a path of emasculated integrity, between the courage to innovate and the urge to scrutinize.

Notes

1 Leviticus Rabbah 22.1 (emphasis added).
2 See for example, Bava Metzia 38b and the name *harifei de Pumbedita* (the bright ones of Pumbedita) which appears in several places in the Babylonian Talmud; for a series of controversies between various *yeshivot* see, for example, Ketubbot 55a.
3 Tosefta Hagigah 2.9.
4 Jerusalem Talmud Hagigah 2.1 77d.
5 Jerusalem Talmud, Sanhedrin 4.2, 22a.
6 Avodah Zarah 58b.
7 Berakhot 8a.
8 Berakhot 3b–4a.
9 Mishnah Hagigah 1.8.
10 Mishnah Sotah 5.2.
11 Sifre Bamidbar 75.
12 Jerusalem Talmud, Pesahim 8.6, 33a.
13 Sanhedrin 51b.
14 Sifra Tazria, Parashat Nega'im, Ch. 13.
15 Jerusalem Talmud, Kiddushin 2.2, 59d.

FOUR   Judaism: Between Religion and Morality

Donniel Hartman

> Is that which is holy loved by the gods because it is holy, or is it
> holy because it is loved by the gods?

This question posed, by Socrates in the Platonic dialogue *Euthyphro*,
constitutes one of the central questions in religious life: is God, and by
implication are God's commandments, the source of that which is ethical, or
do ethical obligations exist independently of God's will? While posed by
Plato in theological terms, the question's significance for religious life lies
primarily not in the way the question impacts on people's understanding of
God, but rather in its implications for the way religious people conduct their
lives. The central issue is whether moral sentiments and considerations that
contradict religious life have any standing and authority for a person
committed to living according to the will of God. Is religious law the sole
source of morality and moral obligation, or are there moral voices and duties
that obligate one, independent of, and even in contradiction, to what is
written or perceived as the word of God?

The aim of this chapter is to explore the inner struggle within the
Jewish tradition around this question. This issue is far from theoretical and in
many ways how it is answered will determine the role religion in general,
and Judaism in particular will and ought to play in civilized society.
Modernity has redefined and reprioritized many of our core moral values.
New sensitivities and guidelines regarding the moral use of power, racial
equality, gender, freedom of conscience, pluralism, tolerance and the
attitude towards the 'other', to name but a few, seriously challenge
traditional religious moral codes and law. The extent to which religious law
feels compelled to both listen and accommodate moral criticism, which is
not founded on or motivated exclusively by its own internal legal traditions
and narrative will determine to what extent these moral values will be
assimilated within modern religious traditions. Where religion is the sole
determining factor in discerning the good and obligating moral behaviour,
contemporary morality is not only irrelevant, but ignoring its moral claims, a
religious duty and sign of piety. However, if religion itself is judged by its
affinity with moral standards that are independent of it, then the moral
obligations of the modern conscience and ethic are significant factors that
people of faith must both address and accommodate.

Were religious law truly capable of being encapsulated in the statement of Hillel, 'What is hateful unto you, do not do to your neighbour, this is the whole Torah and the rest is commentary; go study',[1] the need to preserve the independence of morality from religious law would be superfluous. However, the history of religion in general, and monotheism in particular, has shown how difficult it has been to maintain love of neighbour as the primary defining message. When murder in the name of God has been and continues to be defined by some as an expression of religious piety, the question of the relationship between religion and morality is central not only to religious life, but to the nature and future of the civilized world.

The theological motivation for maintaining the independence of God and religious life from being subjected to 'external' moral standards and judgment is clear. To assume a moral source and authority other than and over God is possibly to contradict the essence of the transcendence and oneness of God, and is in a certain sense akin to idolatry. The divine command need not be intelligible, because its scope and authority are not a function of its perceived affinity to human rationality. The consequence of this position for religious practice is that heeding God's command does not require any measure of personal identification, but only blind obedience. God's command is a kind of closure, a call to cease all ethical discussion and to demand of believers that they overcome *their* moral insights.

In the Jewish tradition, the most prominent exemplar of this view is the story of the binding of Isaac. This act, viewed by tradition as the pinnacle of Abraham's faith, is patently irrational, immoral and inexplicable.

> Sometime afterward, God put Abraham to the test. He said to him, 'Abraham', and he answered, 'Here I am.' And God said, 'Take your son, your favoured one, Isaac, whom you love, and go to the land of Moriah, and offer him there as a burnt offering on one of the heights which I will point out to you.' So early next morning, Abraham saddled his ass and took with him two of his servants and his son Isaac. He split the wood for the burnt offering, and he set out for the place of which God had told him.
> (Genesis 22.1–3)

Regardless of God's prior promises to Abraham that Isaac will inherit him, and the obvious immorality of the command, Abraham piously and possibly even zealously, obeys. He is not only willing to kill his son but, the biblical text states, 'so early next morning.' Abraham neither questions nor tarries. He runs to fulfil the will of God. In addition, precisely because of his faith, blind loyalty and obedience to this command, God rewards Abraham and recommits to their covenant.

> By myself I swear, the Lord declares: because you have done this

and have not withheld your son, your favoured one, I will bestow
my blessing upon you and make your descendents as numerous as
the stars of heaven and sands of the seashore, and your descendants
shall seize the gates of their foes. All the nations of the earth shall
bless themselves by your descendants, because you have obeyed
my command. (Genesis 22.16–18)

Signs of this religious approach permeate the Jewish tradition. From the
scripted and predetermined story of Abraham's descendants' enslavement in
Egypt and the manipulation of Pharaoh culminating in the Exodus drama,
to the story of Job, humanity is often portrayed as the unwilling participant
and even victim in a divine script which we can neither understand nor
question. As God admonishes Job: 'Who is this who darkens counsel,
speaking without knowledge?' (Job 38.2) or, 'Shall one who should be
disciplined complain against Shaddai?' (Job, 40.2). And Job, finally
understanding the duty of the person of faith, responds: 'See I am of
small worth: what can I answer you? I clap my hand to my mouth. I have
spoken once, and will not reply; twice, and will do so no more.' (Job,
40.4–5).

A powerful depiction of this view of the absolute divine authority and
independence over the moral universe is found in the book of
Deuteronomy, which depicts the drama between Moses and God regarding
the divine command that Israel wage war against Sihon the Amorite, king of
Heshbon. God commands:

Begin the occupation: engage him in battle. This day I begin to
put the dread and fear of you upon the people everywhere under
heaven, so that they shall tremble and quake because of you
whenever they hear you mentioned. (Deuteronomy, 2.24–25)

Despite the fact that Heshbon was not part of the Promised Land, God
wants Israel to fight this people, seemingly for public relations reasons so that
the fear of Israel will begin to spread. Moses, however, does not accept this
rationale and ignores God's command:

Then I sent messengers with an offer of peace, as follows, 'Let me
pass through your country. I will keep strictly to the highway,
turning off neither to the right nor to the left. What food I eat you
will supply for money, and what water I drink you will furnish for
money: just let me pass through ... That I may cross the Jordan
into the land that the Lord our God is giving to us.'
(Deuteronomy 2.26–29)

However, Moses' rebellion is not even deemed in the biblical narrative to be worthy of a response, and instead the story continues:

> But King Sihon of Heshbon refused to let us pass through, because the Lord stiffened his will and hardened his heart in order to deliver him into your power. (Deuteronomy 2.30)

The question of what wars Israel will and ought to fight lies solely within the domain of God's will. Humanity may attempt to intervene, but such intervention is destined to be both morally and functionally irrelevant.

A similar religious sentiment is echoed in the rabbinic portrayal of God's response to Moses' questioning of the justice behind Rabbi Akiva's torture and death at the hands of the Romans.

> Then said Moses, 'Lord of the Universe, thou hast shown me his [R. Akiva's] Torah, show me his reward.' 'Turn thee round', said he; and Moses turned round and saw them weighing out his flesh in the market-stalls. 'Lord of the Universe', cried Moses, 'such Torah and such a reward!' He replied, 'Be silent, for such is my decree.'[2]

God's actions and laws are not to be questioned nor judged. The appropriate response of a person of faith is silence and then obedience.

The behaviour of Abraham and the above responses of God to Moses are not posited as extreme and exceptional, but rather serve for some as a paradigm for normative religious piety and everyday acts of worship. Each performance of a commandment, in this view, is a miniature trial, an *akeida*. in which the faithful are challenged to overcome their inclinations, desires and principles in the service of God.

> R. Elazar b. Azarya said: 'From where do we know that a person should not say, "I have no desire to wear *shatnez*, I have no desire to eat the meat of pigs, I have no desire to engage in adultery", but rather, "I do so desire, but what can I do, my father in heaven has so ordered me." It therefore states, "I have set you apart from other people to be mine" (Lev. 20.26), once a person distances themselves from sin, they accept upon themselves the kingship (authority) of heaven.'[3]

According to this tradition, the search for rational foundations and purpose for the commandments is also rejected, for such an effort presupposes that God and humans share a common rationality and standard of the good. Consequently, one finds in the Talmud the position that condemns the associating of rational and moral purposes to the commandments.

One who says 'As far as the nest of a bird do thy mercies reach ... must be silenced.[4]

The Talmud explains the reason for this prohibition.

Because he presents the measures taken by the Holy One, Blessed-be-He, as springing from compassion, whereas they are but decrees.[5]

This person perceives the biblical commandment to send away the mother before taking her offspring as an expression of God's mercy. Such a person errs since God's commandments cannot be explained in relation to human values. Rather, they are decrees of the King to be obeyed and pursued regardless of human principles and values. Thus Rashi in his commentary on the Talmud explains:

God did not give the commandments for the purpose of mercy but rather in order to impose on Israel the rule of his decrees so it will be manifest that they are his servants and keepers of his commandments who follow his decrees even in matters that Satan and the heathens can be critical of and argue that there is no reason in following such a commandment.[6]

Religious piety is judged by a person's ability to dissociate from their moral and intellectual commitments and make the leap of faith to serve God. Shimshon Rafael Hirsch, the leader of German Orthodoxy in the middle and latter part of the nineteenth century, articulates the adoption of this religious position as the central decision facing a person of faith. Explaining the reason for naming the tree of knowledge of good and evil, S. R. Hirsch states as follows:

But rather the tree of knowledge of good and evil, was so designated ... as the tree by which the decision of the knowledge of good and evil was made, through which man would decide how he wished to recognize what was good or bad. There is only one condition for the earth to be able to form a paradise for us, and the condition is this, that we call *that* good, which God stamps as being good, and bad, which he declares as such. But not that we leave the decision between good and bad to our senses. If we place ourselves under the dictate of our sense, the gates of paradise are closed to us and only by the long way round can man regain admittance thereto ...The tree, accordingly, was constantly to remind him of the teaching on which the realization of the whole purity and height of his calling depends ...The teaching that man is to recognize what is good and bad, not by the judgment of his senses or his own mind, but by accepting the will of God when it has been revealed to him, and that he must take such judgment of God as the one guide he is to follow, if he wishes to fulfil his mission on earth and remain worthy for the world to be paradise for him.[7]

Redemption for humanity is only attainable to the extent that humans are willing to accept that the sole determining factor in ascertaining the good is the expressed will of God. Even when all of the humanly discernable evidence points in the opposite direction, the duty of the person of faith is to follow what God determines to be the good.

While the position outlined above has a significant place in Jewish thought, it is but one voice. In the remainder of this chapter, our aim is to outline a different religious sensibility within Judaism, one which views religious individuals as members of a moral community that counts God among its members, and as people who are obligated to examine, and if necessary, criticize God's command. To paraphrase S. R. Hirsch, it is a position that views a religious system that is immune to outside moral review, as one that cannot create paradise on earth, nor guarantee its advocates paradise after life, no matter how noble or self-sacrificing their death. Quite to the contrary; on this view, only a religious system that allows for the correcting mechanism of external moral review can serve as a constructive partner in the civilized moral universe.

The paradigmatic text for this position in the Jewish tradition is Genesis 18, which depicts the dialogue between God and Abraham regarding the justice of God's destroying the whole city of Sodom. When God informs Abraham of his decision and asks for his comments, Abraham does not pause or even question. He stands in defiant criticism of God's decision and states:

> Will you sweep away the innocent along with the guilty? What if there should be fifty innocent within the city; will you wipe out the place and not forgive it for the sake of the innocent fifty who are in it? Far be it from you to do such a thing, to bring death upon the innocent as well the guilty, so that innocent and guilty fare alike. Far be it from you. Shall not the judge of the whole earth deal justly? (Genesis 18.23–25)

In this dialogue between God and Abraham, both God and Abraham view divine will as morally transparent and subject to moral standards discernable by Abraham. In contrast to the position put forth in the story of the *akeida* or by S. R. Hirsch, God's command does not determine the good and does not necessitate blind obedience. For Abraham, he is invited to challenge God for the good is something that God must also comply with: 'shall not the judge of the whole earth deal justly?' The content of 'justly' is one that exists independently of the explicit will of God, and is something to which humanity has access and is obligated by.

This challenging by Abraham is not tantamount to moving outside of the religious system. The issue is not one of dual loyalty. When Abraham argues, 'far be it from you, shall not the judge of the whole earth deal justly', he is arguing that God is not God when God contradicts the good. When religious law violates moral principles, the problem is not one of mere authority, but rather an internal religious dilemma, whereby the religion is articulating and obligating that which is not worthy. The impetus for external moral criticism is a religious one whereby, through this criticism, religion will succeed in exemplifying that for which it ought to yearn.

Evidence of this religious spirit permeates Jewish thought and law. In the Jerusalem Talmud the following discussion between Shimon b. Shatah and his students is recorded:

> Shimon b. Shatah traded in cotton. His students said to him: 'Master, allow us to buy you a donkey so that you will not have to labour so much! They went and bought him a donkey from a certain non-Jew, and found upon it a precious stone. They came and told him: Now you need not labour ever again.' Said he: 'Why so?' They replied: 'We bought you a donkey from a certain non-Jew, and found upon it a precious stone.' He asked: 'Does he know of it?' They replied: 'No.' He told them: 'Go and return it.' 'But (they responded) did not Rav Huna Bivi b. Gozlon say, quoting Rav: It was stated in the presence of Rabbi, even according to the view that stealing from a heathen is forbidden, appropriating his lost property is permitted.' (He responded): 'What, do you think Shimon b. Shatah is a barbarian?'[8]

Regardless of whether Jewish law permits one to keep the lost property of a non-Jew, Shimon b. Shatah assumed that he was bound by a moral code that exists independently of this law. The source for his moral obligation is not the law, but rather his moral conscious. Echoing Abraham, he was not prepared to hide behind the law (or the word of God) to sanction that which he defined as unjust. According to Shimon b. Shatah, one could be a barbarian within the realm of the law, and he saw it as his duty to live by a higher moral standard. Consequently, instead of viewing the precious stone as a reward from God for his piety, his piety made it self-evident to him that his own moral compass had to guide his behaviour.

Following a similar belief, the rabbis rewrite the conclusion of God's response to Moses regarding the war with Heshbon mentioned above. Instead of God ignoring Moses and manipulating the free will of King Sihon of Heshbon, thus forcing upon both sides a war that neither wanted, the rabbis give a new ending to the biblical narrative. According to their new reading, God changed his mind and admitted that Moses was right.

> God replied: 'By your life. I will cancel my opinion (lit. words) and follow yours, as it states (later on in Deuteronomy 20.10) 'when you approach a town to attack it, you shall offer it terms of peace.'[9]

Moses' offering of peace prior to engaging in battle is not only not sidestepped by God, but leads God to change his ruling. 'By your life. I will cancel my opinion', and becomes the new legal paradigm for morality of war.

Throughout Jewish legal discussions, one finds a similar religious sensibility. As Sagi and Statman point out, in the Talmud one finds the widespread saying: 'Why do I need a verse (to validate this position)? Is it based on reason (*sevarah*)?'[10] (See, for instance, BT Tractate Ketubot 22a). When human reason can substantiate a certain legal position, the rabbis argue, there are no grounds for using a biblical verse to do the same. Yet this position is religiously unfounded from the perspective of the view that moral truth and obligation depend on God's will. Could a *sevarah* make God's command redundant? On the contrary: it is the *sevarah* that is religiously and legally superfluous. The Talmud here, however, is actually puzzled by the opposite possibility; it wonders why God would command something that human knowledge could conclude by itself. A conclusion attained through human knowledge is just as valid as a divine command.

This use of human reason as a source for law permeates rabbinic literature. Thus, for example, when the rabbis rule that the preservation of life, while superseding all the commandments, does not supersede the prohibition against murder, they do not base their ruling on a biblical source, but rather on a moral argument based on human reason.

> One came before Raba and said to him: 'The governor of my town has ordered me: go and kill so and so; if not, I will slay you. What shall I do?' He answered him: 'let him rather slay you than that you should commit murder; who knows that your blood is redder? Perhaps his blood is redder.'[11]

No hierarchy exists or is even conceivable that would allow the murder of one human being for the purpose of protecting another. The *sevarah* that you must not commit murder even in order to save life requires no justification, and no theological reflection can call it into question. The trust that halakhah places in the power of moral reasoning emerges in this matter in the clearest possible way: the moral truth that no life is preferable to another enjoys a self-evident halakhic status.

In mediaeval Jewish philosophy, the autonomy of morality appears in the distinction between *mitzvot shimiy'ot*, heavenly commandments, and *mitzvot sikhliyyot*, rational commandments. *Mitzvot sikhliyyot* define a category of rational commandments which, according to a Talmudic statement, humans will pursue even without being commanded. Saadya Gaon, who developed the distinction between rational and non-rational commandments, was even bothered by the question of why we need revelation at all when it touches the ethical domain; after all, we would be obligated to follow such norms even without an explicit revelation.

Similarly, Maimonides limits the above-quoted source from the Sifra that argues that the impetus for religious behaviour should be solely the fact that it is so decreed by God. According to Maimonides, this statement only applies to religious law that has no rational foundation, and which, if it were not for Jewish law, would not be a duty at all. However, those commandments which he classifies under the category of those which 'if they were not commanded, by law they should have been commanded' (BT Tractate Yoma 67b), that is, commandments which have a rational and moral foundation, the impetus for the duty ought not to be the divine command but the rather pious person's aspiration for human perfection.[12]

Nahmanides, the great commentator on the Torah, follows suit, and makes the following point. If all obligations stem exclusively from the explicit expression of God's will, this implies that there is no obligation prior to revelation. Yet, according to the biblical tradition, the world was destroyed by God in the flood because of the corrupt moral behaviour of that generation even prior to receiving instruction regarding this type of behaviour. Nahmanides draws from it an important lesson and states:

> The prohibitions against theft and corruption are rational norms. Their grounding does not need a prophet to declare them as God's will.[13]

Human reason has the power to not only generate ethical obligations independent of revelation, but can also generate religious duty. According to Nahmanides, humanity, in failing to live up to that which they knew to be morally required, sinned as well in the eyes of God, and it is this sin that religiously condemned them and warranted God's response of the flood.

> Is that which is holy loved by the gods because it is holy, or is it holy because it is loved by the gods?

In Judaism, there is no definitive answer. Two different schools of thought and religious sensibilities debate this question from biblical to modern times.

Regardless of how critical one believes it is for religion to have an external moral critic, an Abraham who is ever watching and demanding that the judge of the whole earth deal justly, there is a counter religious voice which religious systems and people have difficulty ignoring. That voice, growing from the deepest core of faith in one God, sees a measure of incongruity if not arrogance in assuming to know something better than God. The decision to believe in and live a life in relationship with the one God seems to many to demand a measure of relinquishing of one's own sense of self and choosing to live under the guidance of One who knows, the One who is true, the One who is just. To either assume to know better or to assume to morally instruct is to perceive oneself as superior to this God, an assumption that is tantamount to idolatry.

The diversity of opinions present in the Jewish tradition on this issue reflects two very distinct and often incompatible religious instincts. We tread on superficial ground when we attempt to discount either the validity or religious sensitivity of either. In many ways, this may be deepest intent of the Bible when it has Abraham embody both. There is the Abraham of Genesis 18 and the Abraham of Genesis 22. They are both present, both equally representative of the will of God.

The presence of both positions, however, has profound practical implications. As stated above, this debate is not merely a theoretical, theological one regarding the nature of divinity, but an issue which determines the direction and meaning of religious life. Each approach not only reflects a different religious sensibility, but also generates different moral responses. How religion will respond to the moral challenges of modernity will be determined in no small measure on which Abraham personifies one's religious ideal.

Will monotheism in general, and Judaism in particular be a force for good, is thus not a question which is easily and definitively answered. It will depend on which vision of religious piety prevails. At the end, the question is less about the nature of Judaism, since both voices are present, but rather a question of education. Here we face a seminal challenge. Unfortunately, while the tradition is ambiguous, religious education or education about religion is more often than not monolithic. It advocates intellectual and moral submissiveness as the sole legitimate expression of serious faith. The Abraham of Genesis 22 is extolled as the model for emulation, while the Abraham of Genesis 18 is ignored or reinterpreted into religious insignificance.

Genesis 22 is a permanent feature of religious life. A life of faith will and must always entail some measure of silence, a measure of submission to the will of God. It cannot, however, be allowed to be the exclusive voice. There is a profound need to educate towards the religious vitality and legitimacy of Genesis 18 as well. Individuals must know that a moral conscience is not the enemy of faith but its greatest ally. They must be taught that religious piety is also expressed in the willingness to stand up and morally criticize one's tradition. They must be taught that a commitment to tradition can also lead one to endeavour to ensure that one's tradition represents the best and noblest of moral principles, and consequently employ legal and interpretative measures to ensure the assimilation of these principles into Judaism.

There is no simple and patent answer as to how one is to balance Genesis 18 and 22. There is no doubt that in certain instances such a balance is impossible. It is then that the religious person must make their most critical choice. Our responsibility is to ensure that the choice is not portrayed as a choice between faith and secularism, but rather as a choice between two Jewish approaches to religious piety and faith in God.

Notes

1 BT Tractate Shabbat 31a.
2 BT Tractate Menahot 29b.
3 Sifra, Kedoshim 10.
4 Mishnah Berakhot 5.3.
5 BT Tractate Berakhot 33b.
6 Rashi, Tractate Berakhot 33b 'Midotav'.
7 S. R. Hirsch, *Commentary on the Torah*, Genesis 2.9.
8 JT Tractate Baba Metzia 8c.
9 Midrash Rabbah, Bamidbar Parshah 19.13.
10 See Sagi, Avi and Statman, Daniel, *Religion and Morality* (1995).
11 BT Tractate Sanhedrin 74a.
12 See Maimonides, *Eight Chapters*, Chapter 6.
13 Nahmanides, *Commentary on the Torah*, Genesis 6.13.

FIVE

Traditional Judaism and the Feminist
Challenge

Chana Safrai

The encounter between Judaism and the feminist world view began as early
as the eighteenth century, at the start of the *Haskala* (Enlightenment)
movement, when the Jewish world and its cultural tradition first encoun-
tered Western culture in Europe. However, only in the latter half of the
twentieth century did the feminist movement begin to clearly delineate its
demands on society and construct a complete world view that existed apart
from the general cultural past, staking out a clear position against the Jewish
cultural world and defiantly challenging its foundations. If we wish to assess
the possible contribution of the feminist movement to the Jewish cultural
world, it is incumbent on us to first appraise the existing encounter on either
side, by first examining the fundamental points of friction between the two
cultures, and then asking where and why Jewish feminist women are
negatively affected in their cultural world. Finally, we must search for
possible ways to build a Jewish world that divides its attention between the
two systems and responds to both of them.

The world of feminist thought posits the principle of equality as an
ethical basis for society. Any show of partiality on the basis of gender is
invalidated from the very start by this world view, which runs counter to
broad cultural norms and attempts to repair legal and social structures so that
they will be closer to the feminist vision. Moreover, social structures that are
contradictory to the supreme value of equality between the sexes, or at least
equal opportunity, are judged to be invalid and unethical, and are therefore
bound for change or elimination. There is no room in feminism for
anything but this basic insight, which is intended to encompass the whole
universe and become an ethical super-value, a constitutional law that cannot
be abolished or compromised. It is the criterion by which every system and
every event is judged.

The world of Jewish thought also stakes a claim to absolute and eternal
truth, which is considered not only ethical at its core, but also sanctified by
heaven and the realm of the Blessed-be-He. The trouble for feminists is that
from the start, Jewish culture posits a clear gender-based hierarchical
structure. This postulate was formulated over many generations for social,
legal and religious structures, and considers itself to be divine in nature. The
Blessed-be-He cannot be other than a masculine image, and therefore the

traditional religious world is directed at Jewish men, obligating them and including them. Study, law, a significant number of *mitzvot* (divine commandments), and prayer are all first and foremost the domain of Jewish men.

Even if it were possible to discover the place of women in some of the literature, though a certain burden of *mitzvah* observance is placed on them and with it they are given a share of holiness, the structure still remains hierarchical, and the place of women on the social and religious ladder is still subject to the male leadership. But because every change is deemed *a priori* an attempt to tamper with the laws of holiness, and would not be recognized in the world of the Blessed-be-He and his Torah, the traditional Jewish cultural world feels no need to listen to new or renewing insights and instead claims for itself the absolute truth, the absolute morality, and most of all, the absolute burden of holiness, which precedes and overshadows any secondary claim, ethical or moral. Before us, then, are two cultures with conflicting social perspectives but with an identical claim to totality. Both, as they understand themselves at their best, are incapable of change, and instead they each negate the other on principle.

What is more, the issue of hierarchy, which is sanctified but also gender-related, influences the encounter between feminist and Jewish perspectives on two basic levels: the leadership and its decision-making process, and the quintessential gender-based culture and its character. One of the main demands of the feminist world view is equality before the law and equality of opportunities in the framework of society, its customs and laws. The feminist movement is internally divided on the issue of how to actually realize these goals, but everyone is in complete agreement that women are entitled to benefit from the rights that modern society grants to its members; that women must be partners in the world in which they live and benefit from the resources allocated to society; and that they must be allowed to contribute their fair share to social development. The debate between various feminist groups and between the generations and stages of awareness of the movement in general is not over the principle but rather over how to achieve it. It is clear that this principle requires that women penetrate the legal and social power centres, whereby they can make their voices heard and clearly articulate their needs. Taking this step requires a complex process of give and take, a process in which quite a few changes are taking place. Definition of the goals has progressed through several different stages, and it now sees itself as a continuing process.

The application of a world view of this sort in the framework of the Jewish cultural world comes up against stubborn opposition from several distinct sources.

Tradition

A tradition that posits sanctified fixation has a hard time welcoming any changes, but progressive changes are particularly difficult. It is easier for the traditionalist individual to be flippant about contrary experiences and to argue that there is no need to contend with them, as any change can *a priori* be considered ephemeral.

Halakhah

The voice of halakhah (Jewish law) and culture is the voice of its sages and rabbis. It is a decidedly masculine voice, which, as already stated, is aimed at men, who are bound by halakhah and its corollaries. The demand to listen to the needs of women is a contradiction in terms for the 'perfect' and sanctified world of halakhah. It is not only a mix of secular and holy, but a mix of wholly different species. The mere demand is conceived of as an attempt to inject alien considerations into the seemingly absolute halakhic consideration, potentially disrupting entirely the order of halakhah and tradition.

Written and Oral Torah

The tradition and authority of halakhah derive from and depend on two fundamental sources: the Blessed-be-He and his Torah (written law), and the sages and their Torah (oral law). This process, in the traditional understanding, is that part of the Torah was given to Moses at Sinai, and was passed down to wise men who studied the Torah. This is the tradition of the sages – men who see themselves as part of a scheme that originated in heaven, who benefit from the original authority of Moses at Sinai. The conventions developed by the sages in prayer and halakhah are binding by virtue of this fundamental authority. In this world view, there is no justification for another voice. The feminist demand to appoint female rabbis, rabbinical judges, arbiters of halakhah, instructors of Torah, and composers of literature is seemingly in absolute contradiction to the principles that lie at the foundation of this perspective. The fundamental feminist claim that the male world gained control over and created these traditional frameworks falls on deaf ears. It seems that there is no encounter or dialogue between the two basic trends.

Furthermore, aside from the political issue of leadership and authority in halakhah, there is the question of the cultural content and means of its expression. The feminist movement charges that the masculine cultural world and the exclusion of women from decision-making and management positions have created a culture that only reconfirms the status of men in the social world: whatever is masculine is relevant and whatever is relevant is masculine. Culture and humanness are masculine, whereas the feminine is the Other, if not the barbaric. Subjects that women find significant do not warrant recognition of status or esteem, and if and when they are recognized by society, such recognition always comes at the expense of their feminine essence.

The world of values in Western society is undergoing immense change. Media, literature, scholarship and religion have all been infused by new concepts, new subjects, and the shifting of key issues in every realm due to a partial but growing response to demands made by women, minorities and children. In the encounter with Jewish culture and its religious tradition, this is an especially discordant demand.

In addition, the language in which the Jewish culture is expressed is a language of masculine character and content. Not only is God himself portrayed as a masculine figure; every expression of commandment in the Torah and halakhic literature and even in the Hebrew language itself, is framed in the masculine gender-form. Though in the Hebrew language the neuter is phrased in the masculine form, the tradition and culture tend to prefer the gendered masculine meaning in their interpretations of the biblical message. Thus 'and you shall teach them to your sons' – the commandment to study Torah in the name of God – becomes a cultural obligation of men, and not of women. This is a tradition that posits that its culture is designated by heaven to men, and only men. The feminist movement argues that a culture must give expression to both sexes, it must not be gender-biased, since then only the men would be reflected and identify with it. The Jewish cultural tradition flaunts its sanctified manifestation, and does not sense in the least the distress of Jewish women. In fact, the tradition has succeeded to a large extent in convincing Jewish women that this stance is proper and justified, such that the feminist encounter with traditional Jewish culture not only falls on the deaf ears of rabbis, but of their wives as well.

In the second part of this chapter, I will attempt to ascertain where it is that women with a feminist consciousness encounter the incapacity of Jewish culture to meet their needs. There are, I suggest, five main, familiar points of friction: Torah study, religious court, personal status, *mitzvah* observance, and the synagogue. Yet it should also be noted that the global Jewish society is not uniform, and that the feminist issue is trickling into various communities and countries in different doses. At present, at the start of the twenty-first century, these issues are familiar to everyone, but not every issue is of equal importance in each place, and even more importantly, some have already found their resolution to one degree or another, at least in some Jewish societies.

It is precisely this variety of existing solutions, as well as the high volume of debates, that dictates some of the suggestions made in the next part of this chapter. For that reason, it is difficult to organize the material in any coherent order, and the given sequence does not represent a chronological or otherwise inherent logic but rather reflects the personal interests and inclinations of the author. Any other sequence could serve as well.

Torah Study

In a society in which learning is the central defining component of identity, the exclusion of women from the obligation to study Torah constitutes not only denial of information, power and leadership, but an outright dismissal of their Jewish social identity. There is not a single individual with a feminist consciousness who does not shudder at the statement of Rabbi Eliezer – 'Whoever teaches his daughter Torah is considered as if he taught her licentiousness'[1] – which serves as a proof-text for the exclusion of women from Jewish culture and knowledge. By keeping women away from this primary resource, they are left lacking the skills needed for essential Jewish experiences, leaving them rootless, culturally meagre, and at the mercy of male commentators.

At the same time, it should be stressed that this important question has already found a partial solution. We are witnessing the establishment of dozens of institutions engaged in making Jewish studies accessible to women, in a variety of shades and styles. Although the majority of these schools are not feminist in nature, in actuality they are performing a decidedly feminist act by providing thousands of women with the opportunity to make Torah study an important part of their lives. And, wonder of wonders, the traditional establishment has not only embraced this religious option, but has made it a substantial part of the lifestyle of the twentieth-century religious woman. Women who learn may be found in every Jewish society, and for several years they have also been teaching, writing, publishing, and becoming part of the general array of compulsory Jewish studies.

The question remains: Will this development make a genuine change in women's status in the traditional social order, or will the male authority find the means to halt their access to other parts of Jewish life? Will these female leaders become Jewish leaders? Will they become arbiters and administrators of the world of culture and halakhah? Will their personal status change as well? Will a Torah be written that will be conscious of the women who study it? Is the Torah capable of being read as a sensitive text suited to feminist consciousness? The evidence from the various Jewish denominations which are engaged in the process for the last century is not as yet conclusive.

The Bet Din *(Religious Court)*

We have already mentioned the absence of women from the leadership and the rabbinate in traditional communities. But another major point of friction is the absence of women as *dayanot* (judges in religious courts) or as witnesses. Similarly, women are absent from the handing down of court verdicts and related proceedings, and the shaping of the law. The status of women – or shall we say the lack of status of women – when it comes to legal pleading in cases of divorce, inheritance and other family matters, as formulated in the traditional Jewish law, constitutes a recurrent source of harm to what are defined as basic human rights.

The Jewish laws of marriage, divorce and inheritance are not egalitarian, and the Bet Din is an exclusively male province, in which the *dayanim* sanctify the traditionalist law. Rabbis and *dayanim* do not understand that the prohibition on women serving as witnesses in Batei Din is not acceptable to the feminist world view. The latter does not view this as protecting the honour or importance of women, or as aid to women, lest their joyous spirit be dampened by the misfortunes and troubles of life. Rather, feminists see this as an injury to their status as human beings responsible for the world in which they live. Feminism assumes an obligation to hold itself responsible for the justice of men and women alike, and a Bet Din of men excludes women from the world of justice. At the same time, it leaves tens of thousands of women stranded as *agunot* ('chained women' whose husbands refuse to grant them a halakhic divorce). Essentially, every encounter with the rabbinical court causes a serious affront to the basic feminist consciousness.

Furthermore, complex Jewish communities tend to compromise and accept in issues of marriage and divorce the standards set by the more conservative denominations. The call for Jewish unity or Jewish social identity is gained quite often at the cost of the feminist values.

Personal Status

A differentiation between the status of men and women is an obvious offence to the feminist world view, but constitutes a basic notion in the halakhic world view. Thus Chapter 1 of Tractate Kiddushin opens with the words: 'A woman is acquired in three ways', whereas Chapter 2 of the same Tractate begins with words 'The man enters marriage'. Herein is the basic calculus of personal status: feminine passivity versus masculine activism.

Similarly, today's marriage ceremonies continue to define the bond between man and woman in a Jewish legal framework in terms of property. The couple enters a hierarchical relationship of dependence between man and woman.

All Jewish denominations have made an attempt, each in its own community, to regulate new terms and conditions for this basic offensive social construct. None have solved the complexity of these notions within the Jewish traditions as yet. All are struggling with large numbers of women awaiting their divorce papers (*Get*), due to the fact that women have a lower legal status and a passive role within the system.

Positive Time-Bound Commandments

A different aspect of personal status relates to the ceremonies of religious Jewish identity. The halakhic tradition does not compel women to observe time-dependent *mitzvot* because, as the argument goes, they do not possess their own time: a daughter or wife is not considered an autonomous entity, and her time is subordinate to the will of the primary man or leader in her private world. When she has neither the time nor the authority to decide for herself on her religious and individual dealings, she is torn between two opposing worlds of values.

Thus the Jewish system renders the hierarchical personal status mentioned above to a regulator of religious life. But the *mitzvot*, and particularly the ceremonial *mitzvot*, are not only part of a religious system but also part of the Jewish lifestyle and identity. With every religious ceremony and blessing first and foremost an obligation on the male, women are pushed again and again to the margins of dynamic Jewish life.

The Synagogue

If minimizing *mitzvah* observance is a blueprint for religious alienation, then minimizing activity in the synagogue is tantamount to repression from Jewish social life and worship. The synagogue is the quintessential public religious creation in the world of Torah – itself the observance of a commandment given by the sages, not God – the expression of the believing Jewish person. However, it is not a 'person' of whom we are speaking, but a 'man'.

The synagogue is the place where the deep connection and meaning between a person and God takes place. But its doors are barred to women. The greatest success of the synagogue, conceptually, is the sense that it is the very centre of Jewish identity worldwide. But a Jewish woman's desire to play a role in this holy place is deemed religious pretentiousness, immodesty and personal conceit, and is met with organized and official derision. In the very place where men experience profound religious elation, women are exempt and often even forbidden. Direct contact with the Torah, either through dancing with it or reading it, the fervour of public prayer and its introduction, and the symbolic connection through the *tefillin* and the *tallit* long ago became archetypical symbols for Jewish religiosity, but all of them are accessible only to men, and hence become a source of suffering and alienation for the women of the Jewish people.

Many Jewish communities are opting for female participation in many of the synagogue activities. It is one of the major sites of change in the last decades. Leaders of all denominations are busy looking for solutions or rejecting them vehemently, all reactions and suggestions no doubt reflecting the pressure from involved feminist Jewish women.

It comes as no surprise that feminism is defined by many upstanding rabbis as an enemy at the gate. And the more that the feminist movement assumes a place for itself in the cultural discourse, the more it is rejected and invalidated in the traditional Jewish discourse. But in my estimation, traditional Judaism has the power to blend with and absorb itself into the social values and sensitivity that the feminist movement represents, and presumably come out rewarded by it. In this section, I shall first discuss the possibilities of a meaningful encounter between feminism and Judaism, then define or classify the fundamental needs required for contending with this major challenge.

In their time, the sages of the oral law (both the Tannaim and Amoraim) consciously fashioned a halakhic and ideological world based on an ancient human feeling that the Torah had to contend with its believers. This dynamic created an old/new world of Torah in which the need for social change and development was recognized alongside a deep commitment to tradition and halakhah.

The sages asserted that God is revealed in different forms to different people at different times:

> Rabbi Levi said: 'In many images they saw him, as someone standing and as someone sitting, as a young man and as an old man. How is this so? When the Blessed-be-He was revealed at the Red Sea to conduct his sons' war and to repay the Egyptians, he looked to them as no more than a young man, since it is only fitting that war be made by a young man, as it says "The Lord is a man of war, the Lord is his name" (Exod. 15.3), and when the Blessed-be-He was revealed on Mount Sinai to give the Torah to Israel, he looked to them like an old man, since it is only fitting that the Torah come from the mouth of an old man (rabbi, sage).'[2]

In other words, human experience dictates the religious sensation, which in turn expresses the human need in godly terms. If to the sages who studied Torah God was depicted as old and wise, then for believing women He will presumably come across as a female being. There is an age-old tradition in the Midrash for the numerous names by which God can be called, preserving both his uniqueness and unity. According to this tradition, new characteristics and other emphases do not pose a risk to his honour, but only enhance the joy of faith, and enlarge the circle of believers. In this spirit, the addition of female names and characteristics should become a natural part within this long tradition, however much opposition it engenders. And along the same lines, the voices of women, along with their worlds of images, their liturgical needs, new ways of singing, praising or expressing belief are not invalid, but can actually become a creative and renewing part of the essence of belief.

A very intricate and complex tradition wrestles with the question of the creation and the workings of the world of the Blessed-be-He. This tradition claims that the existing world is the product of repeated attempts by God to establish the world as we know it, the creation that we ourselves see:

> Rabbi Abahu said: 'How do we know that the Blessed-be-He would create worlds and destroy them until he created this one?' He said: 'I am fond of this one; I am not fond of the previous ones I created.' Rabbi Pinhas said: 'The reason offered by Rabbi Abahu "And God saw everything that He had made, and, behold, it was very good" (Gen. 1.31), I am fond of this one; I am not fond of the previous ones I created.'[3]

In this context, Rabbi Pinhas adds an important additional layer of understanding: 'And Rabbi Pinhas said: "God" (E-L) is your father Israel, just as the Blessed-be-He creates worlds, so too does your father create worlds, just as the Blessed-be-He allocates worlds, so too does your father allocate/destroy worlds'.[4] In other words, the world is not perfect and has to undergo many transformations, first and foremost by God the Creator, and, in his wake, Israel. Israel must emulate the divine act of creating worlds which must then be divided and reorganized. The words contain both an invitation to appraise the quality of God and an obligation to make sure that the world will exist as, and will remain, 'very good'.

It follows that the Amoraim (Talmudic-era scholars) are concerned neither with new creation, nor by change or subdivision, in the same way that they are unconcerned about the influence of the existing world on its own renewal. But on the contrary, the act of renewal via creations is the godly act at its finest. And the human being, or Israel, at any rate, is called upon to take part in this renewal. This is how Rabbi Pinhas understands the substance of the call, 'Hear, O Israel'. In other words, recognition of God's uniqueness is also recognition that there is room for change and upheaval in the world, that radical change in Heaven's name is one of the formative visions of Jewish existence. And in the opinion of Rabbi Pinhas, this is the exact reason that the people of Israel issue the 'Hear, O Israel' call twice every day.

In fact, it was in this spirit that the sages carried out a substantive religious revolution in Jewish tradition. As opposed to the scriptural tradition that places the Temple, the High Priest and an elite leadership echelon at its centre, the tradition of the sages places the Torah and Torah study at the centre of the religious Jewish stage, with the students of Torah, sages and rabbis, as the focal leaders.

For our purposes, the fact that the sages consider themselves a clear and legitimate alternative to the world of the Temple is a crucial concept. It is sufficient to bear in mind one specific statement: 'As long as the Temple exists, the altar in it is atonement for Israel in all their places of habitations, and outside of Israel, sages and the students of sages are atonement for Israel in all their places of habitation ...'[5] In this way, the sages effectively converted the leadership and formed a new rabbinical Jewish world according to their historical and geographical circumstances. But they were not feminists in their times, and therefore today we face the same type of revolution. In their time, the sages essentially abolished the hierarchy between priests and common Jews, making it into a mere symbol. But a gender-based hierarchy still remains in Judaism, obligating us down to the present time.

The way in which the sages chose to act was the way of the Torah. One of the most interesting pursuits in Torah study is tracking the revolutionary interpretive development of Jewish sages over the generations. In each generation, individuals have used creative interpretation and deep, innovative scholarship to shape a renewed world of Torah and to infuse the traditional religious words and concepts with new contents for contemporary Jewish life. They opened an entire world of halakhah and *Aggada* without losing the holiness and importance of the Torah in the Jewish world. In the name of Rabbi Yishmael, we hear – as an interim reckoning – that halakhah bypasses Scripture in three places[6]. Yet there are not only three, but hundreds and thousands of instances in which sages forged a new halakhah on the basis of Torah study and the possibilities it embodies. Not only did the sages learn from the Torah; they also learned against it, bypassed it, uprooted antiquated ideas and forged a living Torah for generations to come. In essence, they shaped a system by which the Torah could be repeatedly adapted and readapted for generations of Jews in the world of the Blessed-be-He. It should be reiterated, however, that

Jewish tradition did not devote much effort to the subject of women's status amidst all this change, and was by no means feminist.

Alongside the interpretive principle, another important holy principle developed in the Mishnah of the Tannaim – namely, the culture of disagreement ('Both views are the living words of the Lord').[7] In a creative interpretive culture, there will necessarily be different opinions and viewpoints. An extensive tradition of the sages advocates the fundamental idea of 'seventy faces to the Torah' and acknowledges the viewpoints of different sages on matters of halakhah. The basic rule in this culture of disagreement did not aspire to reach compromise, but to preserve the religious stances and world views of the rabbinic authorities. In this way, the Tannaim encourage their students and partners to embrace their studies and cultivate their conclusions, and look for ways to live together while acknowledging the diverse positions. Truth is embodied in the expanse of cultural diversity, in the genuine desire to reach the achievable human optimum. The culture of disagreement at its finest assumes that there is truth in every position, and that truth and faith can only be enhanced by the drawing together of all different faces. It emphasizes the importance of real engagement, and wrestles with difficulties that result from the existence of divergent views within families and communities, acknowledging that those who are weak in their faith are liable to fall into a trap and prefer one easy path (or even a stringent one) as a safety measure against errors or mistakes.

As mentioned above, all of these tools were used by the sages over the generations in their efforts to shape a Torah world that obligates the Jewish people to its culture and faith. Everyone has a significant stake in the world of Jewish thought, and everyone long ago became an intrinsic part of the religious Jewish experience. When this culture is understood by the Jewish world as binding, and corroborative of the world of halakhah and Jewish homiletic interpretation, it must also serve in the cultural and ethical encounter of the twenty-first century. All of these tools constitute keystones in our consideration of a new basic question that is creating a storm in our ethical world. They can be used to carefully examine the institutions and traditional statements, and to carry out the requisite changes in order to make the Jewish world consistent with the contemporary world of values. Indeed, for the past few years, as women have made inroads into the Torah world, Jewish tradition has shown a fundamental ability to open its doors and refresh its ranks accordingly. It has taken the opportunity to sort out its world view, through a looking glass of new ethical and social values. Ours is a tradition that recognizes the value of change, although it has made change into a fixated tradition.

Besides the operative devices we have enumerated (and others that we have not, for lack of space), the other side of the coin should also be noted.

It is not enough to use the existing tools. Basic concepts should be cultivated to prepare people to absorb this important social and religious revolution and to grant feminist ideas the language of Jewish culture. Such a revolution would turn feminists from alien beings to assets of the culture of Israel. These concepts (some of which are addressed below) may be found in the basket of Jewish culture, but are in need of refreshing. They are not new in themselves – some have been used by previous thinkers in relation to feminist notions – but nonetheless they deserve a continuous emphasis.

The different variants of Jewish tradition acknowledge that it is possible to select any verse of the Torah and turn it into a foundational principle on which the entire Torah stands. The verse that the Bet Hillel tradition chose for itself, and for good reason, is Leviticus 19.18, 'Thou shalt love thy neighbour as thyself: I am the Eternal.' 'That is the entire Torah', stated Hillel the Elder,[8] or 'This is the fundamental principle of the Torah',[9] which was stated in the name of Rabbi Akiva. Indeed, there exists a tradition that uses this principle to process halakhic judgments, specifically in capital cases, 'Execute him in the nicest way'.[10] It is possible, and perhaps even compulsory, to apply this central principle in our context as well.

Exclusion of women is a sin in light of 'Thou shalt love thy neighbour as thyself.' The feminist challenge contends that this principle should be applied to all human beings, men and women alike. We should transform the world of halakhah, the world of Jewish society, the world of worship of God, into a place where all are 'as thyself' and all part of the divine identity of love. If man was created in the image of God (Gen. 9.6), and the divine essence is defined in Judaism by the choice of the verse 'Thou shalt love', and by the comparison between love for man (Lev. 19.18) and love for God (Deut. 6.5), then this identity between man and God extends to the feminist challenge. It compels bringing religious women to the place of the Blessed-be-He, and requires their inclusion in halakhah and court decisions on social and family matters.

Tanna Devei Eliyahu interprets the love of this verse with a parable:

> To what are the People of Israel compared in this world before their Father in the heavens? To a flesh-and-blood king who has many sons and slaves, has built many homes and many palaces and extensive grounds, without end, conceived an idea and said, I will bring together my children and my slaves and all who love me and fear me, build a courtyard measuring four cubits by four cubits, and make a passage at its entrance that measures four *tefachim* by four *tefachim*, and make a small gate that leads out onto extensive grounds, to receive the king. And his children and slaves came and stood in the courtyard and in the passage, and the king knows in

his mind who loves and fears him, who fears him and does not
love him. He who loves and fears the king troubles himself and
exits the gate that leads to the extensive grounds in order to
receive the king, and he who fears him but does not love him
stands in the courtyard and in the passage. And so the Blessed-be-
He said to Israel, my children – why did I come to receive you,
and you did not come to receive me, as it is said, 'Thou that
dwellest in the gardens, the companions'. (Song of Songs, 8.13)[11]

In the commentator's opinion, the commitment to love requires a
significant effort. The God-fearing individual is left in possession of the
unchanged tradition, seemingly certain that he is doing God's will. But the
Blessed-be-He is expecting that additional voice, the extra effort, and this is
also how He defines the love, as opposed to fear *per se*. What is more, only
the individual who loves, and who makes the effort to open himself or
herself to the 'extensive grounds' that lie beyond the room prepared for him
so long ago – only that individual truly encounters the Lord. The loving
choice claims openness, and a willingness to be daring, and promises a godly
living-space. Not the concern of foreign influence, but rather the challenge
of encountering it and imbuing it with an unmistakably clear Jewish hue –
this is the effort of the believer who is full of love.

Jewish tradition recognized this commitment and gave it clear halakhic
expression. It set for itself the commitment to 'do that which is straight and
good', and considered it necessary to adopt religious and social regulations
'for the purpose of repairing the world'. In other words, to arrange religious
life through the perspective of the social insight in which it exists, as an
insight of straight and good. In the Yavne generation, there was an
exhaustive discussion on the matter of 'And do that which is straight and
good in the eyes of the Lord' (Deut. 6.18):

> 'Good in the eyes of Heaven, and straight in the eyes of man, says
> Rabbi Akiva. Rabbi Yishmael says: The straight in the eyes of
> Heaven, as well. And he says: 'So shalt thou find grace and good
> favour in the eyes of God and man' (Prov. 3.4). The sages decided
> to follow the words of Rabbi Yishmael, as it says: 'Thou shalt do
> that which is right in the eyes of the Lord' (Deut. 21.9), with no
> mention of good. And he says: 'God, God the Lord, He knoweth,
> and Israel he shall know.'[12]

Rabbi Akiva and Rabbi Yishmael are not in disagreement regarding the
human commitment to good and straight, in the same way that they are not
in disagreement regarding the obligation of Israel to know the divine
knowledge, and to do, as much as possible, that which is good. However,

they are very much in disagreement on the question of the place of the individual in the system of good and straight. Rabbi Yishmael, along with the sages biased in favour of his opinion, reduce the human obligation to create the good and straight, whereas Rabbi Akiva sees the importance of the individual as also contributing his or her part in understanding the straight path. Choosing human ethical creation not merely as an imitation of the ways of God, but as a genuine contribution to the world of the Blessed-be-He, is a precept drawn from the school of Rabbi Akiva. This is one of the most favourable Talmudic paths, especially when we come to consider the feminist challenge.

There is no doubt that the traditionalist opponents of feminism's influence on the Torah world have grounds on which to base their argument. The question is not whether the traditional path is acceptable, but whether the possibility of a renewed path exists within that same tradition. The researchers of the Hartman Institute, led by David Hartman, attempt to answer this question, in different spheres of knowledge, with considerable commitment. On the one hand, they carefully analyse the *modus vivendi* of tradition and assess its inherent dual commitment to tradition and to varying social reality. On the other hand, they cultivate values, using the language of tradition, which will constitute an old/new foundation for consideration of new halakhic perspectives. To listen attentively to the diverse and changing voices that exist in tradition is to grant them a new place and status in the halakhic consideration.

The feminist challenge in the social reality of the twenty-first century is not a matter of privilege, and it is not an option that can be rejected. The possibilities the modern world grants to women and men to choose the communities in which they function leaves the culture of Israel no other option than to carefully listen to the 'alien' voice of women, and to cultivate awareness and possibilities that do not lose or cheapen their value. A tradition of values and culture cannot help but hear all of the voices that reverberate within it, and grant them full rights. And the culture of Israel also has a long tradition of responding to real demands for that which is good and straight. It committed a long time ago to change in the spirit of the Torah of Israel, and the feminist challenge is an imperative call to sound the voice of Rachel. We must let the divine entity speak directly to women in their own language, without trepidation, and consider injustices against equality of religious opportunity while also finding their solutions. To include women in the halakhic consideration, and to shape the halakhah such that it will not be gender-based, and enable access of women to holiness and to society, is one of the most essential challenges we face today.

Notes

1 Mishnah Sotah 3.4.
2 Ish-Shalom ed., *Peskita Rabba Parshat Bo.*
3 Genesis Rabbah 3.5.
4 *Ibid.*, 99.2
5 *Tanna Devei Eliyahu Zuta* Ch. 2.
6 Sifre Deuteronomy 122.
7 Eruvin 13b.
8 BT Shabbat 31a.
9 Sifra Kedoshim Parsha 2, 4.12.
10 Tosefta Sanhedrain 9.11.
11 *Tanna Devei Eliyahu Rabbah* 16.
12 Tosefta Shekalim 2.2.

SIX The Changing Status of Women in Liberal Judaism: A Reflective Critique

Rachel Sabath Beit-Halachmi

The Changing Status of Women in Modernity

The age of modernity was a time of great optimism and hope for progress, for people in general and for Jews in particular. As Western societies began to re-examine and expand the freedom and rights exercised by minority groups, Jews and members of other minority religions were great beneficiaries. Throughout the Western world women also benefited significantly from an expanded understanding of their rights in public and private spheres. By the early part of the twentieth century, women began to take on public leadership roles and have more of a visible impact on society. This move towards greater equality in the public sphere laid the foundation for what later became liberal Judaism's model of a just society in which men and women are equal.

As women gained the right to vote in public elections, many Jews argued that women could no longer be denied the same right within Jewish organizations. The interplay between women's increased equality at large and that within the Jewish community is also apparent in regard to study, whereby just as with modernity women could for the first time study in secular universities, within the Jewish community they could finally access and study previously inaccessible sacred Jewish texts. Jewish women's increased involvement and knowledge led to new understandings of gender and religion which in turn dramatically affected two main areas of liberal Jewish life: (1) religious law and practice, and (2) leadership in the synagogue and communal organizational life.

The significant change in the role of Jewish women following the Enlightenment makes modernity a dividing line between two types of intellectual and religious views of Jewish women. The first sees women as primarily responsible for the private sphere characterized by the home and family-centred domain, while the second accords women a full (or nearly full) religious agency in the public domain. This dividing line is especially pronounced in the context of liberal (non-Orthodox) Jewish life. Reform Judaism in particular embraced the expanding role of women by granting women full membership in synagogues as well as voting rights, and by gradually permitting women to perform many public ritual acts previously restricted to men. Reform leaders not only argued that women should be permitted to serve in leadership positions in synagogues, but in 1922 they voted to allow women to be ordained as rabbis – though in practice this did not occur until 1972.

While some may argue that these changes in status provide an answer to the question of the role of women in Jewish life in the modern era, this chapter argues that such changes are in fact only the first two phases of the reform that is necessary in order to fulfil modernity's promise of equality for women. In spite of the fact that Jewish women today have multiple possibilities available to them, we have yet to see the full equality of gender roles and rules in all areas of liberal Jewish communal life. In order to understand the complexities of the 'unfinished business' that remains in order to realize women's quest for equality, as well as the possible conceptual and textual bases it may rest upon within Judaism, we must first conduct a critical evaluation of the changes that have already taken place and the various methodologies according to which such changes were made. Taking into account what we might learn from such a critique as well as the importance of more fully transforming the liberal Jewish community, I will also suggest some directions for thinking about and creating a more inclusive, egalitarian and sustainable Jewish community in the future.

Phase One: Toward Equality through Shifts in Legal Status

There have been many different changes in women's role in the liberal Jewish community and different methods used to achieve them. These changes can be divided into two main phases which parallel, to some degree, various sub-periods in modern Jewish history as well as the different waves of feminist history. The first phase, much like the first wave of feminism, focused primarily on achieving equal access to and participation in the public sphere and equal rights in decision-making power in both the private and public spheres. Embracing the ideas of progress and reason, the arguments made during this first phase (largely from 1870–1970) employed a principle, considered radical at the time, according to which Jewish women should exercise the same rights as Jewish men. Alongside this principle, feminists argued that it would contradict 'the spirit of the age' to prevent women from performing the same religious duties or from studying the same religious texts as men.

Justifications for reform in the two main areas of change – in religious law and practice, on the one hand, and access to leadership in the synagogue and communal organizational life, on the other – rested primarily on prevailing notions of reason and ethics, and on a belief in the supremacy of Judaism's ethical monotheism. Thus the arguments for change often referred to the 'historic veneration of women' and cited Biblical proof-texts and precedent models, such as the prophetesses Deborah (Judges 4.4ff) and Miriam (Exodus 15.20ff) who led the Jewish people in times of crisis and spiritual grandeur. While these arguments also made occasional reference to the 'exalted spiritual status' of the Jewish woman, the central justification for change was the conviction that Judaism at its core is a progressive and ethical religion 'ever striving to be in accord with the postulates of reason' and that it must therefore evolve in accordance with modern notions of ethics and gender equality.[1]

In early discussions regarding the halakhic role of women, Reform thinkers asserted that rabbinic legal literature was no longer absolutely binding, and most argued that it should be used as a source of significant 'guidance rather than governance'.[2] Adopting the era's emphasis on liberation and equality, these *poskim* (religious lawmakers) believed that they had the right to introduce religious reforms especially with regard to the status of Jewish women. They argued for the full equality of women in four areas in particular: (1) religious commandments including time-bound ones traditionally restricted to men according to halakhah; (2) the Jewish prayer quorum (*minyan*); (3) education; and (4) marriage laws (where reforms would work to prevent a woman from becoming an *agunah* – i.e. prevented from remarrying since her husband refuses to grant her a Jewish divorce – and help create an egalitarian marriage contract).

Some of these initial legal changes were made by employing the halakhic principle, echoed by non-religious law, of going 'beyond the letter of the law' (*lifnim mishurat ha-din*); this principle enabled lawmakers to focus on the ethical underpinnings of Judaism and correct laws from earlier periods that contravened these underpinnings. Other changes were made by employing interpretive principles from within rabbinic literature which take into account the influence of different practices among the Jewish people (such as the Talmudic teaching of 'Go out and see what the people are doing' to settle any doubt about a prevailing custom) as well as considering the needs of people within the community in instituting change. In some cases changes were made by taking into account the reality of ongoing evolution of Jewish practice over the ages, together with the extent to which changing contexts demanded accommodation in religious practice.

Halakhic literature itself at times acknowledges the need for change given changing circumstances, even declaring outright: 'In other times we did that, now we do thus', or simply reasoning that 'times have changed'. Wherever the halakhic literature read women out of influential roles because of supposed inherent intellectual or psychological limitations, Reform thinkers adopted a very different understanding of the role of women based on a different conception of women. By employing such meta-halakhic ethical, historical and interpretive principles, Reformers sought and still seek to create a Jewish practice (which some call halakhah) that is 'more lenient, flexible, affirmative of contemporary values, and morally uplifting' than that of non-liberal Judaism[3]. They saw, and continue to see these first-phase changes in women's halakhic status and role as part of an ongoing process of the evolution of halakhah.

While this first phase led to radical changes by significantly expanding the possibilities for women's religious and intellectual activity, including enabling the eventual ordination of women as rabbis, it had its limitations and merits a respectful critique. This phase of change largely created a new reality in which Jewish women who were interested – and who had the necessary skills, training and opportunity – could live Jewish lives as what some have called 'honorary men'. This first phase produced a great ethical achievement, and yet it meant defining women as men and is similar to what feminists call 'formal equality'. With significant exceptions, the extent to which women could be considered and possibly even valued as men was based on the extent to which women acted, thought and communicated like men, as well as the extent to which they accepted men's interpretations of halakhic obligations. Thus, if women wanted to take on the halakhic privileges of men they needed to take on male obligations. In other words, women were allowed to become rabbis but rabbis were hardly allowed to be women. Thus the achievements of this first phase, like those of first-wave feminism, largely assumed male achievements, values and standards as the norms to which women should aspire.

Few efforts were made to envision alternative models for fully integrating women into Judaism. In particular, there was little understanding of the benefits of encouraging women to retain their unique perspective while integrating their experiences of Judaism in the past and present. Few asked what kind of Jewish life could occur if women not only had equal access but could also be interpreters, shapers and leaders from within Jewish culture according to differently defined parameters, values and theology. Yet the first phase is only one approach that modernity enables: ethical equality based on sameness.

Although the term 'honorary men' might carry a negative connotation I do not mean to offer a total critique of this phase, as it was clearly necessary as well as ground-breaking. In order to not only expand the previously limited space permitted to Jewish women in the public sphere but to also allow for women's full equality, it is necessary first to create the possibility of a near-level playing field. If Jewish women were previously denied access to central public activities and sources of communal power in part because they did not have access to the relevant body of knowledge or the possibility of acquiring the necessary skills, then a corrective model in which they could gain full access and master previously male-only arenas was crucial.

Certainly a re-negotiation of the role of Jewish women which permits them to serve as witnesses, be counted as members of prayer quorums, receive *aliyot*, read from the Torah, become *b'not mitzvah*, and serve as *shlichot tzibbur* (prayer leaders) is radically transformative by all pre-modern standards. Thus halakhic status changes and equal access were necessary. Nonetheless, they remain insufficient changes. Moreover they carry with them potentially negative repercussions. Indeed, while liberal Jewish women ostensibly gained equal access during this phase to previously male-only spheres of knowledge and religious activity, in fact they often became pigeon-holed and were expected to represent only women's issues; moreover the few women who were admitted as leaders were often tokens and more often than not failed to receive equal salary and benefits.[6] Through this and other related phenomena, Jewish women have in fact remained effectively marginalized in many spheres of liberal Jewish communal life (how much more troubling such concerns must be among those seeking equality within modern Orthodoxy). Looking at this phase and its results after a century of experience, many questions and problems remain regarding women's role. We must therefore ask what other modes of transformation may still be implemented and what their implications are for the Jewish community.

Phase Two: Expanding Liturgical-Theological Models

A second phase of change has been possible only since the late 1980s and early 1990s, when a significant number of Jewish women began to serve the liberal Jewish community as rabbis, to create prayers and rituals, and to write Jewish feminist theology. With nearly 1,000 women rabbis today, it has been the onset of a critical mass of communally authenticated and legitimated female religious leadership with demonstrated capabilities that has produced an impetus toward a methodology beyond formal equality. The second phase of change has brought a number of achievements: a dramatic increase in the creation of alternate blessings such as those of Marcia Falk; a plethora of new prayers and new ways of turning to God such as those found in the new Reform prayer book *Mishkan Tefillah* published in 2007; and the recovery and incorporation of previously omitted texts from over the centuries.

This phase has also brought the development of dozens of new life-cycle ceremonies designed specifically for liminal or transitional moments in Jewish women's lives, for which previously there was no liturgy and no leadership or religious-spiritual counsel; it has similarly brought about a continual revising of ceremonies and rituals – such as marriage – in which Jewish women and men have only recently established a variety of ways to ensure equal participation. Egalitarian *ketubbot* (marriage contracts), rituals for menopause and for healing from traumas such as rape or mastectomy, baby girl covenant ceremonies, as well as rituals for men and women around marriage and divorce are just a few examples which exemplify this renewed theology. Because of this second phase of change, in mainstream Jewish communities both women and men now turn to God with feminine and feminist language and song, experience how both women and men can lead prayer and creative religious ceremonies, and have access to a greater diversity of models for religious Jewish family and communal life.

A prominent example of Jewish feminist theology from the second phase is Judith Plaskow's *Standing Again at Sinai*.[5] In it Plaskow argues for the reclamation of history and an inclusive creativity which will not only allow for new understandings of divinity but also aim at creating a new and more just religious and social order.[6] She suggests that there will be new possibilities of transformation for the entire Jewish tradition once women are able not only to access but also to interpret Judaism's most sacred concepts.

In some ways the second phase parallels the achievements – and also the problems – of second-wave feminism. There are inherent limitations in achieving equality through rabbinic interpretive methodologies which make it necessary for us to simultaneously seek ways to re-shape Jewish tradition by incorporating women's varied and different voices. For example, Plaskow's theology leaves important questions unaddressed. While it widens our liturgical and theological horizons, it leaves us to transform our community without a clear methodology for determining or sustaining the social and interpretive process of creating a Judaism which has fully evolved to embrace the new challenges of gender in modernity.

The Challenges of Moving Toward a Third Phase

The full realization of equality within Judaism is in many ways still a work-in-progress. For instance, despite significant changes in the role of women in liberal Jewish life, women continue to experience inequality in Jewish professional arenas; many halakhic issues and the approach they reflect remain untouched by the influence of the first and second phases of change; and the underlying hierarchy that privileges men and male-centred frameworks continues to exist within liberal Jewish communities.

Most of the changes that have been made have used male-created and controlled methods and structures of thought and legal decision-making. To a large extent, the worth and authenticity of the contributions of women continue to be evaluated from a pre-feminist or early feminist perspective. In communities where halakhah remains central, the attempts to continue the work of equality are bound by the supremacy of legal precedent and form. We must even ask whether full equality can ever be created while employing these methods.

The necessary scepticism of our age demands the development of new methodologies for continuing this unfinished two-fold project of fully assimilating women into all arenas of Jewish life and drawing out the ways in which the community can meet men's and women's different needs while simultaneously benefiting from their equality.

As theologian Rachel Adler writes, although we have inherited modernity's 'egalitarianism, its faith in the human power to remake society and lavish benefits on all its members ... perhaps its optimism, its belief in a harmonious and balanced universe are no longer theologically convincing'.[7] Not only do we need models of theology that are more 'convincing' in view of the complex and rapidly changing world in which we live, we also need a legal methodology that is constructive and not just deconstructive. We need ways for establishing the institutions and environments that will benefit from the achievements of both phases while ensuring that the ethics of the first and the contributions of the second are not sacrificed.

Part of a more constructive methodology at this stage might emerge from seeking to understand the ways in which the two earlier phases can conflict, and yet harnessing their combined insights in order to move forward. Indeed the first phase's search for equality and the second phase's development of alternative perspectives often produce a conflict, as women's success in the mainstream may currently come at the expense of being able to deepen women's unique contribution while, conversely, developing women's unique voice often comes at the expense of their being able to fully participate in and influence the system. This is not only a theoretical point but an observation of conflicts that Jewish women currently experience. Perhaps what we need now is a way of living both phases simultaneously. This will require being vigilant about safeguarding the achievement of both earlier phases of change while at the same time seeking to envision a third.

The Jewish community might respond to this challenge on two levels. First, on the theoretical level, we now have the experience of two centuries of modern integrative thinking in liberal Judaism which prides itself on seeking ways to live in the nexus of two worlds; in fact, this is something that liberal Judaism has thrived on for more than a century. We should celebrate the challenge and the ways in which living simultaneously in both worlds leads to more creative thinking and experimentation with new models. In fact, for many centuries liberal Jews have succeeded in living as committed ethical humanists as well as committed Jews in spite of the fact that some argue that these two modes of existence are irreconcilable.

The relevant parallel is that it is possible for women to be fully accepted and culturally at home within Jewish community organizations, while at the same time retaining and further developing a sophisticated different voice from 'the outside'. As with modernity and Judaism, an external critical and an internal constructive feminist voice can also be integrated. The teaching institutions of liberal Judaism face this question on a regular basis, and ask how they can teach all the skills necessary to read Talmud and at the same time teach people to read the text through new lenses. Like the challenge facing all new endeavours, we need to devise a way to be sensitive to marginalized voices while at the same time maintaining rigorous and consistent standards regarding merit. These challenges are palpable in the synagogue, in the academy and in most Jewish organizations.

A response on the pragmatic level could include the ongoing development of truly pluralistic and heterogeneous religious communities and institutions which facilitate equal access and representation for all, and where women's full participation in all aspects of community life and leadership is ensured. By guaranteeing equality in practice, such a community would have significantly more internal creative power at its disposal to move forward; previously critical voices heard only from the outside would then be understood as calls from among the Jewish people that must be heeded in order to ensure Judaism's ethical and theological survival.

In an ideal world, such an intensely inclusive, pluralistic Jewish community would fully value the unique perspectives and contributions of women, as well as those of other marginalized groups. This kind of community would embody a reciprocal commitment to the general membership on the one hand, and to particular groups that have access to different visions on the other, something characteristic of a postmodern age. After modernity we know that any identity is multi-layered and reflective of a particular contemporary context, and so too can we understand gender and Jewish identity.

Developing a Third Phase: Textual Grounding & Ethical Vigilance

Once the lessons of the previous two phases are internalized, we can and should find ourselves working out the reality of a third phase of change. An example of such a move might be Rachel Adler's *Engendering Judaism: An Inclusive Theology and Ethics*,[8] which models the central principles of ethics and theology found in the first and second phases while pointing to a possible transformation in understanding the complexity of gender and Judaism. In a postmodern interweaving of disciplines that uses contemporary legal theory as well as literary theory, theology and ethics, Adler shows the limitations of the two phases previously discussed and states that a formal shift in Jewish legal and ritual systems together with new liturgies and theology are necessary, but not sufficient, to provide a full response to the challenge of gender after modernity.

Focusing on the foundational principles of feminist and liberal theology, and building on multiple principles of interpretation offered by rabbinic literature, Adler addresses many of the remaining dilemmas of equality in halakhah and ethics, such as the ethical and legal imbalance between bride and groom in traditional Jewish marriage ceremonies. Adler proposes a new kind of covenant in place of the marriage *ketubbah*, a *Brit Ahuvim* – a Lovers' Covenant – which exemplifies the methodology of transforming a foundational religious element based on new readings of traditional texts. The reclamation of a discarded practice of a covenant of partnership (*shituf*) in place of the traditional *ketubbah*, which many modern sensibilities reject because of its inequality, is an example of the kind of work that a third phase needs to encourage.

A third phase, which can and does operate simultaneously with the previously described phases, continues to seek both halakhic and Aggadic (non-legal) textual grounding and resources in past and present Jewish narratives that can provide new possibilities for the continuing adjustment of Judaism to the constantly shifting roles of men and women after modernity. We must however recognize the potential problems inherent in the work of recovering the teachings of ancient texts and appealing to precedent and continuity. Such legitimizing of past systems may appear to imply acceptance of the entirety of the system. Given the unequivocal ethical and feminist foundations which have taken root in liberal Judaism, I do not believe that we need to be concerned. We are fully capable of engagement with the texts in the fullness of what they represent from the new perspective of the fullness of what we are and the context in which we live.

Another example of such an attempt is that of Talmudic scholar Daniel Boyarin. Rather than focusing on misogyny and the traditional lack of Jewish female power and autonomy – a focus that often serves to reproduce it – Boyarin seeks to show how the 'recovery of those forces of the past that opposed the dominant androcentrisim can help put us on a trajectory of empowerment for transformation'.[9] This is a model where our resources for the future are not only the theory of the present but also a new application of the voices of the past. Instead of only rejecting the negative ways in which women might have been treated in many of the ancient texts, a model like Boyarin's suggests that we find strategies for the future in the suppressed opposition to male dominance and in the more dormant feminine voices, however sparse, of precisely those narratives.

Through reading texts with a critical but generous eye (neither apologetic nor solely negative and therefore allowing for new kinds of understandings, neither a combination nor an averaging out of these two phases but a new posture), we can benefit from the past without being restricted by the limitations of older modes of interpretation. If we embrace rather than reject or immediately reinterpret the texts with solely our ethical autonomous goals in mind, they might better serve us in our project of constructing a new model for how Jewish life adjusts to the fullness of gender and sexual identity, given what we know to be true in our time. Therefore, the third phase is one of re-reading and re-interpreting, from a new perspective, the ancient texts of Judaism in ways that preserve and present to us the resources of their creative and spiritual power.

Authority and Authenticity for a Third Phase

Beyond the cultural value of finding textual resources, there is much to be said for re-thinking the entire halakhic system especially where it leads to unjust situations, such as many that exist regarding women's status. At the same time, we must keep in mind that in many circles of liberal Jews we now witness the playing out of the opposite extreme, namely the failure to achieve Jewish communal norms in a variety of areas of Jewish life, precisely because of our policy of over-privileging of individually defined ethics and autonomy. The absence of shared communal norms continues to impact not only on women's roles but also on questions of Jewish identity altogether, raising new questions about the nature of Jewish peoplehood.

A third phase therefore, must demonstrate how it is possible to seek out a Jewish way of living which has norms and a shared praxis that are morally informed yet based on a serious knowledge of the narrative of our tradition. Part of what will give such a system its authenticity and authority will be precisely its continuity of the past and its ability to participate in a larger non-sectarian communal process of development. At the same time, this third phase must continue to allow for differences in the application of moral and ethical values and in its interpretation of and experience of God as a demanding and commanding reality of any Jewish religious life.

Among the specific goals of this next stage are several elements, some of which were absent or lost in the earlier phases of change: (1) preservation of the most culturally significant and relevant aspects of tradition, especially through the greater activity of women in intensive learning communities, thereby allowing for a greater constructive interweaving of past and future and a greater simultaneous engagement in multiple intellectual and spiritual methodologies; (2) ongoing recovery and creation of rituals and ritual activity for women and men, such as those regarding *mikveh* practices (as modelled in a recent conference on *mikveh* use in Boston); and (3) development of a standard of religious pluralism and trans-denominational activity within the Jewish community and among women in particular which will allow for the ritual practice and text learning which is more prevalent in traditional Jewish communities to impact liberal women, and reciprocally to allow for the greater equality and authority than liberal women already experience, to affect the same processes of transformation in the more traditional communities. Such a model of pluralism would be a redemptive pluralism.

The complex task that remains is the full harnessing of the richness and multi-vocality of Jewish tradition, combined with the knowledge of what a completely different approach and experience of it might teach, in order to create new ways of studying Jewish text and living Jewish lives for both men and women. Such a new approach, if carefully and responsibly developed, will surely contribute to the development of Jewish religious and cultural life as a whole and thus ensure that one of modernity's greatest promises – equality for women – will be met with the evolving wisdom and creativity of all of the Jewish people.[10]

Notes

1 Central Conference of American Rabbis (CCAR), The Pittsburgh Platform 1885.
2 For the use of these terms in the Reform discourse see, for example, Solomon B. Freehof, 'A Code of Ceremonial and Ritual Practice', *CCAR Yearbook 51* (1941), 289–97.
3 M. Washofsky, 'Against Method: On *Halakhah* and Interpretive Communities', in J. Walter (ed.), *Beyond the Letter of the Law: Essays on Diversity in the Halakhah* (Pittsburgh, Rodef Shalom Press, 2004), pp. 17–77.
4 T. Cohen (ed.), *Ma'ayan Report: The Jewish Women's Project* (New York, 2005).
5 J. Plaskow, *Standing Again at Sinai: Judaism from a Feminist Perspective* (San Francisco, Harper & Row, 1990).
6 *Ibid.*, p. 238.
7 R. Adler, 'Feminist Judaism: Past and Future', *Crosscurrents*, winter 2002; 51, 4.
8 R. Adler, *Engendering Judaism: An Inclusive Theology and Ethics* (Boston, Beacon Press, 1998).
9 D. Boyarin, *Carnal Israel* (Berkeley, University of California Press, 1993), p. 227.
10 I am grateful to Prof. David Levine of the Hebrew Union College – Jewish Institute of Religion in Jerusalem, who graciously reviewed this article and offered many helpful suggestions.

SEVEN

Judaism, Feminism and Homosexuality

Jonathan W. Malino and Tamar S. Malino

Culture, Continuity and Change

Like all cultural phenomena, Judaism exhibits a perpetual tension between inertia and dynamism. Jewish existence is everywhere marked by negotiation between contending forces for continuity and change. Even the most superficial review of Jewish history presents these contending forces at play: in Babylonia after the destruction of the First Temple, in Palestine and the Diaspora after the destruction of the Second Temple, in Europe after emancipation, and throughout the Jewish world after the birth of the State of Israel.

One dimension of the negotiation between continuity and change involves the religious elements of Judaism, construed broadly to include the patterns of thought, feeling and action that constitute a Jew's response to the fundamental features of existence. Religious phenomena have both social and psychological reality. Historian Gavin Langmuir refers to the psychological aspects as a person's *religiosity*, while the social aspects, connected with religious authority and expressed publicly in symbols, he calls *religion*. A significant element of the negotiation between continuity and change in the religious arena consists of negotiation between an individual's personal religiosity and the more fixed forms of religion within which an individual's religiosity may be framed.

For the past five decades, the religiosity of many Jews has been decisively shaped by feminism: a belief in the equal worth of men and women and the rejection of unjust discrimination between them. More recently, if to a lesser extent, the acceptance of homosexuality has also laid claim to the religious conscience of many Jews. To grasp the impact on Judaism of these changes in religiosity, it is essential to appreciate how a changing religiosity is experienced. It arises as an empirical and moral awakening, a dawning consciousness that transforms how one perceives, understands and judges the world, especially the social world. In the case of feminism and accepting homosexuality, this transformation has been revolutionary.

All of the major streams within Judaism have struggled and will continue to struggle with these revolutionary transformations in religiosity. The struggles are powerful and painful. Because they are struggles between religion and religiosity, they are carried out on many fronts: within the hearts, minds and souls of individuals; among family members; between friends; and, of course, in the larger, less personal institutional structures which comprise a religion.

The major streams within Judaism are distinguishable by the extent to which they have formally accommodated feminism and accepted homosexuality. The Reform movement has fully embraced feminism, notwithstanding ongoing theological debates like those powerfully presented in Rachel Adler's *Engendering Judaism*.[1] Homosexuality, however, remains contested. Male and female homosexuals are fully welcomed in Reform synagogues and may be ordained as rabbis, yet a resolution permitting Reform rabbis to officiate at same-sex unions was passed only after fierce and acrimonious debate.

The Conservative movement has embraced feminism more equivocally than Reform. While it ordains women rabbis, the *teshuva* that made this possible is decidedly not feminist. Ambivalence remains regarding women serving as witnesses, as well as regarding liturgical change. In the case of homosexuality, debate within the movement is intense and widespread. Homosexuals are to be welcomed in synagogues, but openly gay men and women cannot be ordained as rabbis.[2]

The most painful struggles over both feminism and homosexuality have occurred within the Orthodox world. The profoundly patriarchal character of normative rabbinic Judaism, notwithstanding evidence of progressively evolving views toward women among the ancient sages, suggests that feminism may require a fully fledged transformation of Orthodoxy. Nonetheless, Orthodox feminists actively negotiate changes on many fronts within their religious world. Indeed the most systematic treatment of Judaism and feminism is *Expanding the Palace of Torah: Orthodoxy and Feminism*,[3] by philosopher and Orthodox Jew, Tamar Ross.

When it comes to homosexuality, even more is at stake. With biblical verses (Leviticus 18.22 and 20.13) explicitly condemning male homosexuality as *'toevah'* – abhorrence or abomination – the intense suffering of Orthodox homosexuals interviewed in the documentary *Trembling Before God*[4] comes as no surprise. Yet even within the Orthodox world, one finds efforts, like those of Chaim Rapoport in *Judaism and Homosexuality: An Authentic Orthodox View*,[5] to mitigate the painful consequences of Orthodoxy's uncompromising rejection of homosexuality.

Interlude

We are feminists who embrace homosexuality. Each of us, in different ways and at different stages of our lives, has experienced a profound awakening – born of our religiosity as Jews – to the imperative that women and men, homosexuals and heterosexuals, be treated equally. We are sensitive to the tremendous injustice, in society at large and within Judaism, in denying this equality. We also believe that there is a significant connection within Judaism between biblical and rabbinic misogyny and the abhorrence of male homosexuality. In what follows we will explain our attitude toward homosexuality, sketch the connection we see between misogyny and the abhorrence of homosexuality, and draw out its significance for the contemporary Jewish debate over homosexuality.

Embracing Homosexuality

Understanding fully what is involved in embracing homosexuality requires articulating a Jewish sexual ethic. It is not surprising that both Conservative and Reform movements, as they have grappled with homosexuality (and with other rapidly changing sexual mores), have chosen to formulate new statements about Judaism and sexuality. We do not have the space to spell out our own views on Jewish sexual ethics, nor is it necessary in order to explain what we mean by 'embracing homosexuality'. To embrace homosexuality is to treat homosexuality and heterosexuality, and male and female homosexuality, identically within one's sexual ethics.

Consider, for example, whether one's Jewish sexual ethics ought to condemn intercourse among unmarried people. In our view this question must be addressed identically for heterosexuals and homosexuals. If heterosexual intercourse is acceptable between unmarried couples, then so is homosexual intercourse. If homosexual intercourse is acceptable only within loving monogamous relationships, the same must be true for heterosexual intercourse. We reject any effort to constrain acceptable homosexual sex within boundaries not applied equally to heterosexuals.

A more controversial implication of our principle is our rejection of the common reliance on the biological fixity of sexual orientation to legitimate homosexuality. Many people have been moved to accept homosexuality by the realization that a person's sexual orientation is substantially rooted in genetics. Such people, even if they recognize that sexual conduct is not fixed in the way sexual orientation is, hesitate to condemn homosexual behaviour, because the orientation from which it flows is beyond choice. On this view, heterosexuality remains the norm, not only statistically, but also morally. Were we all capable of *being* heterosexual, that would be the way we should be.

Those who advocate this view accept or tolerate homosexuality, but they do not embrace it. In embracing homosexuality we insist that the only asymmetry between heterosexuality and homosexuality is the lesser frequency of the latter. Should a person be bisexual and choose to live as a homosexual, such a person would have the same religious standing as one whose homosexual orientation was in no significant way a matter of choice. Homosexuality and heterosexuality are forms of human diversity, worthy of appreciation as are the many other forms of diversity among human beings and cultures.

Finally, we make no moral or religious distinction between male and female homosexuality, in sharp contrast to both Jewish and pagan cultures. Leviticus speaks explicitly only of male homosexuality, and references to female homosexuality in rabbinic literature are few and far between. Whatever the reasons, it has led Jewish law to condemn male homosexuality far more forcefully than female homosexuality. In Roman culture, where male homosexuality was accepted – indeed expected – under certain circumstances, female homosexuality was roundly condemned. Neither Jewish nor Roman culture embraced homosexuality as we do.

Feminism and Male Homosexuality

In his book, *Wrestling with God and Men: Homosexuality in the Jewish Tradition*,[6] Steven Greenberg discusses at length what he considers to be the main rationales for the Orthodox Jewish prohibition against homosexuality. One of these, 'Humiliation and Violence', strikes us as particularly important, because it connects the two revolutionary changes in religiosity we discussed above, and because the connection has important implications for how rejecting misogyny can undermine a fundamental obstacle to accepting, if not embracing, homosexuality.

Greenberg focuses on the two biblical verses condemning male homosexuality: Lev. 18.22, 'Do not lie with a male as one lies with a woman: it is an abhorrence (*toevah*)'; and Lev. 20.13, 'If a man lies with a male as one lies with a woman, the two of them have done an abhorrent thing; they shall be put to death – their bloodguilt is upon them.' In an effort to understand what is being proscribed in these verses, Greenberg convincingly draws on midrashic and halakhic sources, as well as recent research into the ancient West, to illuminate the relationship between the rabbinic and Graeco-Roman understandings (in contemporary terminology, 'social constructs') of gender and sexuality. Anyone familiar with the acceptance of homosexuality within the pagan world will recognize the profound difference between it and the Jewish world. What Greenberg shows, however, is that both worlds share fundamental features. In both, sexual penetration is ultimately about domination, in both there is a hierarchy of men over women, and in both, having anal intercourse with an equal (in Judaism, any male) automatically amounts to violent humiliation and degradation by feminizing the male. The meaning of male anal intercourse does not depend on the motives of either participant, or whether the intercourse is consensual or even marked by positive emotion. The social construct of gender and sexuality gives the act meaning: *humiliation through feminization.*

After sketching his understanding of sexual relations which forms the backdrop to Lev. 18.22 and 20.13 – at least as the rabbis understood them – Greenberg rephrases Lev. 18.22 as 'You shall not humiliate a fellow male by the kind of penetrations men do with women; it is abhorrent.' In rephrasing the text in this way, Greenberg has gone beyond identifying a rationale for prohibiting abhorrent male intercourse. He has revealed the inferiority of women to men to be inherent in the very meaning of the verse, just as it is inherent in the very meaning of the sexual act.

Not every proposed rationale for forbidding male intercourse can be understood in this way. Consider, for example, the idea that male intercourse is forbidden because it cannot be procreative. The non-procreative character of male homosexuality does not thereby become part of the meaning of the verse in Leviticus, nor is it part of the meaning of the act. It is a feature of the act, just as it may be a rationale for prohibiting the act, but it lacks the intrinsic connection found in the rationale of humiliation.

It is the special character of the rationale of humiliation that leads us to our main point: *there is no biblical prohibition against homosexuality for a feminist.* As Greenberg makes amply plain, the rationale of violence and humiliation is mediated by misogyny. Misogyny too is tied intrinsically to the meaning of male intercourse. What happens, then, if one is a feminist for whom misogyny is itself abhorrent, indeed as abhorrent as the incestuous *toevot* enumerated in Leviticus 18? For a feminist, male intercourse *cannot* possess the meaning that it has for one who is a misogynist. If one rejects the inferior status of women, male intercourse simply cannot be automatically dominating, violent, humiliating and degrading on the grounds that men are engaging in the kind of penetrating men do with women. Hence, from the perspective of the feminist, what Leviticus prohibits cannot take place. The prohibition is empty.

To appreciate the point we are making, let us return to the rationale of procreation. According to this rationale, the value the Torah puts on procreation leads to forbidding a form of sexuality that cannot be procreative. Suppose that just as the feminist rejects the inferiority of women, one were to reject the value the Torah puts on procreation. One might, in consequence, no longer prohibit non-procreative male intercourse. But it would not follow that the prohibition could no longer be violated or was empty. One who did not value procreation simply would not object to its violation.

Before considering the significance of our argument, we want to distinguish it from a similar-sounding argument advanced by a number of liberal Conservative rabbis who have sought to challenge the dominant view that Leviticus prohibits all male homosexuality. According to this argument, the Torah only 'knew of coercive non-loving male homosexual relations'. Hence when it prohibited male homosexuality, it was only prohibiting coercive, non-loving relations, for the Torah could not prohibit what it did not know. Hence there is no prohibition in the Torah against non-coercive, loving homosexual relations.

Suppose that the Torah knew only of coercive, non-loving homo-sexuality – not because the meaning of homosexual intercourse, within the biblical social construct of sexuality and gender, is independent of the intentions and feelings of those involved, but because the Torah never contemplated consensual male relationships with loving feelings. What would follow? Nothing. For it certainly cannot be true that the Torah prohibits only what it 'knows about'. Rabbinic Judaism depends on just the opposite, on the possibility that the Torah is applicable to circumstances far removed from anything the Torah 'knew about'. Perhaps, then, the argument should be rephrased as follows. Since the Torah only knew of coercive, non-loving homosexual relations, its rationale for prohibiting homosexuality could only be in order to prohibit coercive, non-loving relations. But this would still be a *non sequitur*. What the Torah knew about cannot be transformed directly into a statement of the Torah's rationale for its prohibition. It could, however, be proposed as the basis for a reasonable hypothesis about the Torah's rationale. So understood, the argument might have some force, although the force would be lessened if the hypothesized rational were assumed to be the *sole* rationale. In any case, the rationale would be extrinsic to the meaning of the prohibited act, and consequently would not be automatically voided in cases where the rationale did not apply.

Feminism and Female Homosexuality

Our conception of 'embracing homosexuality' rejects any normative distinction between male and female homosexuality. Since Jewish law distinguishes them and since our argument has been rooted in passages in Leviticus that address only male homosexuality, it is relevant to ask whether our argument has any force against Judaism's prohibition of female homosexuality. The answer is not easy to ascertain.

We know that the rabbis expressed a far more easygoing attitude toward female homoeroticism than to male intercourse (in marked contrast to the pagan world). It is possible that this difference, like the prohibition of male intercourse, was predicated on misogyny: women are inferior to men, hence women's sexuality is inferior to men's sexuality, hence female homosexuality is less 'worthy' of condemnation than male homosexuality. Were this reconstruction plausible, our argument would indeed apply, and would entail that prohibitions against female homosexuality are as empty – for a feminist – as those against male homosexuality.

Not all opposition to female (or male) homosexuality need presuppose misogyny. By mediaeval times, Jewish law reflected the influence of biblical, Hellenistic, Roman, Christian and Islamic cultures. Its sexual attitudes were likely an amalgam of varied conceptions and considerations. Female homosexuality might have been condemned as unnatural, non-procreative and undignified. Against such considerations, our argument would have no bite. Its significance is not diminished, however, by its inability to undermine (even for a feminist) every objection to (even female) homosexuality.

Conclusion

We are under no illusion (neither is Greenberg) that our reading of Leviticus is unquestionably the 'right' reading, though we find it as reasonable as any other. Even less do we believe that were our reading unchallengeable, it would magically remove the resistance to embracing homosexuality which lies so deep in the history of both Judaism and Christianity, and hence the West. Our goal has been to show that one obstacle to accepting homosexuality, the biblical texts in Leviticus, should carry no weight for a feminist.

It should not be surprising that the feminist religious awakening would carry other religious awakenings in its wake. Nonetheless it might be hard to imagine that a prohibition, nestled among prohibitions against incest whose grip upon us has not weakened, could be neutralized by feminism. This is the failure of imagination expressed in the accusation that one who embraces homosexuality is bound to slide down a slippery slope to embracing bestiality. It is also the failure to imagine the profound abhorrence misogyny deserves.

We believe that many Jews who see themselves as feminists in the modest sense identified earlier in the chapter still refuse to accept, no less embrace, homosexuality. To the extent that their refusal is linked to Leviticus, we hope their refusal will be weakened by our argument. May we go from awakening to awakening![7]

Notes

1 R. Adler, *Engendering Judaism: An Inclusive Theology and Ethics* (Boston, Beacon Press, 1998).

2 This was written before the Conservative movement's recent decisions concerning gays. These have narrowed the gap between the Conservative and Reform movements substantially, although even the most liberal *teshuua* adopted by the Law Committee of the Rabbinical Assembly explicitily rejects the attitude towards homosecuality we advocate.

3 T. Ross, *Expanding the Palace of Torah: Orthodoxy and Feminism* (Lebanon NH, University Press of New England, 2004).

4 S. S. Dubowski (Director), *Trembling Before God* (New Yorker studio).

5 C. Rapoport, *Judaism and Homosexuality: An Authentic Orthodox View* (London, Vallentine Mitchell, 2004).

6 S. Greenberg, *Wrestling with God and Men: Homosexuality in the Jewish Tradition* (Wisconsin, University of Wisconsin Press, 2005).

7 Thanks to Yehuda Gellman and Tova Hartman for criticism and encouragement.

Part II: The Challenge of Diversity

EIGHT

The Religious Significance of Religious
Pluralism

David Hartman

Religious pluralism would seem to be such a simple and natural ideal to
accept today, yet many people express scepticism and even antagonism to
pluralism as a framework of personal commitment and faith. While
acknowledging and promoting tolerance and freedom of religious expression as practical norms, they are convinced there is no place for diversity in
respect of the fundamental truth claims of religious life. While genuinely
believing in the need to safeguard the rights of 'the other' in the legal and
interpersonal domains, they believe that pluralism is incompatible with the
essential nature of religious faith in general and of Judaism in particular.

The denial of religious pluralism in general is often based on the
assumption that all faith communities necessarily believe in the final
vindication of their particular traditions over those of their rivals. In his
article on the relationship between Judaism and other faith traditions,
'Confrontation', Rabbi Joseph B. Soloveitchik claims:

> Each faith community is unyielding in its eschatological expect-
> ations. It perceives the events at the end of time with exultant
> certainty and expects man, by surrender of selfish pettiness and by
> consecration to the great destiny of life, to embrace the faith that
> this community has been preaching throughout the millennia ...
> the waiving of eschatological claims spell[s] the end of the vibrant
> and great faith experience of any religious community.[1]

In addition to this kind of *a priori* argument about the exclusivist nature of
faith traditions in general, many Jews also believe that the Biblical tradition
itself expressly supports the idea of the supremacy of one faith above all
others. Historically, monotheistic faith traditions rooted in the Bible used
the biblical paradigm of divine selection/rejection to justify their
triumphalist claims. The classical biblical paradigm of God's relationship
to human history is the selection of one child to the exclusion of the others.
In the book of Genesis, the hatred between the brothers, Jacob and Esau, is
kindled by the realization that the divine blessing is sufficient for only one
child. And, according to many, this exclusionary mode culminates in the
book of Exodus where God, at Sinai, reveals the true way of worship to his
elect people. Regardless of whether divine election ends with Israel at Sinai

or with the New Israel of the *New Testament* or with the calling of Mohammed in the *Koran*, the biblical tradition, according to this interpretation, is the source of a religious outlook that is clearly incompatible with a pluralistic sensibility.

In addition to expressing these philosophical and ideological arguments in defense of their opposition to religious pluralism, some proponents of religious exclusivity seem to be personally threatened by the presence of religious diversity. Living with others committed to different forms of worship upsets them because the commitment of others calls their own commitment into question. The 'other' exposes them to the uncomfortable thought that their particular tradition may be just that, a particular expression of religious faith with no assurance of absolute truth and universality. Pluralism thus endangers their passionate relationship with God.

This chapter will address these issues by providing an alternative understanding of some of the main theological and narratives themes of Judaism. In contrast to the exclusivist interpretation of the biblical world view, we will present an interpretation of biblical theology and of two of its central themes, creation and revelation, which supports a pluralistic, rather than an exclusivist, religious sensibility. Our purpose is to show how the concept of revelation can be understood as an affirmation of the possibility of multiple ways of worshipping God.

We shall also question the *a priori* association of religious passion with exclusivity and triumphalism by showing the religious and theological significance of pluralism. Finally, we will argue the emotional antipathy to pluralism is often less due to religious and philosophical considerations than to an underlying psychological need for control and an inability to tolerate uncertainty.

The Religious Significance of Religious Pluralism

There is a profound religious significance to affirming pluralism. First and foremost, it expresses the rich plentitude of God. The diversity of forms of worship and expressions of belief and love for God reflect the boundless reality of a living God, a God who cannot be contained within any single cognitive and expressive framework, a God for whom ultimately 'silence is praise'.

On the human side, religious pluralism confirms the fact that in our love for God we can never escape the constraints of the human condition. We cannot transcend the inherent limits of our particular form of worship nor can we conceal its particularity by negating the validity of others' forms of worship.

Religious pluralism is thus a positive expression of a distinct religious sensibility, a sensibility that celebrates the infinite plenitude of the divine reality, on the one hand, while affirming human finitude, limitation and vulnerability, on the other hand. These two complementary motifs are the organizing principles of my understanding of covenantal Judaism. To show this, we shall present an analysis of biblical theology and certain aspects of rabbinic Judaism, which exemplify the values and spiritual orientation of a pluralistic form of covenantal Judaism.

The Scandal of Biblical Theology and the Covenant Idea

In contrast to the self-sufficient god of Aristotle, the biblical God was considered philosophically scandalous because of the image of a God who was emotionally involved, vulnerable and deeply affected by human behaviour. Aristotle's god was perfect, unchanging and oblivious to human beings, whereas the biblical God, as A. J. Heshel wrote, was passionately 'in search of man'.[2]

In the biblical tradition the concept of perfection is a relational category involving both implicit and explicit types of interdependence. From the very beginning of the Bible, in the Creation narrative in Genesis, God is dramatically presented in relational, anthropomorphic terms. In the course of the account of creation, the idyllic description of an omnipotent God whose will is realized effortlessly in the natural world – 'Let there be …' – abruptly changes with the creation of human beings who brazenly challenge and oppose God's design. The expression of God's will, is, as it were, constrained by human freedom; God is no longer the only actor in the scene, as he was with respect to the creation of nature. This idea is at the heart of the relational, or what I call the covenantal, framework of biblical theology.

The concept of covenantal religion develops in the Bible in parallel to the transition in the character of God from an independent, unilateral actor to a God who recognizes that only through human cooperation can the divine plan for history be realized. As the scope of divine power contracts, the role and status of finite human beings expands.

Divine Self-Limitation and Human Empowerment

Abraham can be described as the first covenantal figure because of the mutuality of his relationship with God, especially in his dialogue with God concerning Sodom. Abraham appeals to independent principles of morality in his argument with God about the fate of the people of Sodom. 'Far be it from you to do such a thing, to bring death upon the innocent as well as the guilty, so that innocent and guilty fare alike. Far be it from you! Shall not the judge of all the earth deal justly?' (Gen. 18.25)

Abraham's use of a moral argument not grounded in revelation or other authoritative source against God's declared intention to destroy Sodom reflects the dignity and self-assurance of a person who trusts in his own natural sense of justice and morality. It is this sense of confidence, self-respect and absence of intimidation that characterizes a covenantal relationship.

The covenant with Abraham and the covenant with the People of Israel at Sinai express the same fundamental principle of covenantal theology: divine self-limitation makes room for human empowerment in determining the direction of human history. The God we meet in history and in our personal lives is not an omnipotent, absolute, overwhelming presence that crushes a person's sense of worth and dignity. Covenantal consciousness begins with the awareness that God stands in a relationship with human beings who are accepted as they are yet burdened with the task of becoming the carriers of the divine vision for human history.

The Two Poles of Covenantal Thought: Creation and Revelation

The two complementary organizing frameworks of covenantal religious experience are Sinai (revelation, history) and Creation (nature, being). The historical narratives describing God's relationship with the people of Israel are characterized by their intimacy and particularity. God addresses Israel as 'my people' while Israel refers to God as 'my God'. The covenant at Sinai establishes the relational framework between the God of revelation and a particular people.

The 'election' of Israel conveys the sense of intimacy of close, personal relationships without denigrating others' relationships of the same kind. This intimate relational framework is balanced by the very different, less personal framework of Creation, where the universal God of Creation is related to all of humanity.

While the historical narratives in the Bible are the main focus of the sacred literature that defines the Jewish people's identity, the Creation story also shapes Jewish consciousness. The references to Creation in the Jewish liturgy, especially on the Sabbath, indicate that the Jewish perspective on life is nurtured not only by collective memories of Jewish history but also by an awareness of the universal human condition that all human beings share because of the gift of having been created in God's image.

Unlike the Sinai revelation, the Creation story is not about the people of Israel, but about the common origin and condition of all human beings. The biblical description of the creation of the first human being is transformed by the Jewish tradition into a normative principle: beloved is every human being who was created in the image of God.

Covenantal Judaism is informed by a continuous dialectic between the intimate particularity of one's relationship to God and one's people, on the one hand, and the shared universality of God's relationship to all human beings, on the other. As a created human being, the Jew is part of and responsible for the general history of the world and not only the particular history of the Jewish people.

The dialectic between the Jew's particular and universal identities, between the God of Israel and the God of Creation, makes Jewish identity a dynamic, challenging experience. The particularity and intimacy of our relationship to the God of Israel must never overpower or diminish our awareness of the God of Creation who commands us to build a shared world of values with all human beings.

The challenge of religious pluralism is to integrate the Creation motif into the revelatory religious mindset so as to develop a religious sensibility where genuine appreciation and respect for diversity reflect one's basic religious beliefs and instincts.

The State of Israel and the Challenge of Pluralism

The tension between the universal spirit of creation and the intimacy of one's particular tradition is acutely felt in the state of Israel today. Living in Jerusalem makes one realize that something radically new is demanded of the Judaic spirit. Although it is hard to articulate clearly what is required, the 'ingathering of the exiles' and the establishment of the third Jewish commonwealth in the land of Israel have created a powerful and explosive new reality.

On the one hand, Jews from around the world have come home. Jews no longer need to wait and pray for their return to Zion. On the other hand, the home to which they returned was not the ideal messianic reality of their dreams and prayers. In returning home, we discovered we were not a united, loving family. We were divided, conflicted and often incapable of accommodating our differences peacefully. The slogan 'we are one!' sounds ludicrous when our prime minister talks about the possibility of civil war.

Conflicts over how to interpret the concept of the holiness of the land have created bitter polarization, anger and cynicism between whole sectors of our society. Is returning land a betrayal of the covenantal tradition? Are we meant to be the exclusive sovereigns of the land or can a Jewish state exist alongside a Palestinian one?

Not only are we estranged from one another, but the violent struggle with the Palestinians has created suspicion and distrust of 'the stranger in our midst'.

In returning to the land of Zion, we thought we had returned to our homeland where we were free to fulfil our long-held dream of national and political self-expression, only to discover that there were Arabs here who also felt a deep connection to the land. In addition to having to re-examine our claims to our home, we also were confronted with groups whose beliefs and traditions challenge us to reconsider many of our traditional ideas and attitudes.

Jerusalem is a living symbol of diversity. Walking through Jerusalem today, one hears the sounds of different religions, which once fought holy wars for control of this city, and one is reminded that this city cannot be divorced from its history. One hears muezzins calling Muslims to their mosques, church bells tolling as Christians make their way along the Via Dolorosa to the Church of the Holy Sepulchre, and Hasidic Jews rushing to pray at the Western Wall.

When I look at this teeming diversity, I think of that puzzling name God disclosed to Moses, *Ehyeh Asher Ehyeh*. When asked by Moses how to respond to the people's question, 'What is his name?' God answered: *Ehyeh Asher Ehyeh*, 'I will be who I will be' (Exod. 3.14). I cannot think of a better way of describing the feeling of being called upon to relate to our tradition in a new way than by evoking the sense of innovation, newness and becoming conveyed by this enigmatic name. There is something unprecedented happening to us because of our forced involvement with the 'other' in our lives. Our self-definition is in a state of becoming, of moving towards a new religious understanding of history.

Religion without Salvation

The flowering of Jewish particularity in the city of Jerusalem can be seen as an opportunity for developing the pluralistic implications of covenantal Judaism. Whereas the universality of the Creation story derives from the idea of the common fatherhood of God, the universal significance of the revelation narrative relates to the relationship of God with finite human beings. The particularity of the covenant between God and Israel is itself an indication of God's affirmation and acceptance of finite human beings with their limited, imperfect natures.

This idea can shape our understanding of the significance of our commitment to Jewish particularity and to the presence of religious diversity in Jerusalem today. In this city, where religions often fought bloody 'holy wars' to gain exclusive control, we, the Jewish people, can bear witness to the dignity of religious particularity and to the importance of celebrating the partial and the incomplete.

The challenge to our identity and tradition is implicit in the kind of questions we are being forced to confront. Can a committed believer develop an identity in which other traditions are acknowledged and valued as valid expressions of faith? Must a religious Jew believe that he or she possesses the exclusive truth in order to be passionately committed to the Jewish tradition?

In order to do this, we must develop a religious sensibility devoid of an obsessive concern with salvation and eternity. We must overcome the longing to be saved from history.

The story of Creation expresses an affirmation not of eternity but of temporality. God's Creation is deemed good without any reference to redemption or eternal salvation. The Gnostics could not accept the world as it is as being the manifestation of a loving god. Human suffering and death could not be expressions of a loving god. Consequently they believed that one must get away from this imperfect, tragic world in order to encounter the true god of love. As long as the world was seen as sinful and evil, God could only be experienced through a drama of eternal salvation.

By contrast, Judaism taught that the world with all its imperfections was good in the eyes of God (as was said repeatedly in the first chapter of Genesis). God affirms our humanity in spite of our vulnerabilities, our weaknesses and our finitude. Although we are fragile, corporeal creatures, who experience pain, deprivation and tragedy, human life is not inherently sinful. 'God saw all that He had made and behold it was good.' What this means is that we do not have to escape our human finitude in order to feel dignified. We do not have to go beyond the concrete and the temporal to live authentically before God.

The revelation and covenant narratives express this idea as well. The affirmation of imperfect human beings is the essence of the covenantal message. The covenant does not relate to yearning for salvation and redemption. On the contrary, God's gracious love is expressed in the divine acceptance of humanity in its finite, temporal condition. The God of the Covenant wishes to enter the sanctuary and the Temple, to be housed in the concrete forms human beings comprehend and find meaningful. God does not ask that the Temple be immersed in the quest for eternal salvation.

Although the yearning for salvation from sin is not alien to biblical spirituality, the themes of human failure and rebellion against God are related repeatedly throughout the Bible. Human failure is a constant, inescapable feature of life. What I am arguing is that the idea of salvation as the yearning to go beyond the human condition is antithetical to biblical covenantal spirituality.

The Psychological Obstacles to Religious Pluralism

The acceptance of others and the ability to live with human diversity would seem to be so very natural and simple. Why, therefore, do people feel so threatened by the implications of religious pluralism? One reason, I suggest, is related to the compelling need for certainty and salvation that pluralism undermines.

Just as the fear and anxiety of death is due, in no small measure, to feelings of helplessness and lack of control, similarly acknowledging the 'other' who cannot be absorbed into our own familiar categories undermines the certainty and stability we crave.

The crucial question of religious pluralism is: can we live with uncertainty? Must we long for the absolute, ironclad truth of God telling us, 'This is my way; follow it and you are saved, deviate from it and you are lost'? Do we need absolute assurance that our way is God's way in order to build our spiritual lives and infuse passion into our religious behaviour? Must I believe that the 'other' is mistaken or, as Maimonides claims, an instrument for my redemption (*Mishneh Torah*, Melakhim, xi, 4 (uncensored version))?

A Religious Tradition without Absolute Certainty

I believe there is an alternative religious sensibility within the Judaic tradition that does not rest on the need for absolute certainty and exclusivity. There is a famous passage in the Babylonian Talmud about the controversies of the schools of Bet Hillel and Bet Shammai. The Talmud says that their disagreements were so intense that the Torah was in danger of becoming two *Torot* (i.e. the community was being split into warring factions). This state of discord ended when a heavenly voice was heard saying, 'These and these are the words of the living God.' Though deeply divided over many issues, the schools of Hillel and Shammai both embody the living word of God. 'However, with respect to practice, the law is according to Hillel.'

'And why did God side with Hillel?' asks the Talmud. 'Because when he (Hillel) presented his views in the bet midrash, the academy of learning, he presented Shammai's position before his own.' When Hillel addressed his students, he first presented the arguments of the opposing point of view and only then did he present his own position. In other words, he did not teach Torah as if his viewpoint was the only valid position, as if he possessed the sole truth. Hillel believed and taught that there was more than one plausible, justifiable opinion.

The codification of one opinion as official law does not affect the pluralistic legal epistemology expressed in 'These and these are the words of the living God.' Deciding which opinion becomes law by the principle of majority rule or some other procedural technique does not determine the relative truths of the rival opinions. Majority rule may reflect a practical procedure for enforcing uniform practice when rational argumentation alone fails to produce unanimity. Therefore, when a law is codified according to the majority, the minority viewpoint is not discarded as being no longer relevant or significant. The prospect of overturning the codified law in the future and accepting the minority opinion remains a permanent possibility (see Eduyot 1.5).

Living by the codified law offers no assurance that one's religious life accords with the absolute truth. For those who require complete religious certainty, the absolute truth, Judaism is bound to be disappointing because of its insistence on the religious validity of controversy and alternative viewpoints. This is the result of building a spiritual way of life on learning and discussion between scholars and not only on the revealed word of God.

In the rabbinic tradition, the Jew is claimed by the revealed word of God, yet that word is filtered through the minds of finite human beings whose arguments, interpretations and decisions largely determine the substantive content of God's word in daily life. Rational persuasion, rather than dogmatic certainty, mediates the covenantal word of God.

Two Forms of Love: The Challenge of Covenantal Pluralism

The Torah refers to two types of love: love of one's neighbour and love of the stranger. In neighbourly love we interact with a person with whom we share common values. When we love our neighbour, we extend the self and expand communal solidarity. In loving the stranger, however, we meet the 'other', the different one, the one who cannot be subsumed easily under our familiar categories.

With respect to the love of the stranger, the Torah makes explicit reference to the Jewish people's historical experience of suffering under a tyrannical regime that oppressed them for being different. Our differences were a source of fear and hatred.

In contrast to the xenophobia we experienced in Egypt, we are told to recall our enslavement and suffering and to empathize with, rather than feel threatened by, the stranger. 'And you shall love the stranger because you were strangers in the land of Egypt' (Deut. 10.19).

Jews throughout history were a stumbling block to those who wished to impose a monolithic framework on the social and political orders. Jewish history reveals that we were often reviled for embodying 'the scandal' of particularity. The Sinai revelation represented our particular way of life and our intimate relationship to God.

My analysis of the universal significance of revelation and the covenant in terms of the affirmation of particularity and human finitude underlies my claim that the covenant as a religious paradigm does not aim at universalizing a particular faith tradition by denying the validity of others. My basic distinction is between a universalistic religious impulse that celebrates the partial and the particular, and a universalistic impulse that believes in the supremacy of one tradition through the elimination of all others.

Given the conceptual distinctions discussed in this chapter, universality should be confined to creation rather than revelation. In other words, it is not the content of revelation but the ethical consciousness grounded in creation that should be universalized. Creation places limits upon and should act as a corrective to the normative content of revelation. No community can fully realize itself if the ethical norms of creation ('Beloved is every human being created in the image of God') fail to become embedded in human consciousness.

The fulfilment of any particular community's tradition is conditional on the universalization of the ethical. The messianic dream must be of a world in which all human beings realize that they are created in the image of God and that all of life is sacred. Only then can the God of creation reign in history.

Revelation implies that God accepts our human limitations and recognizes that human beings realize their potential only within particular communities. For the committed Jew, loving Judaism means loving one's people's memories, one's parent's songs, and one's community's tradition. In embracing Jewish particularity (revelation, history), we also long for the day when human beings will give up war and acknowledge the sacredness of every human being (creation). Until the universal triumph of the ethical, history will remain a hostile environment. We will be condemned to endless violence and war as long as we are frightened to acknowledge and affirm the dignity of the 'other' and to learn to love the stranger and not only the neighbour.

Notes

1 J. B. Soloveitchik, 'Confrontation', *Tradition*, 6/2, 1964, 5–29.
2 A. J. Heshel, *God in Search of Man: A Philosophy of Judaism* (London, Octagon Books, 1978).

NINE   Monotheism and Violence

Moshe Halbertal

In his *Dialogue on Religion*,[1] David Hume draws an important and disturbing distinction between paganism and monotheism. Paganism, says Hume, is by nature pluralistic. The recognition of a multitude of gods limits the imperialistic impulses of paganism from the attempt to dictate a particular way of life. Just as in paganism there is no single and exclusive god, but rather a multitude of forces acting alongside one another, so too it does not demand an exclusive, obligatory and true life style, but allows for a multitude of forms of religion and cult. The pagan believer is like an investor who diversifies his investments. He does not place them all in one basket, but worships a number of gods alongside one another, and these gods accept with equanimity the existence of other forces alongside themselves. Unlike paganism, claims Hume, monotheism is intolerant and posits a single, absolute God. It thus presents one exclusive truth and hence one exclusive way of life. It is not surprising, therefore, that crusades, jihads, and religious wars originated in monotheistic patterns of thought.

In line with this monotheistic logic, the Bible orders the destruction of the pagan religions found in the land of Israel, because it does not allow for the existence of competing gods. For the adherents of monotheistic religions, it is not only important that the God that they represent be admired and worshipped; it is also important that he be the one and only God. The biblical God does not tolerate the worship of other gods alongside himself; he is a jealous God and as such he commands: 'you shall have no other gods before me'. The internal nexus between monotheism and exclusivity might lead to violence and intolerance. How do adherents of monotheistic faith confront the demand for exclusivity, particularly when accompanied by the call for total war against its rivals? This question became sharpened and exacerbated at the beginning of the present century, during which it seems possible that two monotheistic civilizations – Islam and Christianity – might stand against one another in a violent confrontation. Is it indeed correct to say that there is a connection between the structure of monotheism, and intolerance and violence? Is there a place in which monotheistic religions could move on from a clash of civilizations to a collaboration between civilizations? The negation of idolatry is the ultimate basis of Judaism. What is a possible approach of Judaism to this painful and complex subject? Is there an understanding of the war against idolatry that opposes the exclusivist violent potential within the monotheistic religions?

Before examining this question from the viewpoint of an approach that prohibits the worship of idols, another line of inquiry that might be fruitful is one which focuses on the distinction between exclusivism and particularism. Such a distinction rests upon an interpretation of Judaism that opens a certain possibility for dealing with this question because, despite the fact that the one God stands in the very centre of its being, it seemingly does not insist upon one single way to the one God. Judaism is a particularistic religion, and as such does not aspire to impose its own way of life upon all of humankind. Moses Mendelssohn, in his book *Jerusalem*,[2] noted the possibility for religious tolerance opened by the particularistic nature of Judaism. According to his approach, the non-universal nature of Judaism, specifically, gives it a certain advantage over universal monotheistic religions. Mendelssohn argues that, as opposed to Christianity, which claims that a person's salvation is dependent upon his joining the Christian religion, Judaism does not claim any monopoly on the path to salvation. Mendelssohn brings support to such a claim mainly from rabbinic sources that state that righteous Gentiles have a place in the world to come (Tosefta Sanhedrin 13, 2). It seems, following this approach, that the highest religious reward and virtue can also be achieved outside the boundaries of the Jewish tradition, and that there are valid and religiously legitimate forms of worship that are regarded virtuous in the eyes of God. According to this approach, the meaning of the election of Israel is not exclusivist, but particularistic. Whereas the exclusivist approach posits a monopoly over meaningful spiritual life, the particularistic approach argues that there is not only a single way to serve the one God.

Mendelssohn's greatness lay in his revealing the possible connection that exists between universalism and intolerance. On the face of it universalism, which addresses all of humanity, presents all human beings as equal before God, but because of its universal stance it strives to impose itself as the one and only legitimate way to serve God. The weakness of Judaism, according to the universal approach, is that not only does it demand the worship of one God, but it chooses a specific, single group to stand before the one God. Mendelssohn transformed this weakness into a source of strength by interpreting the concept of Israel's election from the perspective of particularism rather than from that of its exclusivism. The challenge posed by Judaism to the other religions, as the mother monotheistic religion, is that it states that one may address the one God in different ways and manners.

Mendelssohn's argument contributes an important dimension to the issue, yet it does not fully resolve our dilemma concerning the nature of monotheism and the prohibition against idolatry as such. After all, though Judaism might allow for the flourishing of many ways to God, they are still all addressed to the one God. To what degree is this absolute and exclusive claim susceptible to violence and inherently intolerant? In order to give an initial response to this concern we have to examine the complex nature of the monotheistic claim. Alongside the prohibition, 'You shall have no other God's before me,' there is an additional proscription: 'You shall not make for yourself a graven image or any likeness.' This prohibition is a second component within the definition of idolatry, which adds a new and complex dimension to the structure of monotheistic thought. Examining the second component of monotheism will reveal a counter voice which points to limitations on truth claims and power positing the absolute transcendence of God.

The prohibition against making any graven image or likeness turns the emphasis away from the worship of other gods, to the suitable or unsuitable manner of representation of God himself. In the second commandment concerning idolatry we learn not only that it is forbidden to worship alien gods, but that it is also forbidden to represent the God of Israel himself in visual representations, sculpture or two-dimensional imagery. What is the significance of this second prohibition? The restrictions imposed on the manner of visual representation of God are connected to the notion that representation is a form of control. To represent something means to make it present, as is indeed implicit in the English verb 'to re-present'. The presumption involved in representation is inherent in its attempt to capture in a two-dimensional image or in a statue the essence of that which is represented, to capture its inner essence and to make it transparent. The prohibition, 'you shall not make for yourself a graven image or any likeness' states that the transcendent and holy God is he who by his very nature is not subject to full representation, and that we are unable to capture him or to make him present. The connection between representation and profanation explains the distinction made by the biblical tradition between visual and verbal representation. Whereas visual representation of God is totally forbidden, his representation in language is definitely permitted. The same biblical text that prohibits the making of images allows the word, and indeed floods us with linguistic representations of God. In the liturgical poem *Anim Zemirot*, which many Jewish congregations are accustomed to reciting every Sabbath, the worshippers depict the damp curls of God's hair – but it would be inconceivable to imagine the worshippers in any Jewish community commissioning an artist to paint God's locks on the ceiling of the synagogue or to depict God creating man, as is done in the Sistine Chapel in the Vatican. The source of the biblical distinction between visual representation and linguistic representation lies in the fact that the picture does not leave any gaps, but attempts to create a fullness of representation – unlike the case of language. As opposed to the presumption of the visual and the plastic, the vacuums left by language transform it into the only medium with which it is fitting to represent God.

One may also define the distinction between language and image in a different manner. The picture depicts a static situation, one that catches its subject and transforms it into an object that freezes its presence. By contrast, voice and word are by nature dynamic: the speaker expresses himself through their means, but they do not create a stable object that is likely to substitute for that which is represented. The picture attempts to control that which is represented, because it freezes it in a certain state, and it is this capturing that, in the final analysis, creates the error of substitution, the substitution of the represented by its representation. The graven image and likeness that are meant to point at something beyond themselves are therefore likely to become an independent focus of the cult; the making of an image or a statue is accompanied by the worship of the image and statue. The cult of representation nullifies their character as representative, and changes them into that which comes instead of that which is represented. The statue, one might say, assumes the characteristics of that which it represents; it is transformed from something that represents God to something which substitutes for him. Thus, the visual representation contains two dimensions that distinguish it from the linguistic representation – exposure and substitution. These two dimensions thus connect between representation and control, and profanation, and are hence the reason for the sharp boundary in which it is stated that the image is prohibited and language is permitted.

The prohibition against making a graven image or likeness establishes the transcendence of God, his being distinct from the human world, his being an entity that cannot be subject to full actualization, a hidden essence that it is impossible to represent or to fully control. This prohibition determines the absolute boundary between the human and the divine. It follows, therefore, that whereas the former prohibition, 'you shall have no other God's before me,' determines the exclusivity of God, 'you shall not make for yourself a graven image or any likeness' establishes the transcendence of God. How is the second prohibition of idolatry related to the question of the connection between monotheism and violence and to the relationship of monotheism to politics? In order to spell out the full meaning of the important implication to politics, an examination of the concept of deification is necessary. In articulating the strict rejection of deification, the relationship between monotheism and violence will be cast in different light.

The substantive sin that the second prohibition of idolatry comes to prevent is deification – the crossing of the boundary between a human being and the divine. Deification is the gravest political sin, because it means the granting of absolute authority to the system of human rule, to the point of deification. Deification is the conveying of titles and gestures that are unique to God to a human being, human institution or human value. The establishment of a firm boundary between the divine and the human has an immense impact on Jewish understandings of politics. It sets itself against pagan conceptions of politics. In its attempt to draw the boundary between the divine and the human in relationship to the realm of politics, the Jewish tradition struggled with the following question regarding what constitutes deification. The problem can be formulated in the following manner: At what point does the ceremonial acceptance of authority in politics become actual worship? The first and most natural candidate for this realm is that of the cult itself. It is forbidden to pray, to offer sacrifices, incense or libations, to any factor other than God himself. Nevertheless, the boundaries of deification are not clear. A person may, for example, honour his father through all kinds of gestures that express a relation of standing before an authority. If, however, he were to offer him incense it would be said that he has turned his father into a god. At what point does a gesture of respect and of acknowledging authority become deification? Within the political realm, this question is a crucial one and there are extreme answers offered to it. For the enlightened pagans of Rome, the cult of the emperor – even offering sacrifices to his image – was a minor matter of civil religion, no more than an expression of loyalty to the state. At the other extreme, the Jewish zealots who led the great rebellion against the Romans saw an ordinary civil obligation such as paying taxes to the emperor as a form of acknowledgement of and service to an alien god. What then is the boundary that separates authority and deification? What titles are exclusive to divinities, such that attributing them to a political figure or institution establishes an alien god? The broader the realm of the titles, the gestures and the political functions that are attributed in an exclusive way to the divinity, the narrower the possibility of establishing any political authority that will not be considered idolatrous.

It is possible to explain in a preliminary manner the connection between politics and deification and the internal tension regarding the boundaries of deification by examining the attitude to the category of the kingship of God. There is a struggle in the Bible between two understandings of the idea of the kingship of God. The one claims that God is king; the other claims that the king is not God. According to the former claim, kingship is an exclusive characteristic of God. Transferring the function to a human being is tantamount to deification. This is what Gideon said to the people when they wished to set up a royal dynasty: 'I will not rule over you, and my son will not rule over you; the Lord will rule over you' (Judg. 8.23). On the same note, the wish of the elders to set up a king at the end of Samuel's life is perceived by God as treason, tantamount to other forms of idolatry:

> For they have not rejected you, but they have rejected me from being king over them. According to all the deeds which they have done from the day I brought them up out of Egypt even to this day, forsaking me and serving other gods, so they are also doing to you. (1 Sam. 8.7–8)

The only form of human leadership that is consistent with this understanding of the kingship of God is the non-institutionalized leadership of the judges, created *ad hoc* for the needs of the moment. As charismatic leaders – earlier versions of crisis managers – the judges never set up a permanent army financed by taxation. But even with the limited nature of their task, God was insistent upon demonstrating his direct rule in an open manner. He instructed Gideon to reduce the number of troops he had assembled for the battle with Midian: 'The people with you are too many for me to give the Midianites into their hands, lest Israel vaunt themselves against me, saying, my own hand has delivered me' (Judg. 7.2). In the prophetic polemics against making defence alliances with such superpowers as Egypt or Assyria, one can see a further restriction placed upon *realpolitik*, deriving from the political monopoly of God. God is, in the final analysis, the master and the giver of protection, and Israel is his vassal, not that of Egypt or Assyria: 'Woe to those who go down to Egypt for help, and rely upon horses, who trust in chariots because they are many, and in horsemen because they are very strong, but do not look to the Holy One of Israel, or consult the Lord' (Isa. 31.1).

At the heart of the claim that God is king lies the idea that political submission is a form of cult, and that granting royal authority to any human being is tantamount to his deification. Yet this political ideology is vulnerable to a sharp criticism. Without the state's monopoly over the use of power, the weak will become completely vulnerable. The anarchist's 'state of nature' will not be a community of free individuals each respecting the rights of his neighbour, but will lead to total chaos or to the arbitrary rule of the strong. The final verse of the Book of Judges is a summary of the opposition position regarding what may be learned from the social attempt at anarchy: 'In those days there was no king in Israel, every man did what was right in his own eyes' (Judg. 21.25). When a community of this type of holy anarchy confronts threats on the part of organized states with strong standing armies, as inevitably happens, it quickly collapses. Hence the elders of Israel present their request: 'We will have a king over us, that we also may be like all the nations, and that our king may govern us, and go out before us and fight our battles' (1 Sam. 8.19–20).

The alternative understanding of the kingship of God, which grows out of such criticism, is that the king is not God. According to this understanding, which represents the mainstream of biblical political thinking, God does not assume a monopoly upon politics as his exclusive realm; instead, he imposes restrictions upon the demands that may be made by politics. The attribution of kingship to human beings is not an act of deification; it is only the myth of kingship as an ahistorical institution rooted in the nature of things, it is only the claim that the king is God that constitutes deification. When the king is not only a warrior, a legislator or a judge, but also the one who causes the Nile to flood its banks or the sun to rise – then the boundary between the human and the divine is crossed. The kingship of God, according to this approach, is recognizable in the struggle against transforming the political into the cosmological and the historical into the mythic.

In the final analysis, the Book of Samuel accepts the institution of kingship so long as the king does not deny his dependence upon God, as may be seen from the critical stance of the prophet further on (for example, in 1 Samuel 12–15). The view that the king is not God allows the existence of earthly politics, but strives to assure that the political does not transgress its own boundaries. The king must fear God, not become a God himself: 'That his heart may not be lifted up above his brethren, and that he may not turn aside from the commandment, either to the right hand or to the left' (Deut. 17.20). The advantage of paganism over monotheism was, as mentioned, in the possibility of multiplicity that it represents. However, its great and profound lack is that it does not draw a boundary between the human and the divine, and that it therefore allows the deification of the political system itself. In the history of paganism we repeatedly find the deification of political forces, from the Egyptian pharaohs who were considered gods, via the Babylonian kings who saw themselves as divine incarnations, through the Roman emperors who, from the days of Augustus on, underwent a process of deification including the establishment of the cult of the emperor.

In the biblical tradition, deification is treated not only as idolatry but as the primary sin of Adam because of which he was expelled from the Garden of Eden. The first chapters of the book of Genesis are concerned with setting the limits to deification. After the expulsion from Eden which befell the first human couple because of their desire to become God-like, there is another attempt, this time collective, to cross the boundary between the human and the divine. In its early stages of history humans understood the infinite power of collective effort, attempting at communal self-deification in the Tower of Babel. The seductive force of deification is inherent in the duality in human nature as such. Humans are part of their environment, yet they dominate and shape it at will. In that respect they are creators and God-like: 'Be fruitful and multiply, fill the earth and subdue it' symbolizes not only man's capability, but also his responsibility. However 'playing God' is the ultimate political sin humans have committed. In modernity, where technology allows almost unlimited expansion of the capacity to control, deification poses itself as a far more crucial concern. In the twentieth century, humans have developed the means to destroy all organic life through nuclear war. It seems very plausible and not accidental that in the twenty-first century humans will develop the means to direct and determine all organic life through genetic engineering. The attempt of humans to gain full control of their reality and be God-like turns against humanity itself. In their effort to reach such a state, people attempt to make everything predictable. The deepest danger of that state is that humanity will end up erasing what Hannah Arendt describes as the human condition itself. The project of total domination which is the aim of totalitarian deificatory politics sets as its main enemy the features of spontaneity, plurality and unpredictability, which define human beings. In this sense, affirming the ultimate transcendence of God and the strict boundary between the human and the divine has become the major political concern of modernity. Humans need to recognize that within their sublime freedom of action there are also the principles of limit and finitude. Human beings must distinguish between their obligation to imitate God and to walk in his ways, and the arrogance and pretence of being like God.

Let us now return to the basic question with which we began: the relationship between monotheism and violence. The prohibition against idolatry, as we have seen, involves two different components. The first commandment, 'you shall have no others gods before me,' dictates the absolute demand for exclusivity. The second one, 'you shall not make for yourself a graven image or any likeness,' establishes the boundaries of representation and the making present of God himself; it postulates God's transcendence. There is a profound tension between these two commandments. One major feature of such a violation of the boundary is the growing voices which speak in politics as if they are articulating God's absolute point of view. Those who speak 'in the name of God', who carry 'his word' into the world by presuming to know and to transmit the absolute truth about him, injure the transcendence of God. Just as it is impossible to represent God through graven image or likeness, so it is impossible to find the way to him through a single, exclusive and absolute path. The limited and violent playing out of zealous exclusivity damages the awesome transcendence of God himself. Awareness of man's finitude means the recognition that we do not have the absolute truth about him, that we can never represent him in a transparent and complete manner.

In recent years we have witnessed the transformation of political conflicts into religious wars. The Israeli-Palestinian conflict is in danger of sliding into a Jewish-Muslim conflict, and some observers claim that the West and Islam are on the brink of a clash of civilizations. The use and abuse of religion in such a conflict serves the aim of making relative claims absolute. Claims for territory, water and security can be compromised as invoking the idea of the sacred blocking the possibility of settlement, since what is sacred is indivisible. The appeal to what is sacred serves to entrench human instrumental interests and concerns in the realm of the absolute. Yet monotheism, with its quest for transcendence, has to aim in the opposite direction. The role of monotheistic tradition in its war against idolatry has to function as a force that makes absolute claims relative rather than absolutizing relative claims. The ultimate destiny of the relations between monotheism and violence depends, among other things, on the following question: which voice within the monotheistic tradition will become dominant, the voice of exclusivity or the voice of transcendence?

Notes

1 D. Hume, *Dialogues Concerning Natural Religion* (Indianapolis, Hackett Publishing Company, 1980).
2 M. Mendelssohn (trans. A. Arkush, ed. A. Altmann), *Jerusalem or On Religious Power and Judaism* (Hanover NH, 1983).

TEN Who is a Jew?
Membership and Admission Policies in the
Jewish Community

Donniel Hartman

Introduction

As an ideal construct, a community is constituted by a collection of individuals who share something in common. What they share serves as the foundation and locus of their shared cultural space and gives their community its distinct place and identity. Within the context of this ideal paradigm, a central vehicle for expressing and maintaining this shared space is through membership policies. These policies are determined in accordance with the content of what the fellow members of the community hold in common and by virtue of which the community has come into existence and inhabits a space of its own. Through its policies of admission and subsequent ability to exclude, a community is empowered to determine and govern its collective character and identity.

In reality, however, it is not a common cultural space or collective ethos that defines most communities, but, at best, the search for this shared space and ethos. More often than not, communities do not pick most of their members; they inherit them, and with this diverse membership body come differing notions of the *telos* of their collective enterprise. The challenge real communities face is how to develop a shared collective identity despite this diversity.

In this context, the search for a membership policy is a complex and often bifurcating experience. The allocation of membership presupposes an agreed-upon common *telos* and shared identity which the membership policy both reflects and supports. Once this agreement is lacking, any particular membership policy will only reflect the will and understanding of one part of the community. When this happens those whose understanding of the collective identity is excluded from the proposed admissions policy, even though their membership is not contested and often 'grand-fathered in', feel marginalized. When the condition for new members is that they embody the particular perspective of only one segment of the society, then the community is in essence declaring that all other members are second-class citizens, an inherited aberration which they hope will one day disappear. The proliferation of these types of divisive feelings amongst fellow members undermines a community's collective life.

Herein lies the challenge and difficulty with admissions policies in the messy, diverse and multi-cultural communities within which we find ourselves. On the one hand, all membership or admission policies must be representative of the lived reality of the community and the actual make-up of its members. However, given the lack of a collective shared identity, admissions polices will invariably have a prescriptive quality to them. Depending on the extent of the ideal nature of the policy, ever-increasing numbers of members will find themselves alienated from the community within which they live.

This is the predicament in which the modern Jewish community with its membership policies finds itself. Over the last two centuries, diversity, along with a subsequent denominationalism of unprecedented scope, have taken root within the community. As a result, it has become increasingly difficult to ascertain a shared ethos around which the Jewish community can remain unified. Within this context, it is not surprising then, that one of the more pointed and salient expressions of this denominationalism is the bitter contentiousness to which any discussion of membership and admission policies inevitably devolves. As a people divided over the question of what constitutes Judaism, we have been unable to reach anything approaching a consensus around the question of 'who is a Jew?', and all current attempts seem to only further the divisive nature of contemporary Jewish collective life.

The aim of this article is to review the foundations for this contentious reality and to offer some suggestions as to how to begin to alleviate it. To this end, I will first review the essential features of Judaism's classical membership policies and assess their implications for the complex reality of contemporary Jewish life.

From the opening statement to the Jewish people's founding father, Abraham: 'Go forth from your native land and from your father's house to the land that I will show you. I will make of you a great nation,' the question of membership surfaces (Gen. 12.1–2). Who will constitute this 'great nation'? Jewish law identifies three different criteria used for allocating membership: birth, marriage to a male Jew, and conversion. While all three were present to varying degrees throughout different periods of Jewish legal discussion, they do not exist together at any one historical moment. Thus, for example, in the biblical period, conversion was not a mechanism of membership. From the period of Ezra and Nehemiah, marriage to a male member had ceased to bind one to the community. From the rabbinic period onwards, birth and conversion became the two exclusive methods for acquiring membership.

Jewishness as Shared Ethnicity

In the Bible, the first criterion outlined for admission into Abraham's 'great nation' was birth; more specifically, being one of Abraham's offspring:

> The Lord appeared to Abram and said, 'I will assign this land to your *offspring*.' (Gen. 12.7; emphasis added)

> I will maintain my covenant between me and you, and your *offspring* to come, as an everlasting covenant throughout the ages, to be God to you and to your *offspring* to come. I assign the land you sojourn in to you and to your *offspring* to come, all the land of Canaan, as an everlasting holding. I will be their God. (Gen. 17.7–8; emphasis added)

As both a symptom and symbol of its ethnic foundation, the 'great nation' bears the name of Abraham's grandson, Jacob (also called Israel): *Bnei Yisrael*. In its most literal, racial expression, members in Israel are referred to as the sole carriers of a common 'holy seed' (Ezra 9.2), a notion that is predicated on the presence of a common lineage. The mediaeval Jewish philosopher and poet, Judah ha-Levi (1086–1145), similarly grounded the election of Abraham and his offspring on a myth of a unique common genetic ancestry that originated in Adam.[1]

Matrilineal and Patrilineal Descent

If birth defines Jewishness, the question of who, father or mother, determines this lineage becomes increasingly significant in modern times, as rising intermarriage rates yield higher percentages of children with only one Jewish parent.

In the Bible, ethnic affiliation and consequently membership status is transmitted to the offspring of Jewish fathers. Thus, *Bnei Yisrael* are the offspring of the *male* children of the *male* grandchild of Abraham. Regardless of the wife's identity, it is the father who determines one's membership, tribal affiliation, share in the land and legal status in the ritual life of the community.

This policy for determining ethnicity remained in effect as long as intermarriage was considered legal. Once it was banned, first by Ezra and then in rabbinic law, the exclusive power of patrilineal ethnicity was curtailed. Henceforth, a policy that combined patrilineality and matrilineality was adopted. Where Jewish law legally sanctioned the marriage, membership was determined in accordance with the father's affiliation.

'Wherever there is an act of marriage (*kiddushin*) and there is no sin, the offspring follows the father'.[2]

Thus, for example, whether one is a Cohen, Levite or Israelite is determined in accordance with the father's status. However, where the marriage is unconstitutional and consequently legally a non-reality, the mother's affiliation determines the child's nationality. In those cases where the mother has no valid marriage claim with the father of the child, the offspring follows the mother.[3]

The primary implication of this shift to matrilineal ties as the determining factor for Jewishness involves the case of intermarriage between a Jew and non-Jew. While permitted in certain circumstances in the Bible, in rabbinic and in subsequent legal literature, this case is not simply prohibited but divested of all legal significance, and thus deemed essentially a non-act. A Jew and non-Jew, in other words, cannot enter into a marriage bond, and their connection has no recognized legal ramifications. As a result, when the husband/father is a member of a different faith community from the wife/mother, he has no legally enforceable responsibilities or ties to either the wife/mother or their child. In such instances, the bond of the mother to the child is given precedence over that of the father. Consequently, the rabbis ruled that in such cases, Jewishness is determined by matrilineal descent.

This position remained in effect for close to 2,000 years and is still applied by the Orthodox and Conservative movements, the Reform movement outside the United States, traditional and secular Israelis, and by the laws of the State of Israel as represented in Israel's Law of Return. Reform Judaism in the United States however, in 1983, formally adopted the position that *either* matrilineal or patrilineal descent is sufficient to determine and confer membership in the Jewish nation so long as the child is brought up Jewish.

Shared Ethnicity as a Sufficient or Necessary Condition

A central issue regarding the allocation of Jewish membership on the basis of a person's ethnicity is whether birth, while clearly necessary in the Bible, is also viewed as sufficient unto itself to confer membership. That is, granting that the community's foundations are ethnic, does shared ethnicity also serve as the central defining characteristic? Or does membership require other factors as well, such as shared faith and behaviour? Two distinct answers to this question are found in the tradition, each with far-reaching consequences for both the question of membership in general and for the viability of collective Jewish life in the modern era in particular.

One perspective views birth not only as a necessary but also as a sufficient condition for membership. Thus, the land is guaranteed unconditionally to Abraham's offspring, by virtue of this biological fact alone. Accordingly, even when the people are deemed unworthy, the state of election and its attendant promises remain in effect:

> And when the Lord your God has thrust them from your path, say not to yourselves, 'The Lord has enabled us to possess this land because of our virtues'; ... but it is because of their wickedness that the Lord your God is dispossessing those nations before you, and in order to fulfil the oath that the Lord made to your *fathers* Abraham, Isaac and Jacob. (Deut. 9.4–5; emphasis added)

Indeed, even when Israel's sins result in exile, most biblical narratives see the exile as temporary, with redemption and return a historical inevitability:

> Yet, even then, when they are in the land of their enemies, I will not reject them or spurn them so as to destroy them, annulling my covenant with them: for I the Lord am their God. (Lev. 26.41–44)

The covenant with Israel, founded on the promise of God to Abraham, Isaac and Jacob to their descendants, is inviolable, regardless of Israel's behaviour. Children may stray, but they never cease to be one's children.

In post-biblical writing, the paradigmatic source on the irrevocability of the covenant is the rabbinic statement, accepted in the Middle Ages almost universally as law: 'Israel has sinned' (Josh. 7.11), Rabbi Abba son of Zavda said: Even though he has sinned, he is still an Israelite.[4] Where shared ethnicity is viewed as both necessary and sufficient, there is a basic sense of belonging that transcends faith and behaviour, and is unaffected by ideological differences or sin. Current divisions and debates aside, a Jew is a Jew is a Jew. While profoundly divided, the community still has a foundation of commonality that it can call upon and count on to consolidate its basic unity.

This notion of birth as the foundational criterion in allocating membership, however, is not the only voice emanating from the Bible and Jewish law. It is interesting to note that, beginning with Isaac and Jacob, the 'offspring' status alone is clearly not viewed as sufficient. Isaac and Ishmael shared the same father; Jacob and Esau the same father *and* mother, yet neither Ishmael nor Esau was considered a forefather of the Jewish people, nor were they or their offspring included in the Israelite nation. Some additional condition, then, beyond biological descent and ethnic ancestry, seems to be a factor in the Bible's definition of membership. What this condition is, however, is not explicated.

Rabbinic commentaries, attempting to fill this gap, pointed to the faith and piety of the elected offspring, or conversely to the moral and spiritual shortcomings of those not chosen. Thus Ishmael, the disinherited son, is portrayed alternately as an idolater, adulterer and murderer.[5] Already as embryos, the Midrash explains, Esau pursued idolatry while Jacob pined after the study of Torah.[6] As an adult, Esau is depicted as an adulterer, murderer, and heretic.[7] While these characterizations are found nowhere in the biblical narrative, they do reflect the notion, found in the election narrative of Isaac and Jacob, that common ethnicity alone was viewed as insufficient. In many ways, the paradigm for the piety-based admission policy is found in Abraham himself. Abraham's election begins with, and is conditioned upon, his taking a leap of faith: 'Go forth from your native land ... I will make of you a great nation' (Gen. 12.1–2). Furthermore, throughout his life, Abraham was ushered through a battery of loyalty tests and challenges to his faith in order to justify his status as the elected one. Only after he passes the final test of the *akeida*, the Binding of Isaac, does God state: 'By myself I swear, the Lord declares: *Because you have done* this and not withheld your son your favoured one, *I will* bestow my blessing upon you' (Gen. 22.13; emphasis added). The initial promise of Genesis 12 needed to be ratified by a life of fidelity to and faith in God.

Nevertheless, it is interesting to note that while Abraham, Isaac and Jacob require another factor beyond birth to substantiate their election, subsequently the requirement seems to disappear. All of Jacob's male children, without exception, are classified as members and no one outside of the family either goes down to Egypt or is calculated within the national census.

The issue, however, is far from resolved. With the completion of the Exodus, where God declares the election of Israel unconditionally – 'I will take you to be my people, and I will be your God' (Exod. 6.7) – the biblical text abandons its exclusive narrative form and weaves in a legal code which serves to regulate the belief and practices of Israel. Being God's people is not simply an inheritance acquired at birth and vouchsafed for life, but a dynamic identity composed of requirements and expectations:

> The Lord called to him from the mountain, saying, 'Thus shall you say to the house of Jacob and declare to the children of Israel: You have seen what I did to the Egyptians, how I bore you on eagle's wings and brought you to me. Now, then, if you will obey me faithfully and keep my covenant, you shall be my treasured possession among all the peoples.' (Exod. 19.3–6)

To be God's 'holy nation' and 'treasured possession' requires more than certification as Abraham's offspring. Israel must 'obey me faithfully and keep my covenant'.

More than a requirement for maintaining Israel's elected status, covenantal fidelity is portrayed as the ultimate purpose of election itself. As Isaiah states:

> My witnesses are you – declares the Lord – my servant, *whom I have chosen. To the end* that you may take thought, and believe in me, and understand that I am he: Before me no god was formed, and after me none shall exist ... So you are my witnesses – declares the Lord and I am God. (Isa. 43.10–11; emphasis added)

Israel does not simply inherit a promise – they inherit a purpose. The fulfilment of this purpose then becomes a condition, which, if rejected by Israel, abrogates the covenant:

> You shall be left a scant few, after having been as numerous as the stars in the skies, because you did not heed the command of the Lord your God. And as the Lord once delighted in making you prosperous and many, so will the Lord now delight in causing you to *perish* and in *wiping you out*. (Deut. 28.62–63; emphasis added)

Furthermore, even those texts that speak of the non-violability of the covenant base this promise not on Israel's genetic roots alone, but on a vision of their subsequent, inevitable, return to God:

> Those of you who survive shall be heartsick over the iniquity in the land of your enemies; more, they shall be heartsick over the iniquities of their fathers; and they shall confess their iniquity and the iniquity of their fathers, in that they trespassed against me, yea, were hostile to me. When I, in turn have been hostile to them and have removed them into the land of their enemies, then at last shall their obdurate heart humble itself, and they shall atone for their iniquity. *Then* will I remember my covenant with Jacob; I will remember also my covenant with Isaac, and also my covenant with Abraham. (Lev. 26.39–42; emphasis added)

While Israel is elected by virtue of their ancestry, they must earn and justify this election to make it permanently their own. Only after they repent will God then re-activate his covenant. Israel is an ethnic community, but shared ethnicity does not exhaust the definition of its collective space. Together with ethnicity there is a system of faith and behaviour by which Israel must abide if they are to remain Israel.

One of the more extreme expressions of this conditionality of membership is found in Maimonides' writings, where in a number of places, he takes the position that not only is ethnicity insufficient, it is in fact hardly relevant. The central and necessary condition for membership is faith:

> *When* all these foundations are perfectly understood and believed in by a person, *he enters the community of Israel* and one is obligated to love and pity him and to act towards him in all ways in which

the Creator has commanded that one should act towards his
brother, with love and fraternity. Even were he to commit every
possible transgression, because of lust and because of being
overpowered by evil inclination, he will be punished according to
his rebelliousness, but he has a portion [of the world to come]; he
is one of the sinners of Israel. *But if a man doubts any of these
foundations, he leaves the community [of Israel]*, denies the fundamental, and is called a sectarian, *apikorus*, and one who cuts among
the plantings. One is required to hate him and destroy him.[8]

According to Maimonides, membership in Israel is contingent on the
acceptance of certain principles of faith. One who takes these on is
considered part of Israel, while one who rejects them, regardless of his
ethnic roots, is cast out of Israel's shared cultural space.

Membership through Marriage

The second option for acquiring membership in Israel, present prior to the
sixth century BCE, when it was deemed illegal by Ezra, is through marriage
to a Jew, or more precisely, a Jewish male. The ethnic family unit, while
commonly defined as an exclusive entity open only to those who have
blood ties, is in fact open to 'outsiders' through the institution of marriage.
Bnei Yisrael were not constituted by men and women of Israelite descent
alone, but often by Israelite men and non-Israelite women who married into
the community. Given the patrilineal bias of the Bible, the avenue of
membership through marriage was available only to women. Since a woman
did not transmit ethnicity, she could not transmit Jewishness to a non-Jewish
spouse. The first evidence of this process of acquiring membership appears
when the matriarchs and the subsequent wives of the sons of Jacob are
integrated as members, despite their non-Abrahamic ancestry. Dinah the
daughter of Jacob, in contrast, since she has no Israelite man to marry (other
than her brothers), ultimately disappears from the story, and both she and
her possible descendants are not mentioned amongst the Israelites who
descended to Egypt (Exodus 1).

While marriage with a non-Israelite was clearly acceptable and
prevalent, it was not without limitations. The first evidence of restrictions
is found with Abraham's instruction to his servant 'Put your hand under my
thigh and I will make you swear by the Lord, the God of heaven and the
God of earth, that you will not take a wife for my son from the daughters of
the Canaanites among whom I dwell, but will go to the land of my birth and
get a wife for my son Isaac' (Gen. 24.2–4). The preference for women from
Ur of the Chaldees, Abraham's birthplace, over Canaanite women, could

not have been the result of an ideological affinity with the former as distinct from the latter, for both were equally idolatrous. Nor is it based on familial ties, for as seen above, the covenant is with Abraham's descendants. The Bible, however, provides no explicit explanation for this restriction.

This limitation on intermarriage with local Canaanite women, followed also by Jacob although not by his sons, is made mandatory for Israel when they inherit the land.

> When the Lord your God brings you into the land that you are about to enter and possess, and he dislodges the Hittites, Girgashites, Amorites, Canaanites, Perezzites, Hivites, and Jebusites, seven nations much larger than you – and the Lord your God delivers them to you and you defeat them, you must doom them to destruction: grant them no terms and give them no quarter. You shall not intermarry with them: do not give your daughters to their sons or take their daughters for your sons. For they will turn your children away from me to worship other gods, and the Lord's anger will blaze forth against you and he will promptly wipe you out. Instead this is what you shall do to them: you shall tear down their altars, smash their pillars, cut down their sacred posts, and consign their images to the fire. (Deut. 7.1–5)

The biblical prohibition against intermarriage, similar to Abraham's instruction to his servant, is framed by geographical boundaries. As a rule, intermarriage with non-Israelite women is not forbidden. In fact if it was, there would have been no need to specifically prohibit the seven Canaanite nations. The reason for the geographical restraint, as explicated here in Deuteronomy, is the result of the fear of influence from the idolatrous spouse: 'For they will turn your children away from me to worship other gods.' This influence, however, is geographically sensitive, for the power of idolatry is also geographically sensitive, and by definition limited to a specific locale. The idol of a foreign land has no power or authority over the inhabitants of the land of Israel. It is only indigenous idolatry that can serve as an alternative to the worship of God. Furthermore, the proximity to the idolater's family further exacerbates the dangers of influence. These fears may also have been at the root of Abraham's instruction.

Given the limited prohibition against intermarriage, one can articulate the following rule: intermarriage is permitted and is a process of acquiring membership so long as the non-Jewish spouse will be integrated into the Israelite religious and national context. Where there is a danger of the opposite occurring, i.e. the Israelite being integrated into the idolater's religious and national milieu, then intermarriage is forbidden. Thus the marriage of Israelite women to non-Israelite men and marriage with idolaters indigenous to the land of Israel are both outlawed.

Membership through marriage is thus an extension of the approach that viewed shared ethnicity as a necessary though not sufficient category for membership. Through the bonds of marriage, a non-Israelite woman receives the affiliation of her spouse. She does so, however, not simply through the legal consequences of marriage, as found, for example, in both the laws of Nuremberg and the State of Israel's Law of Return. She joins Israel because marriage involves acceptance of the religious and national affiliation of one's spouse. Where this does not or will not occur, then the marriage alone is not sufficient to confer membership and is, in fact, banned.

The biblical allocation of membership through marriage is thus conceptually a precursor to the rabbinic allocation of membership through conversion. However, in the Bible, this conversion of identity is achieved without a formal process of identity and membership transformation. A paradigm for this marriage/conversion is found in the Book of Ruth, with Ruth often mistakenly identified as the first convert. Ruth the Moabite marries one of Elimelech and Naomi's sons while they are sojourning in Moab. The intermarriage is mentioned as a matter of fact, with no explicit or implicit censure. The nature of Ruth's status and relationship to the religion and people of Israel while in Moab is not discussed. However, when upon Naomi's return to Israel after the deaths of her husband and two sons, and the end of the famine there, both sisters-in-law are urged by Naomi to return to their mother's house. Naomi depicts the sister-in-law who opts to stay in Moab and return to her family as not simply leaving Naomi's family, but rather as returning to 'her people and her gods' (Ruth 1.15). By implication, their prior life with Naomi's sons entailed a connection to a different people and a different god. What the Bible portrays as laudatory with regard to Ruth is the fact that she remains loyal to Naomi. The consequence of this loyalty and of her return with Naomi to the land of Israel is the preservation of Ruth's association with the God and people of Israel.

> But Ruth replied, 'Do not urge me leave you, to turn back and not follow you. For wherever you go, I will go; wherever you lodge I will lodge; your people are my people, and your God my God.' (Ruth 1.16)

While later rabbinic sources saw this statement as a conversion moment, Ruth did not convert in any formal sense, never undergoing an official process of changing her religious and national identity (unless of course one identifies her mother-in-law, Naomi, as the first female rabbi). Rather, she joins the community and its religion through marriage and remains there despite her husband's death. As such, to use the words of the Book of Ruth, she is like 'Rachel and Leah, both of whom built up the House of Israel' (Ruth 4.11).

In the Book of Ezra and subsequently in rabbinic sources, intermarriage becomes forbidden. In what is portrayed as the first Midrash, the Book of Ezra expands the prohibition of intermarriage to the new inhabitants of the land of Israel, 'whose abhorrent practices *are like* those of the Canaanites, the Hittites, the Perizzites, the Jebusites, the Ammonites, the Moabites, the Egyptians, and the Amorites' (Ezra 9.1; emphasis added). Consequently, all who have married local women are forced to annul the marriage, there being no other solution as conversion was not yet available. From the period of Ezra onwards, both intermarriage and the allocation of membership it entailed were universally abrogated.

Given the prevalence of intermarriage in the contemporary Jewish community, however, it is not unreasonable to project that in the near future there will be a position advocating its return, possibly making the same distinction present in the Bible. When a couple chooses Judaism as their and their children's religion, then intermarriage is permitted. Intermarriage will only be prohibited when the non-Jew's religion or lack of religious/national affiliation determines the family's identity. In many ways it may come to be viewed as a logical extension of the United States Reform Movement's position, according to which Jewishness is dependent on either patrilineal or matrilineal descent on condition that the child is given a Jewish education and identity. Where the marriage is viewed as creating a Jewish family unit capable of conferring Jewish membership and identity, it is difficult to sustain a policy of rejection of the marriage itself, as well as the status of the non-Jewish spouse as outside the community. In fact, with the prevalence of intermarriage, the Jewish people around the world have already informally begun this process.

Membership through Conversion

The third avenue for acquiring membership is conversion, first deemed legal in the Second Temple period. This was an outgrowth of the idea that Jewish identity transcended pure ethnicity and, as stated, a formalization of the process which non-Israelite wives went through when marrying their Israelite husbands. An exclusivist, ethnocentric perspective on Jewishness would not have allowed for the possibility of conversion, as proven in the Book of Ezra.

Once conversion came to be incorporated into the legal tradition, the question of what would constitute a valid rite of passage arose. It is possible to identify in Jewish law two distinct schools of thought regarding this process. The first, dominant in rabbinic and subsequent halakhic literature prior to the nineteenth century, views conversion as a formal rite in which a non-member becomes a member with little consideration given to his or her prospective future commitment and fidelity to Jewish law. This position views conversion itself in somewhat minimalist terms, as a gateway to membership but not as the primary arena for determining the nature and quality of Jewish life. Just as a born member of a religion can choose to deviate and sin, so too can a convert become a sinning member. A convert is subject to the same consequences for sin as a born Jew: sanctions and policies of marginalization and exclusion.

A paradigmatic example of this view can be found in the Talmudic discussion of Hillel the Elder's approach to the conversion process:

> Our rabbis taught: A certain heathen once came before Shammai and asked him, 'How many Torahs have you?' 'Two', he replied, 'the Written Torah and the Oral Torah'. 'I believe you with respect to the Written, but not with respect to the Oral Torah; make me a proselyte on condition that you teach me the Written Torah [only].' [But] he scolded and repulsed him in anger. When he went before Hillel, he converted him. On the first day, he taught him, Aleph, Beth, Gimmel, Daleth [The first four letters of the Hebrew alphabet]; the following day he reversed [the order] to him. 'But yesterday you did not teach them to me thus,' he protested. 'Must you then not rely upon me? Then rely upon me with respect to the Oral [Torah] too.'

> On another occasion it happened that a certain heathen came before Shammai and said to him, 'Make me a proselyte, on condition that you teach me the whole Torah while I stand on one foot.' Thereupon he repulsed him with the builder's cubit which was in his hand. When he went before Hillel, he converted him. He then said to him, 'What is hateful to you, do not to your neighbour: that is the whole Torah, while the rest is the commentary thereof; go and learn it.'

> On another occasion it happened that a certain heathen was passing behind a House of Learning, when he heard the voice of a teacher reciting, 'And these are the garments which they shall make; a breastplate, and an ephod'. Said he, 'For whom are these?' 'For the High Priest', he was told. Then said that heathen to himself, 'I will go and become a proselyte, that I may be appointed a High Priest.' So he went before Shammai and said to

him, 'Make me a proselyte on condition that you appoint me a High Priest.' But he repulsed him with the builders cubit which was in his hand. He then went before Hillel, who converted him.[9]

In each of the above cases, Hillel converts the individual in question even though his commitment to observe Jewish law (to say nothing of his motivation for conversion) is highly suspect. In the first case, despite the fact that the vast majority of Jewish law is rooted in the Oral Torah, Hillel is yet willing to convert the individual who rejects that Torah in its entirety. In the second case, the individual who is willing to convert so long as the process does not take more than a few moments is not only uncommitted to observance, but makes a mockery of the process. In all probability, he is converting as a favour to his spouse or her family. In the last case, the individual wants to convert simply because he believes that he will acquire some financial gain. Neither the laws nor the faith of Judaism are of any consequence to him. In none of these cases does Hillel raise an objection or precondition before assenting to the prospective convert's request. For him, the mere desire to convert is sufficient. Only after the conversion is *complete* does the education process begin; a process which, according to the text, Hillel himself immediately initiates with each new Jew.

The central legal source, which defines the process of conversion in the Talmud, is found in Tractate Yevamot. Like Hillel's approach, it does not make prior commitment to faith or practice a condition for becoming a Jew. Where it differs is in placing an emphasis on ensuring that the convert knows what he is getting into. A valid conversion process does not have to guarantee future observance, but it must make very clear to the individual what he is taking upon himself, politically, religiously and legally:

> Our rabbis taught: If at the present time a man desires to become a proselyte, he is to be addressed as follows: 'What reason have you for desiring to become a proselyte; do you not know that Israel at the present time are persecuted and oppressed, despised, harassed and overcome by afflictions?' If he replies, 'I know and yet am unworthy,' he is accepted forthwith, and is given instruction in some of the minor and some of the major commandments. He is informed of the sin [of the neglect of the commandments of] Gleanings, the Forgotten Sheaf, the Corner and the Poor Man's Tithe. He is also told of the punishment for the transgression of the commandments. Furthermore, he is addressed thus: 'Be it known to you that before you came to this condition, if you had eaten suet you would not have been punishable with *karet*, if you had profaned the Sabbath you would not have been punishable with stoning; but now were you to eat suet you would be

punished with *karet*; were you to profane the Sabbath you would be punished with stoning.' And as he is informed of the punishment for the transgression of the commandments, so is he informed of the reward granted for their fulfilment. He is told, 'Be it known to you that the world to come was made only for the righteous, and that Israel at the present time are unable to bear either too much prosperity or too much suffering.' He is not, however, to be persuaded or dissuaded too much. If he accepted, he is circumcised forthwith. Should any shreds which render the circumcision invalid remain, he is to be circumcised a second time. As soon as he is healed arrangements are made for his immediate ablution, when two learned men must stand by his side and acquaint him with some of the minor commandments and with some of the major ones. When he comes up after his ablution he is deemed to be an Israelite in all respects.[10]

The rabbis and subsequently the three major mediaeval codifications of Jewish law set one condition for the convert's acceptance: it must be clear to him that conversion to Judaism joins him not merely to God in a new relationship, but to a particular community, whose members have been suffering as a consequence of their affiliation. Once the aspiring convert indicates his understanding and acceptance of this shift, the Talmud and all subsequent codifications acknowledge that 'he is accepted forthwith'.

The subsequent process of absorption into the faith is geared towards making the convert aware of certain factors that might influence his decision. These include a cursory knowledge of Jewish law and, in particular, of the sin of not fulfiling the obligations to the poor and the consequences of transgression. This last point is important, as its purpose is not to elicit a commitment to observance – quite the contrary. Given the fact that the level or quality of the potential convert's observance is not predetermined or pre-committed, it is important that he or she be aware of the implications of any decision to violate the law. Prior to conversion, the person could eat what he or she wanted, observe the Sabbath in any chosen manner, etc. Once a Jew, the convert will be held liable, like all other Jews, for deviance from the legal system. The purpose of all these latter instructions, which occur after 'he is accepted forthwith', is to provide information that might influence and possibly sway the convert's decision to continue. From the perspective of Jewish law, however, he or she has already been accepted.

As distinct from this unconditional approach to conversion, the minority opinion in rabbinic and mediaeval Jewish law requires of potential converts a prior commitment of fidelity to all or much of Jewish law. In other words, conversion is only granted to those committed to becoming ideal citizens. One of the earliest representations of this position is found in the Sifra on Leviticus 19.34. Leviticus states: 'The *ger* (lit. stranger, but interpreted by the Midrash to denote the convert) who resides with you shall be to you as one of your citizens.' The Sifra then states:

> 'Citizen' – this refers to a citizen who has accepted upon himself (as binding) all of the words of the Torah. So too the convert refers to one who has accepted upon himself (as binding) all the words of the Torah. From here they said: A convert who accepted upon himself (as binding) all the words of the Torah with the exception of one, is not accepted. Rabbi Yossi son of Rabbi Yehudah said: Even if (the exception) is a minor matter of Rabbinic minuteness.[11]

This Midrash advances a model of conversion that is conditional on the convert's full acceptance of *all* of Jewish law. While an ethnic Jew may reject the law yet remain a Jew by virtue of his ethnicity, a convert can only join to the extent that he or she embodies the ideal notion of the shared ethos or 'cultural space' of the Jewish community. Given the lack of ethnic roots, the convert can only join by accepting the ideals, values and way of life of a Jew.

This latter approach to conversion, while still debated, has become more prevalent in contemporary Orthodoxy since the middle of the nineteenth century. One exemplar of this position, Rabbi Moshe Feinstein, a leading Orthodox halakhic authority of the twentieth century, rules as follows:

> As to what his honour debated regarding the status of a convert who did not accept upon himself *mitzvot*, whether he is considered a convert, it is simple and clear that he is not a convert at all, even [if we only find out that he did not accept *mitzvot*] after the fact ... And even if he verbally stated that he accepts the commandments, but we know that this acceptance is not truthful, [the conversion] is void ... And in general, I do not understand the reasoning of the rabbis who err on this matter, for according to them, what benefit are they producing by doing so to the community of Israel by accepting converts such as these, regarding whom it is certain that God and the people of Israel are not pleased that converts such as these will assimilate into Israel. Legally, is it simply that he is not a convert at all.[12]

Irrespective of what one thinks about the sufficiency of shared ethnicity or what constitutes a valid conversion, these two avenues of admission represent differing visions of the core identity of the Jewish people. One views Jewish identity primarily as a collective whose members are first and foremost bound by ties of shared ethnicity, while the other sees Jewish collective identity embodied in a set of common values, ideals and practices. By adopting both as avenues for admission, the Jewish tradition refused to select one over the other and chose instead to live with an internal and in many ways irresolvable tension. On the one hand, the ethnic roots of the community create a notion of Jewishness as family, a people bound together with ties of loyalty and responsibility regardless of their practices and beliefs. Israelites, although they have sinned, are still Israelites. At the same time, by emphasizing its shared *telos* – accepting converts and limiting the ties of loyalty in certain extreme cases of deviance – the community is stating that ethnicity, while a foundation, is not sufficient to define all that Jewishness entails. While one becomes a Jew through birth, and that fact cannot (in most cases) be undone, the Jewish community chose to define itself in terms that transcend racial categories alone.

The Modern Situation

One of the more troubling and challenging aspects of contemporary Jewish collective life is its inability to reach a consensus on the rules that govern *any* of the above-mentioned admission criteria. Regarding shared ethnicity, since the United States Reform Movement's adoption of patrilineality as an avenue for admission, the question of who is born a Jew debated for the first time in Jewish history. With regard to membership through intermarriage, the disagreement is more subtle but also more pervasive. Officially, all the Jewish denominations are united in their rejection of this avenue of acquiring membership. However, while Jewish officialdom is for once united, close to fifty per cent of the Jewish people outside Israel are acting differently. From being a marginal act that symbolized a rejection of Judaism and the Jewish people, intermarriage has entered mainstream Jewish life. Not only is intermarriage not viewed negatively, but the non-Jewish spouse often affiliates with both Judaism and the Jewish people. Ignoring the policy of the rabbis and the more traditional Jews, a large segment of the Jewish people have begun a process of re-instituting the biblical notion of membership through intermarriage. Finally, regarding admission through conversion, there is no agreed-upon understanding of what the process must entail, particularly as the result of Orthodoxy's adoption of a conversion policy that sets Orthodox faith and observance as preconditions. If an individual can become a member through conversion only to the extent that he or she fully embodies the ideals, values and practices of Jewish life, as understood by Orthodoxy, then by definition, Conservative, Reform and Reconstructionist conversions are meaningless according to Orthodoxy.

The above disagreements challenge Jewish collective life in different ways. While the disagreement over conversion is seemingly less significant, given the relatively small number of converts involved, it is not by accident that it has become the source of some of the most divisive and rancorous inter-denominational debates. As stated above, particular admissions policies that reflect the understanding of one group of members alone serve to marginalize all others who do not share this understanding. Thus, a policy that legitimizes only those converts who are willing to be Orthodox does not affect converts alone, but all those who are not Orthodox. Through this policy, non-Orthodox Jews feel that they are being disinherited. When this policy is further connected to the State of Israel and its Law of Return, then non-Orthodox Jews feel that Israel, the focus of Jewish collective identity and memory, is being taken from them. The proliferation of these feelings generates strong forces of bifurcation that threaten Jewish collective unity.

The disagreements on birth and intermarriage pose an even greater threat. While birth may not have been viewed as sufficient to express Jewish collective identity, throughout the ages it provided a form of safety net for the community. Even if we disagreed with each other regarding issues of faith and law, these disagreements rarely generated calls for mutual expulsion. An Israelite, even though he or she had sinned, was still considered an Israelite. By debating who is a Jew by birth, with roughly half of the Jewish children born today in the United States having only one Jewish parent, the contemporary Jewish community has lost its safety net. Now, as stated above, complex communities are rarely defined by that which the various and diverse members hold in common. More often than not, they can at best aspire to be united by a search for that elusive collective identity. This search, however, presupposes an agreement regarding the make-up of the individuals who are building a common life. When Jews disagree on the issue of who is born a Jew, the disagreement extends to the question of with whom we have to debate the issue of Jewish collective identity. If one side sees the other as outsiders, they do not need to take their opinion seriously, for the search for a collective identity is conducted amongst insiders alone. In such a reality, there is no hope for reaching some form of collective understanding of the boundaries, meaning and *telos* of the Jewish collective enterprise.

Furthermore, a consequence of the absence of a basic agreement as to who is a member is that marriage between Jews of different denominations may be increasingly threatened. The acceptance of each other as marriage partners is the most minimal sense of mutual accommodation, an expression of our willingness to consider each other as Jewish despite our disagreements. Once this is removed, the community as one united entity will officially cease to exist.

Where does this leave us? The process of ideological diversity and denominationalism, which began some 200 years ago, has reached its critical stage and developed into a widespread division regarding membership itself – not merely with regards to who *ought* to be in but who *is* in. Such a condition cannot be ignored for much longer and it requires the urgent attention of all Jews of all denominations. We must decide whether we want to be a part of one people, to share and live together as partners in the same 'house', or whether we want to move out and create separate communities. If we want to stay, then it will require both our shared attention and a common willingness to do something about it.

Were it possible to envisage a compromise that would require of every side to relinquish something of their denominational 'truth' for the sake of the people, we could begin the process of rectifying the current situation and begin to build a shared membership policy. The problem is that it is hard to envision what such a compromise would look like. Reform Judaism is not about to repeal its decision on patrilineality, Orthodoxy is not going to recognize non-Orthodox conversion procedures or rabbinic courts, and intermarriage as an acceptable marriage option for Jews is here to stay.

The threat to our collective life is real and it is our religious responsibility to respond. Given the absence of a shared admission policy, I would suggest the adoption of the policy that membership ought to be determined in accordance with any of the traditional membership policies outlined above. At issue is not whether I personally accept matrilineal or patrilineal descent or this or that conversion process, but rather that we all must recognize that we cannot determine the membership policies of the whole people on the basis of our own denominational affiliations. A community's shared collective space must be determined by the members of the community as a whole, and our community – whether we like it or not – is a divided one. We have listened to the 3,000–4,000-year diverse narrative of how individuals have joined our people and have reached different conclusions. So long as one remains within the boundaries of this narrative, absent a consensus, I believe it is our duty to recognize the legitimacy of his or her claim to membership in the Jewish people.

I am not naïve, however, and the same denominational reality that prevented us from reaching a shared consensus will greet the above suggestion with broad condemnation. We do need, however, to ignore the initial criticism and unpack the arguments more carefully to see whether, in fact, its scope cannot be limited. Adopting this policy and allocating membership to individuals whose status is contested need not be an issue in most areas of Jewish collective life. First, the State of Israel, as the home of a diverse Jewish population and the centre of Jewish life for Jews of all denominations from around the world, has to be the first to abide by this policy. Citizenship in the State is not a halakhic category as is evident by the non-Jewish citizens who live there. In essence, Israel's Law of Return already follows similar lines, and we must renew our commitment both to not change it and to expand the rights of all denominations to confer Jewish membership within the State. In Jewish communities around the world, on an institutional level – be it synagogues, Jewish federations, JCCs, day schools, camps, or the like – with the exception of the allocation of certain ritual roles, there are no legal impediments to its broad application either. Even these ritual roles themselves, such as being counted in a *minyan* and receiving an *aliyah*, do not warrant the institution of membership-checking procedures with the subsequent pain, embarrassment and factionalism they will engender. In addition, there is no halakhic reason why a child of patrilineal descent whose parents want to send him or her to a Conservative or Orthodox day school should be prevented from doing so. The right to a Jewish education need not be limited to one's denominational definition of members alone. The same is the case for leadership positions in all of the above. As a general rule of thumb, all Jewish institutions, including the State of Israel, should be willing to allocate Jewish membership in accordance with the same criteria they already use for awarding honours for financial contributions. Whoever is Jewish enough for us to accept their money (or to make the personal sacrifice of serving in the Israeli Defence Forces), should be counted as insiders for membership purposes as well.

In fact, the only area where there remains a real problem is marriage, where the differences of opinion about membership lead to a boundary that many believe cannot be overcome. While one may welcome another's child into a school, or sit with them on a board, diverse denominational policies vis-à-vis conversion, for example, will lead many to refrain from marrying each other. While in theory this is of grave consequence, on a collective level in reality this situation need not necessarily require a communal solution. At the end of the day most Jews in fact currently abide by the above-suggested policy. Where the majority of Jews are not willing to marry outside the faith, they are certainly willing to accept patrilineality and conversion, even through a denomination other than their own. This is also the case amongst many who insist on their marriage partner being of the Jewish faith. Where the problem is more acute is in more traditional circles, in particular in Orthodoxy. Here too, the problem in most cases has a functional solution. One who marries into Orthodoxy in all probability accepts Orthodox definitions of membership and is willing to undergo a conversion. If Orthodoxy does not want to find itself with a shrinking potential marriage pool and completely separated from the rest of the Jewish community, it will utilize in these cases the precedent set by Hillel and adopt conversion processes which are welcoming and sensitive. Over the years it will become common knowledge that dating and subsequent marriage to an Orthodox Jew may ultimately require this, and only those so inclined will embark on this path. In the event that the individual does not want to convert, the couple is still left with plenty of other Jewish options if they nevertheless choose to marry. There may be cases that will end in individual tragedies, and while I am not belittling the personal suffering that may ensue, the extent will be sufficiently small to avoid implications on the future of Jewish collective life.

There is then one question that we face, and that is whether we are committed enough to the Jewish people to cease playing denominational politics with our future. While a shared and common membership policy is preferred, it is in no way a necessity. All that is needed is for us to internalize that Judaism is a collective enterprise and that our people is larger than any one of our individual denominations. What we have to learn is that accepting this axiom does not require the violation of any halakhic commitments or principles of faith; neither does it presuppose some idyllic consensus on these issues. We are an ideologically divided people and such we will stay. What we need to do is separate ideological commitments from the need for political posturing, and halakhic principles from the need to constantly delegitimize each other. Once we do this we will realize that in most areas, and in fact in the most important areas of our collective life, we can accept each other as Jews even though we each disagree with the Judaism the other professes. While in theory we have been taught by our denominational loyalties that this compromise is impossible, as argued above, in almost every instance it is eminently and functionally doable, and where it is not, in most cases there are *ad hoc* solutions available. All that is needed is a healthy will to survive, not as individuals, but as one people.

Notes

1 J. Ha-Levi (trans. N. D. Korobkin), *The Book of the Kuzari* (Northvale, Jason Aronson, 1988), 1.95, 103.
2 Mishnah Kiddushin 3.12.
3 *Ibid.*
4 BT Tractate Sanhedrin 44a.
5 Tosefta Sotah Ch. 6.
6 Genesis Rabbah 63.
7 BT Tractate Baba Batra 16b.
8 Maimonides, *Introduction to Perek Helek*, in M. Kneller, *Dogma in Medieval Thought* (Oxford, Oxford University Press, 1986), p. 16 (emphasis added). See also Maimonides, Laws Pertaining to Idolatry, 2.5.
9 BT Tractate Shabbat 31a.
10 BT Tractate Yevamot 47a-b.
11 Sifra Kiddushin 8.3 on Leviticus 19.34.
12 M. Feinstein, *Responsa Igrot Moshe*, Yoreh Deah (New York, Rabbi M. Feinstein, 1974), 1.157.

ELEVEN

The Anomalies of Jewish Political
Identity

Michael Walzer

We all know how anomalous Jewish identity is, and we all know the
reasons; so I am going to begin this chapter by reciting what we all know. I
hope this will be a useful exercise: to make explicit what is mostly informal
knowledge, common sense, or intuitive understanding can help us think
about things more clearly.

So: the Jews are a people, a nation, for a long time a stateless nation,
but nonetheless a collective of a familiar kind. There are many nations, and
we are one among them. And, at the same time, the Jews are a religious
community, a community of faith, as we say in the United States – which is
another collective of a familiar kind. There are many religions, and ours is
one among them. The anomaly is that these two collectives are not of the
same kind, and they don't ordinarily or, better, they don't, except in the
Jewish case, coincide. Other peoples or nations include members of
different religious communities. Other religious communities extend across
national boundaries and include members of different peoples or nations.

Consider first how we differ from other peoples. The French people,
for example, includes Catholics and Protestants and now Muslims – and
Jews too, who would certainly resent being denied membership. But the
Jewish people does not include Christians or Muslims. It does indeed
include secular Jews and also distinct denominations of religious Jews, and so
one can say that there exists among the Jewish people a range of religious
sensibility (and insensibility). But it is commonly understood, even among
the irreligious, and it is established law in the State of Israel, that formal
conversion to another religion excludes the convert from membership in
the Jewish people. But aren't there Jewish Buddhists nowadays? And what
about Jews for Jesus – aren't they still Jews? Maybe so, but these identities
seem to involve something considerably short of formal conversion. Their
status is up in the air. What is clear is that there are no Jewish Catholics,
Baptists, Methodists or Presbyterians. However pro-Israeli American
Pentacostalists are, they can't join the Jewish people without giving up
their Christianity – which they don't have to do to join any other people.
So the Jews are not a 'people' like the others. Zionism aimed to produce a
'normal' people, and given the conditions of our exile, that project was

certainly a healthy one; the Zionist passion for normalcy has real achievements to its credit. But it hasn't made us like everyone else.

Nor is our religion like all the other religions. The Catholic Church, for example, is a universal religious community that includes men and women who are members of the French, Italian, Irish, Nigerian and Korean peoples, and many others, too. The Jewish religious community isn't like that, even though it does include men and women who are French, English, Russian, and so on – because Jews are French, English, and Russian with a difference. The pre-Zionist and then anti-Zionist campaign to create a normal religious community, consisting of Frenchmen, say, or Germans, of the 'Mosaic faith', seems to me less healthy than Zionism was, but, still, it was an understandable response to the conditions of our exile. And it, too, has proven futile: French Jews continue to be Jewish in both the religious and the national sense. However 'French' they are or think themselves to be, they are as anomalous as ever.

In the United States, it was Jewish advocates of cultural pluralism, Horace Kallen the most important, who invented the idea of hyphenated Americans, so that we could add 'American' to our identity without giving up 'Jewish': we are not Americans who happen to be of the Jewish religion; we are both American Jews (religiously) and Jewish-Americans (nationally). We pretend that we are like American Catholics, on the one hand, and like Italian-Americans, on the other. But the analogy doesn't work in either case. Many American Catholics, for example, are not Italian, and some Italian-Americans are not Catholic, while our religious and national identities continue, anomalously, to coincide. Even those of us who aren't personally religious are Jewish in both these senses.

The existence of the State of Israel makes things even more complicated. Here is a Jewish state that has a large and growing number of non-Jewish citizens. Some Jews inside and outside of Israel claim that the state doesn't belong to its citizens, in the way all other states do, but to the Jewish people as a whole, including Jews who are citizens of other states. This would be a greater anomaly than any of those I have discussed so far, but it isn't true except in a very special sense of 'belong'. Normally I have decision-making authority over things that belong to me, but the Jewish people as a whole doesn't have decision-making authority over the State of Israel. The state is a democracy, and democracies belong, in the normal sense of that word, to their citizens. So Israel belongs to its citizens, including its non-Jewish citizens.

Perhaps Zionist normalcy would be realized if and when 'Israeli' became a nationality – for this nationality would extend to members of different religious communities, Jewish, Muslim and Christian. Doesn't it do that already? But it also extends to members of different national communities, Arabs and Jews, and it doesn't yet offer a superseding nationality. One day being an Israeli might be more important than being an Arab or a Jew, and then there would be a normal Israeli nation, with a state of its own. But this state would not 'belong' to the Jewish people in any sense of the word – as that's precisely what would make it normal. We might need, maybe we already need, a new hyphenated identity, Jewish-Israeli, to designate those citizens of the Jewish (national) state who are also (religious) Jews.

So far, the normalizing projects have failed to overcome the weight of history and tradition. But they haven't failed definitively; they might one day be revived with greater success. And I can see the point of experimenting right now with what might be called bits and pieces of normalcy. Consider the question of how one joins the Jewish people/ religion. Right now there is only a religious way in. But why shouldn't it be possible for prospective Jews to choose whether they say 'Your people shall be my people' *or* 'Your God shall be my God'? Why do they have to say both together, even in cases where one or the other isn't what they really mean? The search for a naturalization process that might sit alongside the conversion process seems to me entirely legitimate, even sensible, though it is unlikely to succeed in the near future.

But there are motives for normalization that should make us uneasy: the hope, for example, that other people might like us better if we were more like them. Anomaly isn't popular. People find us hard to understand. Because neither our national nor our religious community is inclusive in the standard way, we are accused of being parochial, hostile to outsiders, exclusionary, chauvinist, and, in any group except our own, disloyal and subversive. Indeed, we have all heard accusations of these kinds, and sometimes, since we are very good at self-criticism, we are driven to ask ourselves whether, or to what extent, they might be true. Still, we should not take responsibility on ourselves for the hatred we inspire among (some) of our neighbours. We need not make excuses to the people who accuse us. We have a simple position to defend, before we move on to self-criticism: it really isn't all that hard for our neighbours to live with our anomalies, if they are minded to do so, and they should be so minded. In a world where there are many ways of being different, an extraordinary diversity of customs and beliefs, what justice requires (from us, in the Diaspora and in Israel, and from everyone else too) is respect for difference – and our own differences are among those that demand respect.

To make that demand effective, we must respect ourselves, and that means, right now, embracing the anomalies. This doesn't seem to me the right time for any large-scale revival of the normalizing projects. We are what we are, and we need to make a secure place for ourselves in the world

– a place for ourselves *as we are*. If we do that, one or another kind of normalcy might follow in time (or it might not).

As a free-thinking reader, what would it mean to embrace the anomalies? We are a single religious community, many of whose members are irreligious, and all of whose members constitute a single people. We belong in two places at once (leaving geography aside). We have a cultural heritage that is, as Ahad Ha-am wrote in his controversy with Brenner, 'filled with the religious spirit, which free-thinkers cannot embrace'[1] – but which many free-thinkers do embrace. I mean, they recognize the value of that heritage, even if their engagement with it is critical or oppositionist. And similarly, quoting Ahad Ha-am again, they recognize the God of Israel 'as a historical force that gave vitality to our people and influenced ... the progress of its life over millennia',[2] even if they deny that the God of Israel exists. It is possible or, at least, among Jews it is possible, to stand within the community of faith without sharing the faith – another example of our anomalies. I suspect that more Jews have found themselves in that position over the centuries than the faithful today will acknowledge. Freethinking Jews have a religious identity because we inherit a religiously inspired culture – in which we find much to admire and appropriate. We can't convert to another religion and remain members of the Jewish nation, but (mostly) we don't want to do that.

Similarly religious Jews have a secular/national identity because they live as members of a people that is organized and whose affairs are administered, in both the Diaspora and in Israel, by 'lay leaders' chosen by political processes – which is to say, not chosen either directly or indirectly by God. And they accept and enjoy the benefits of this identity. They can't leave the people without giving up their religion, but (mostly) they don't want to leave. As a free-thinking reader of the Bible, I would say that something like this was also true in ancient times. The ancient Israelite kingdoms were 'like the other nations', exactly as the elders who came to Samuel asking for a king intended them to be. Remember how the prophets complained about the political prudence of kings like Hezekiah – who lacked, they said, faith in God. Yet prophets and kings were members of the same nation and the same religious community. Then as now, the national and religious communities coincided in membership, even though they were different in kind. And then as now the political community included people with different (non-Israelite/non-Jewish) national and religious identities. The biblical writers either denied or tried to eliminate these differences, but we cannot do that today. This commitment is crucial to our political rebirth: that the members of other nations and religions, citizens of the modern Jewish state, must not suffer because of our anomalies.

The constant mixing of incongruous elements *is* our history, and this is what I would teach to our children. They must learn that our national history is also a religious history, which has its beginning in a covenant with God, which was regularly violated by the people who made it. And they must learn that our religious history is also a national history, driven by political and economic forces, subject to environmental and demographic constraints, exactly like all the other nations. Religious children must study secular texts; secular children must study religious texts. They must all be taught that though the memberships coincide, nation and religion are not the same thing (or else there would be no anomalies). We live differently in each. In the religious community, we associate with Reform, Conservative, Orthodox and Ultra-Orthodox Jews, and also with sceptics and free-thinkers – and then with Christians, Muslims, and so on outside the community. In the nation, we associate with Jewish-Americans, and Jewish-Italians, and Jewish-Russians and Jewish-Israelis – and then with Americans, Italians, Russians and Israelis outside the nation.

Moving among these different associations requires constant changes of style and sensibility. Jews have become pretty good at making these changes, and I think that we should celebrate this ancestral talent, rather than trying to reject and replace it – as if it would be better to be always the same, to possess a singular identity, to overcome the anomalies. Of course, we should insist that the world allow us to be what we are; we should act honestly in front of the others. But anomalous is what we really are.

Notes

1 Ahad Ha-am, 'Torah from Zion', in M. Walzer, M. Loberbaum, N. Zohar and A. Ackerman, *The Jewish Political Tradition, Volume Two: Membership* (New Haven, Yale University Press, 2003), pp. 409–10.
2 *Ibid.*

Part III: The Challenge of Statehood

TWELVE

The Significance of Israel for the Future
of Judaism

David Hartman

Throughout history many people, both in Israel and abroad, believed – and
continue to believe – that the fundamental purpose of the State of Israel was
to solve the condition of Jewish suffering by providing a national home for
Jews. Although persecution and suffering played a major role in the national
quest for Jewish political independence, treating Israel solely as a haven
against persecution is, I believe, incomplete and inadequate for understanding the significance and importance of the rebirth of Israel.

The Zionist revolution was deeply infused by utopian social, political
and cultural longings. Many dreamed of a new Jew, a transformation of the
Jewish psyche. The return to the land was envisioned not only in terms of
physical safety, but also as a healing process that would liberate Jews from
the negative self-image they had internalized over centuries of oppression
and powerlessness. For religious thinkers such as Rabbi Abraham Isaac
Kook, the Zionist revolution was destined to release spiritual energies that
had been repressed by the unnatural condition of *galut* (exile). Rabbi Kook
looked forward to the emergence of a new Jewish prototype as a result of
the secular, often atheistic, Zionist enterprise.

Jerusalem specifically has always been the receptacle of Jewish historical
hopes and dreams. Israel generally invites ideological passions because it
connects Jews to the historic memories and aspirations of the Jewish people.
One cannot relate to or live in Israel without being affected by the visions of
Isaiah and Amos, the passion of Rabbi Akiva, the age-old longing of Jews to
return to Jerusalem where justice and human fulfilment would be realized.

It is, therefore, not surprising that the urgent practical questions of
security and the economy are not the sole preoccupations of Israelis. To the
outsider it seems strange that an embattled, besieged country such as Israel is
always embroiled in internal controversies that have little to do with security
and survival. For example, entire government coalitions are formed and in
turn collapse over issues related to how one applies halakhah (Jewish law) to
society.

It is not accidental that, starting from the early years of statehood, the
Bible was the national literature of this country. Despite a strong disavowal
of the Bible's theological foundations, there was – and, I believe, still is – a
profound identification with the biblical outlook in terms of human types

and values, and prophetic moral and social aspirations. I am not suggesting that a biblical religious pathos infuses the country, but only that Jewish life in Israel is imbued with some of the broader historical conditions and perspectives present in the biblical outlook. In Israel, in contrast to the Diaspora, the synagogue and Jewish family life cannot generate a sufficient sense of vitality in order to make Judaism a viable option for modern Jews.

Our return to the land has not only recreated some of the existential conditions that informed the biblical, covenantal foundations of Judaism but it has also provided Jews with an exciting opportunity to recapture some of the salient features of their biblical foundations. The acceptance of responsibility for Jewish national existence can be understood as a progressive extension of the rabbinic understanding of the covenantal relationship between God and Israel. In order to explore this topic, I will first describe the three main approaches to the establishment of the State of Israel and then outline my own understanding of a covenantal perspective on Zionism.

Secular Zionism in Revolt

Zionism began over a century ago as a revolt against the conception of the Jewish people as a community of prayer and learning. The traditional waiting posture for liberation from exile was inspired by the biblical account of the Exodus from Egypt. The Exodus story served as a key paradigm of Jewish historical hope by emphasizing that despite the utter helplessness of the community, the Jewish people could rely on the redemptive power of God. Zionism taught that only if Jews were to take responsibility for their future would history change. This stood in sharp contrast to the biblical belief that Jews were not the masters of their own history. Exile was the result of sin and only through *teshuvah* (a return to God) and the *mitzvot* (commandments) would their exilic condition come to an end by the grace of God. The courage of traditional religious Jews to persevere under all conditions of history was sustained by their belief that Israel was God's elect people and that God would not permanently abandon Israel. The early Zionists rejected this approach to Jewish history and hope.

Nevertheless, the early Zionists by no means rejected Jewish heritage in its entirety. In many cases, they treated the Bible not only as the greatest literary treasure of the revived Hebrew language, but also as a major source of the ethical norms that would guide Jews in rebuilding their ancient homeland.

The early Zionists spanned every imaginable extent of the theological domain. Many were avowed atheists, others wanted to restore a biblical faith untrammelled by the rabbinic tradition, and others were devotees of land mysticism or a religion of labour. Many agreed, for example, on the need to create new formats with which to celebrate traditional Jewish festivals. In Israel today, there are still kibbutzim that celebrate Passover as a 'spring festival' using new language and forms of ritual, but non-religious families typically hold a traditional Passover meal with all the usual customs, even without religious commitment.

This is not, however, perceived by most Zionists as a serious problem. If one strips away the external trappings of traditional sentimentality found in many Zionists' appreciation of Jewish customs, one discovers the belief that concern for the survival of the Jewish people and commitment to the State of Israel are the new substitutes for traditional Judaism. The mainstream Zionist thinkers rejected the traditional view that the covenant with God at Sinai was constitutive of Jewish self-understanding. For many Zionists, identification with the historical destiny of the nation was not only necessary for being a Jew, it was also sufficient. Judaism during the exile had instrumental value in preserving this nation from disintegration, but the new nationalistic spirit provided a more effective instrument with which to make possible the continued existence of the Jewish people.

Religious Anti-Zionism

While the security of the State of Israel concerns the vast majority of Jews, not all Jews share the same appreciation of the Jewish state's significance for Jewish life and identity. At one end of the spectrum of views are those who deny any positive religious significance to the rebirth of Israel. For them, the establishment of a Jewish state represents a serious infringement on the role of God and Torah in Jewish history.

The reaction of traditional religious circles to early Zionism was intensely hostile. The fact that various European nations were regaining their independence had no significance for them. They believed that the third Jewish commonwealth could not arise out of political developments in the secular world, but should only result from God's redemptive intervention into history. They were not waiting for handfuls of pioneers to come and drain the swamps, but for a Jewish restoration of the sort described in the Jerusalem Talmud: 'Although your fathers were redeemed, they returned to being subjugated; but when you are redeemed, you shall never again be subjugated' (Kiddushin 2.1).

Today the same scepticism about Zionism is maintained by the *haredi* (Ultra-Orthodox) population, which rationalizes its representation in Israel's parliament and its participation in coalitions by pointing to how much its educational institutions benefit from government support. In Israel as elsewhere, they cooperate with the secular powers that be, but this should not be taken as implying that they ascribe religious significance to the rebirth of Israel. Their academies of learning do not celebrate Israel's Independence Day nor do they offer prayers of thanksgiving, *Hallel*, for the re-establishment of Jewish national autonomy, although prayers may be offered for the safety of those fighting in Israel's Defence Forces.

Not only do these religious anti-Zionists refuse to ascribe any spiritual significance to the State of Israel, but they also regard the state *per se* as a threat to the future of Judaism. For them, self-government grounded in secular politics and social institutions is the arch-enemy of traditional Jewish spirituality. As they see it, Israel offers the Jewish people a new kind of Jewish identity. Nationalism, Zionist history and folklore, the Hebrew language, Israeli culture, Israeli geography and archaeology, etc., are elements of an alternative way of life meant to displace God, Torah and classical Jewish teachings. In addition, they believe that Jewish political autonomy has engendered a psychological shift towards assertiveness and self-reliance, thereby alienating Jews from their traditional obedient posture to the Jewish faith. The Zionist ethos stands in sharp contrast to the traditional attitude of waiting patiently for the Messiah.

Messianic Religious Zionism

Diametrically opposed to the religious anti-Zionist approach are those who celebrate Israel within the context of a messianic, redemptive orientation to Jewish history. Their experience of Jewish life is filled with vitality and excitement. For them, the birth of Israel represents the end of exile and the beginning of the fulfilment of the prophetic visions of Jewish history.

When the return to the land of Israel gathered pace, religious elements began joining the secular Zionist revolution. In order to justify their participation in the Jewish march toward political independence, some of them began claiming that Zionism was a prelude to the coming of the Messiah. As argued above, for traditional Jews the only alternative political category to exile was the establishment of a messianic society. Consequently, any attempt to abolish the situation of exile had to be justified within the framework of the messianic promise. The best-known attempt of this kind was provided by the philosophy of Rabbi Kook. He offered an argument similar to Hegel's 'cunning of reason'. Although the secular Zionists believed their efforts would lead to a socialistic Jewish state where Judaism would be an anachronism, God would divert the course of events so as to turn Jews into 'a kingdom of priests and a holy nation' (Exod. 19.6). Who is to judge how the Lord of history chooses to bring about his ultimate design for the world? With this argument, Rabbi Kook justified the decision of observant Jews to join forces with a secular political movement that purported to supersede halakhah and Jewish covenantal consciousness.

Theological presuppositions of this kind enabled religious elements to forge a partnership with socialist Zionists during both the British Mandate and the early decades of the State of Israel. The political implications of such presuppositions, however, became apparent after the Six Day War, which unleashed the potential force of these messianic longings among a considerable number of religious Jews.

The expansion of Israeli control over most of the Promised Land was seen as confirmation that the establishment of the messianic kingdom was in the process of realization. There was a rush to set up rudimentary settlements in large numbers of places on the assumption that the ingathering of the exiles would shortly swamp Israel. As with all previous messianic expectations, reality proved otherwise. The reverses of the Yom Kippur War, the drying-up of Jewish immigration, and the disillusionment accompanying the final stages of the withdrawal from Sinai weakened their messianic fervour.

In spite of the progressive deterioration of the ecstatic mood of the Six Day War, the dominant religious ideological perspective of religious Zionism today is still Rabbi Kook's messianic theology. The vitality of religious youth movements is still nurtured by teachings from the Kook tradition. In contrast to Rabbi Kook, I would argue that religious Zionism does not need to treat the rise of Israel as a divine ruse leading towards the messianic kingdom. There is an alternative perspective from which to embrace religiously the secular Zionist revolution, namely the observation that Israel expands the possible range of halakhic involvement in human affairs beyond the circumscribed frameworks of home and synagogue. Jews in Israel are given the opportunity to bring economic, social and political issues into the centre of their religious consciousness. The moral quality of the army, social and economic disparities and deprivations, the exercise of power moderated by moral sensitivities, attitudes toward minorities, foreign workers, the stranger, tolerance and freedom of conscience – all these are areas that challenge our sense of covenantal responsibility.

The existence of the State of Israel, from this perspective, prevents Judaism from being confined exclusively to a culture of learning and prayer. The realm of symbolic holy time – the Sabbath, the festivals – is no longer the exclusive defining framework of Jewish identity. In returning to the land, we have created the conditions through which everyday life can mediate the biblical foundations of our covenantal destiny.

At first glance, the claim that the Zionist revolution has brought the demands of the covenant of action back to Jewish spiritual consciousness seems totally unrelated to the lived reality of Israeli society. Religious self-consciousness in Israel is found chiefly in two camps: either the traditional ghetto-like spirituality that has characterized Judaism for the past several centuries, or the messianic religious passion expressed by the adherents of Rabbi Kook's theology of history.

The halakhic tendencies in the former camp reflect a conscious repudiation of modernity. There is not an atmosphere of celebration of the new religious opportunities that statehood has made possible, but rather an outright disregard of them. The bulk of their halakhic *responsa* deals with the same halakhic questions that occupied religious leaders during our long exilic history, such as *kashrut* (Jewish dietary laws) and marriage. Even the sabbatical and Jubilee years, which touch on the social and economic vision of Judaism, have been reduced to questions of what type of food one is permitted to eat in the sabbatical year.

Furthermore, the establishment of the State of Israel has not in any way affected religious practices in the community. It would not be far-fetched to say that Israel is the last haven in the world for a secular Jew to feel comfortable in his or her secular perspective on life. In contrast to the Diaspora, there is a much sharper repudiation of traditional Judaism in Israeli Jewish society than in many other Jewish communities. If anything, anti-religious sentiment has been growing in response to the political assertiveness of certain groups of observant Jews.

As for the second camp, those who claim that Israel is part of a necessary messianic drama need not be disturbed by the prevalence of secularism in Israel. On the contrary, Rabbi Kook's theology of history enables them to regard the secular revolution as merely a temporary phase in God's scheme for bringing about the eventual establishment of a messianic Jewish society. The belief in the inevitability of the messianic redemptive process enables many religious Zionists to minimize the importance of the widespread lack of serious religious observance and sensitivity in the country. One can dance with Ariel Sharon on religious festivals with the same enthusiasm as yeshivah students dance with their Torah teachers. Army generals who lead us to victory serve the same messianic process. What makes an act religious is not necessarily the motivation of the agent but the consequences that result from this act. Many atheists or religiously indifferent persons in both the army and political life are perceived as pawns in the hands of the Lord of history, who has seen fit to utilize the military and political power of a secular Zionist state to bring about the triumph of the divine messianic scheme.

How then can I give some plausibility to my own perspective in spite of what seems to be such overwhelming evidence to the contrary? My answer will present a conceptual analysis of how I believe secular Zionism has enriched Jewish covenantal consciousness, thereby providing a new framework in which to experience and develop Judaism in the modern world.

Creation, Divine Self-Limitation and the Covenant

The Creation story in Genesis provides the theological and anthropological framework for understanding the concept of the covenant at Sinai. According to the first chapters of Genesis, God initially believed that humans would reflect divinity by virtue of God's magnificent powers as Creator. Man and woman were made in God's image. Precisely this act, however, contains the seeds of alienation and rebellion against God. Because human beings are endowed with freedom of choice, mirroring God's own freedom, they are not automatons that necessarily mirror the divine hope for human history.

God's will meets no opposition in the creation of nature, but it meets opposition in the creation of humans. This is the fundamental significance of the story of the Garden of Eden, Cain and Abel, and the sequel up to the destruction wrought by the Flood. The Flood expresses the divine rage when God's will is frustrated:

> The Lord saw how great was man's wickedness on earth, and how every plan devised by his mind was nothing but evil all the time. And the Lord regretted that he had made man on earth, and his heart was saddened. And the Lord said: 'I will destroy man ... both man and beast ...' (Gen. 6.5–7)

These verses should be contrasted with the earlier chapters of Genesis where the Lord takes pleasure in all of creation including human beings: 'And God saw all that he had made, and found it very good' (Gen. 1.31). In the Creation drama, man and woman are the culmination. If they fail, all of creation loses its significance for God. After the Flood, God promises Noah that he will separate his ongoing activity as the Creator of nature from the behaviour of human beings:

> Then Noah built an altar to the Lord and, taking of every clean animal and of every clean bird, he offered burnt offerings on the altar. The Lord smelled the pleasing odour, and the Lord said to himself: 'Never again will I doom the earth because of man, since the devisings of man's mind are evil from his youth; nor will I ever again destroy every living being, as I have done. As long as the earth endures, seedtime and harvest, cold and heat, summer and winter, day and night shall not cease'. (Gen. 8.20–22)

Nature is now endowed with intrinsic significance as a creation of God independent of human behaviour. God will no longer destroy nature because of humanity. The Creator of the universe further differentiates between nature and human history by setting self-imposed limits that distance God from human beings. God moves from Creator to covenant-maker when he accepts that the divine will alone does not ensure that the human world will mirror his vision for history. This change is revealed in the contrast between Abraham and Noah.

Abraham's prayer for the people of Sodom reflects the decision of the all-powerful God of Creation to become the limited Lord of history. Abraham stands at Sodom as God's responsible and dignified 'other'. The rabbis noted this in contrasting the behaviour of Abraham and Noah. When God told Noah that he was about to destroy the world, Noah accepted God's decree passively. But when God told Abraham that he was about to destroy two evil cities, Abraham pleaded at length on behalf of the innocent who might be destroyed with the guilty (Gen. 18.23–33). In the case of Abraham, God felt obliged to consult his covenantal partner before implementing his plan:

> Shall I hide from Abraham what I am about to do, since Abraham is to become a great and populous nation and all the nations of the earth are to bless themselves by him? For I have singled him out, that he may instruct his children and his posterity to keep the way of the Lord by doing what is just and right, in order that the Lord may bring about for Abraham what he has promised him. (Gen. 18.17–19)

The development toward covenantal responsibility reaches its quintessential expression in the moment of Sinai, when a whole nation is commissioned to implement in its total way of life the will of God as expressed in the *mitzvot*. In contrast to nature where the will of God is expressed as absolute power, at Sinai the community is called to share responsibility for history. The covenant mediated by the *mitzvot* continues the shift of the frame of reference from a theocentric drama in which God seeks to maintain total control (the Creation and Exodus stories) to a covenantal drama in which a human community is charged with the responsibility of building a society that will reveal the presence of God in human life: 'And I shall be sanctified in the midst of the community of Israel' (Lev. 22.32).

The Covenant and Human Responsibility

From a Talmudic perspective in which God is mediated in halakhic action, it would be legitimate to claim that any event that challenges us to widen the application of the normative halakhic system intensifies the sense of God's presence in daily life. I wish, however, to make the stronger claim that the rejection of the traditional posture of waiting for messianic redemption can itself be seen as a further elaboration and intensification of the spirit of covenantal responsibility found in the covenantal patriarchal and Sinai narratives and, above all, in the rabbinic tradition. I am not claiming that this is what the Zionist founders intended, but that rebuilding and renewing the community's national life extended and developed further the rabbinic tradition's understanding of the role assigned to human beings in the covenant.

In the rabbinic tradition, Israel is not only called upon to implement covenantal norms, but also to analyse, define and expand their content. No longer is God the final interpreter of his own law as in the biblical tradition. Now he is prepared to accept the verdict of scholars in the rabbinic academy who declared that Torah is 'not in heaven' (Deut. 30.12). In the rabbinic tradition revelation alone does not define how Torah is understood and applied in concrete situations.

The rabbinic tradition loosened the grip of the biblical paradigm of revelation and the need for prophecy by empowering human beings to reveal and expand the meaning of Torah through rational reflection and legal argumentation. In the classic Talmudic story of the dispute regarding the ritual status of the 'oven of Aknai', R. Eliezer invoked divine assistance in order to persuade the sages to accept his position after failing to convince them with legal arguments. After several miracles failed to win the sages over to his point of view:

> ... he [R. Eliezer] said to them: 'if the law is as I say, let it be proved from heaven!' Whereupon a heavenly voice cried out: 'Why do you dispute with Rabbi Eliezer, seeing that in all matters the law is as he says!' But Rabbi Joshua arose and exclaimed: 'It is not in heaven' [Deut. 30.12]. What did he mean by this? Said Rabbi Jeremiah: 'That the Torah had already been given at Mount Sinai; we pay no attention to a heavenly voice, because thou has long since written in the Torah at Mount Sinai, "After the majority must one incline". (Exod. 23.2)[1]

The rabbis understood 'It is not in heaven' to mean that human beings could define and expand the meaning of God's word without the need for prophesy or miraculous divine intervention. Yet, while firmly maintaining that Torah was not in heaven, rabbinic Judaism remained committed to the biblical idea that history was in heaven. Jewish history on the national level continued to be perceived in terms of the model of the Exodus from Egypt, where the all-powerful Lord of history miraculously redeems a powerless people.

The covenantal community takes upon itself responsibility for what the word of God means. Learning becomes a dominant new expression of religious passion. Rabbi Akiva, one of the forerunners of the intellectually dynamic and bold interpretative tradition of the Talmud, who in his life expressed total commitment and love for God, claimed that the paradigmatic book for understanding Israel and God was the Song of Songs. 'All the books of the Bible are holy; the Song of Songs is the holy of holies' (Yadayim 3.5). In the rabbinic period, God as teacher and lover became the central metaphors of the covenantal relationship with the God of Israel.

Despite this human-oriented transformation of the roles of prophecy and miracles in mediating God's love and intimacy, the rabbinic tradition did not similarly neutralize the need for divine miraculous intervention with respect to the Jewish people's national political existence. Attitudes to history continued to be characterized by a prayer-like longing for divine intervention in history that would solve the suffering of Jewish exile and national insecurity. Jewish political liberation, Israel's return to its ancient national homeland, was conceived in terms of the biblical paradigm of the Exodus from Egypt: 'May he who performed miracles for our ancestors redeeming them from slavery to freedom, redeem us soon and gather our dispersed from the four corners of the earth ...' (Prayer for the New Month).

Jews waited for redemption. Liberation would come from a power beyond and independent of human initiative. In contrast to the culture of the *bet midrash* (the Torah academy), where Jews felt no need for revelatory intervention to know how to apply Torah, and God's power was absolute and supreme, here Jews had to wait patiently for God's intervention. Although Torah was not in heaven, Jewish historical destiny was.

The Zionist revolution expanded the rabbinic spirit of confidence and trust in human initiative to new dimensions by liberating Jews from the traditional passive orientation to historical hope grounded in helpless dependency on the Lord of history. According to what I call a covenantal approach to Judaism, the dramatic significance of the establishment of the State of Israel is not a sign of the imminent unfolding of religious eschatology, but is an exciting new stage in a process that began at Sinai where Israel was prepared to accept God's self-limiting love as the central theological principle of its religious way of life.

Today, Jews are in a position to move further in the development of the covenantal concept that began at Sinai by expanding our covenantal consciousness to include responsibility for our fate in history. The covenantal community is called upon to complete the process that began at Sinai by bearing witness to the idea that without divine self-limitation there can be no mature, responsible historical role for Israel in the covenantal relationship with God.

One can summarize the different stages of this covenantal process in the following way: the Bible liberated the will of the individual to act with responsibility with the words 'I have put before you life and death, blessing and curse. Choose life – if you and your offspring would live – by loving the Lord your God, heeding His commands, and holding fast to Him' (Deut. 30.19–20); the Talmud liberated the intellect to define the contents of Torah; Zionism liberated the will of the nation to become politically responsible, to promote the 'ingathering of the exiles' and to re-establish Israel as a covenantal nation in history without relying on a divine rupture into human history.

The State of Israel is, therefore, the main catalyst for rethinking the meaning of God as the Lord of history. The future of Judaism depends on our ability to discover meaningful ways of relating to God's love and power in a world where history, and not only Torah, is not in heaven.

Notes

1 BT Baba Metzia 59b.

THIRTEEN   Religion and State in Israel

Menachem Lorberbaum

The problem of religion and state has plagued the politics of the State of
Israel since its creation. It has been a constant source of destabilization of
Israeli coalition politics, given especially the tie-breaker role assumed by
Orthodox parties such as the National Religious Party, the Ultra-Orthodox
Agudah and more recently, the Sephardi Orthodox Shas party. The
disproportionate power amassed by Orthodox parties, and their manner of
wielding it in terms of budgetary allocations and legislation, have long been
perceived by secular Israelis as political blackmail. But the coalitional politics
of religion in Israel are indicative of a much deeper cultural rift. Indeed, the
cultural divide in Israel is rooted in the very foundational moments of the
Zionist movement and its pre-state congresses. Zionism was a movement of
Jewish national rejuvenation initiated by mostly secular, yet nationally
committed Jews. The very legitimacy of secular Zionism, and by extension
the very legitimacy of its progeny – the State of Israel conceived of in
worldly, not religious terms – has been an anathema to many religious Jews
(regardless of denomination) for decades. It is the crux of Jewish identity
politics.

A status quo of religious observance in Israel was articulated in a letter
sent by David Ben Gurion in 1947 to the representatives of the Agudah
party. The letter ensured that Agudah would join in signing the Declaration
of Independence of the new state. Among other points, the letter promised
that marriage in Israel would be in accordance with Torah law, that Shabbat
would be the day of rest, and that kosher food would be served in the
military. Its ongoing obligatory status has been ensconced in coalition
agreements of successive governments.

For decades, the status quo established in 1947 served as the general
guideline for questions of religion and state. The religious parties satisfied in
this achievement did not view a constitution as necessary or even helpful for
ensuring Orthodox freedom of religious practice. On the contrary, if
anything, a constitution would threaten to call into question the religious
and ritualistic commitments the state had undertaken at the expense of the
freedom from religion of those of its citizens that wished for it. So even
though a constitutional process had begun in the early 1950s, the Orthodox
parties were one of the principal groups (though not the only ones) that had
little interest in its coming to fruition.

A status quo, however, is nothing but the armistice line of warring parties. It is not a moral document. It could therefore not ensure the long-term commitment that a value-laden constitutional agreement aspires to. Indeed, in the course of the 1990s the weight of the status quo waned as the renewed development of constitutional legislation in Israel gained momentum. New basic laws were added to the slowly advancing (but incomplete) constitutional process, most notably the basic law of 'Human Dignity and Liberty'. To be sure, these laws tried to take into account the complexity of Israeli identity politics. After declaring that 'Basic human rights are founded upon recognition of the values of human beings, of the sanctity of their lives and of their being free,' the basic law 'Human Dignity and Liberty' then turns to expound its purpose: 'The purpose of this basic law is to protect human dignity and liberty so as to anchor in a basic law the values of the State of Israel as a Jewish and democratic state.' The very legislation of 'basic' laws seemed to signify what Chief Justice Aharon Barak declared to be a 'constitutional revolution', equipping the Supreme Court with the legitimacy it needed for judicial review.

Though the religious parties supported the legislation of the basic laws, they feared the implications heralded by the activist liberal chief justice in the final decade of the twentieth century. The relations between religion and state in Israel thus entered a new phase, governed by an incomplete constitution and a no longer existing status quo. This void was one of the factors leading to the most vigorous theocratic attacks against the sovereignty of the State of Israel in the name of the Jewish religion it had ever experienced in the fifty years of its existence. The *haredi* (Ultra-Orthodox) community attacked the authority of the Supreme Court to sit in judgment, while the religious Zionist community attacked the legitimacy of the state to exercise sovereignty over matters of territory. Religious Zionism combined with Ultra-Orthodoxy to undermine classic expressions of sovereignty with regard to policy and justice. These attacks not only aimed at the democratic character of the state but critiqued the very formation of human political agendas that are not religiously sanctioned. It was as much an attack on politics as worldly and prudential as upon democracy. Politics, on their account, must be guided and constrained by a divine agenda they are privy to.

These theocratically inclined renunciations of state legitimacy were the immediate background for the assassination of Prime Minister Yitzhak Rabin. But while it is true that this primal act of violence, and later the outburst of the second Intifada, caused these communities to recoil at the consequences of their respective agendas, their withdrawal may yet prove merely temporary. For the accumulating efforts of the de-legitimization of state sovereignty revealed the fact that the State of Israel has not succeeded in adequately addressing the place of religion in its political society. Despite the unique achievements of the creation of a thriving society, in economic and cultural terms, and of a state-sponsored thriving of religious learning and of religious communities, both secular and religious Israelis have come to the point that they do not understand what a 'Jewish and democratic state' might even mean. Rather than signal the common denominator of Jewish Israelis, this definition in fact highlights the depths of their sense of disillusionment.

Furthermore, in order to thrive, political ideologies are in need of contributing circumstances. In the case of Israel, it is the state itself that has provided circumstances beneficial to the growth of anti-political and anti-democratic theocratic religiosity and done little to curb these tendencies. Israel is the only Western democracy that generously funds educational systems that teach students to disregard the authority of state law and that rewards the graduates of this educational system by exempting them from civil service. Given the consequences, we might argue that the Israeli political system's continuous reluctance to address the adequate place of religion in the polity is nothing short of criminal.

There is no doubt that the specific character of the Israeli parliamentary coalition system encourages sectarian politics and enhances the power of minority interests as opposed to the common weal. Even small improvements, such as raising the electoral threshold, can contribute greatly to the elimination of splinter groups from the parliamentary debate. Awareness of such technical avenues also serves to caution us against focusing too much on ideological differences, a vice to which the highly rhetorical Israeli political discourse is all too prone. Bloated ideological rhetoric is the best camouflage for political neglect. At the same time, we must identify the debates that seriously affect the very legitimacy of political society.

Our approach to questions of religion and state must therefore address both fundamental Jewish and political values on the one hand, and the constitutional structures of the state that provide the circumstances conditioning the political realization of values, on the other. I will not argue here against any specific ideology. Rather my purpose is to outline those values and institutional formulas that would enhance the stability, cohesiveness and justice of the State of Israel as a state of Jews but of non-Jews too, and one with a deeply rich and variegated ethnic, religious and cultural population.

'Separation of Church and State'

A classic modern solution for dealing with the tensions between religion and state is to call for a separation of the two. The creation of the modern republic has been inseparable from a renewed conception of the domains of politics and religion. Mediaeval empires and later, absolute monarchies, sought political legitimacy in the church and theories of divine right. Modern republics, by contrast, are worldly in their conceptions of politics and in their sources of legitimacy. Therefore, constitutionally speaking, they have for the most part espoused a separation of church and state. Such a separation is understood to be beneficial for politics but no less for religion. It certainly helps ensure freedom of worship as a basic right in the liberal republics.

Yet even so, a cursory look at the constitutions of modern polities reveals that there is no one formula for the adequate arrangement of the relations of church and state. Consider the following examples:

France is a secular republic. The church and indeed all forms of religion are barred from the public domain. A young Muslim woman's wish to attend a public school wearing a scarf gives rise to a constitutional debate. The public domain here is not neutral with regard to religion but rather secularly committed. Religious symbols and affiliations must be kept out of the civil domain.

In contradistinction, the United States is not a secular polity. The Fourth Amendment declares that Congress shall not establish a church. Yet this institutional separation of church and state is meant to allow for an enriching interplay between religion and politics: 'In God we trust.' Today, it is impossible to conceive of a candidate for the American presidency who is not religiously committed. Furthermore, the profound Protestant character of the American polity is obvious when we consider that in its entire history the United States has had only one Catholic president.

Britain differs radically from both France and the United States. It is a constitutional monarchy, and the monarch is, by virtue of office, head of the Church of England. Britain knows no constitutional separation of church and state. Yet it is a liberal society in so far as citizenship is not premised on religious affiliation and the state respects the freedom of religious association.

In contrast to an existing fundamental agreement with regard to specific civil rights, the constitutions of modern republics are radically divided as to the best arrangement of the religious and the political. Different countries have different histories, and various religions give rise to different practices and cultures. The institutional arrangements of church and state derive from the particular historical and cultural backgrounds of the people who are the citizens of the republic.

This holds true for the State of Israel, too. Simply calling for a separation of religion and state in Israel is not enough. More has to be said about the Jewish religion, the nature of the Israeli polity, and the specific nature of the hoped-for separation in order to judge what the best arrangement might be and to understand why this indeed is the case.

'A Kingdom of Priests and a Holy People'

John Locke's *Letter Concerning Toleration*[1] is the founding document of the separationist position. Locke's predecessors, Thomas Hobbes and Baruch Spinoza, had cautioned vigorously of the dangers of an independent church, and espoused therefore a position of sovereign supremacy over the church. In contradistinction to these predecessors, Locke maintained that if the church agreed to accept the limitations incumbent upon a non-governmental organization, the sovereign could afford, on his side, to relinquish the imposition of supremacy. Locke advocated turning the church from an institution with a stake in ruling to what we would recognize today as a Non-Governmental Organization (NGO).

Locke argued that two religious groups seemed to be principally unable to accept such an arrangement. Catholics, he argued, maintained not only a religious but a political loyalty to the Pope in Rome and were therefore suspect of a split loyalty with regard to the state. Similarly, Jews, because of the specifically political character of their religious commitment, could not countenance a separation of the civil and religious realms:

> For the commonwealth of the Jews, different in that from all others, was an absolute theocracy; nor was there, or could there be, any difference between that commonwealth and the church. The laws established there concerning the worship of one invisible Deity were the civil laws of that people, and a part of their political government, in which God himself was the legislator.[2]

Locke identifies the structural peculiarity of the Jewish religion. The Torah is a political project. Ordering the polity and prescribing the requisite ritual are complementary spheres of the one law aimed at creating a 'kingdom of priests and a holy nation' (Exod. 19.6). The constitutional character of the 'commonwealth of the Jews' is in turn derived from a specific political theology according to which 'God Himself was legislator', or in other words, God was sovereign.

Locke thus makes three important arguments about the Jewish religion: (1) The Jewish religion is committed to a specific political theology wherein God is conceived of in political terms. He is sovereign. (And this presumably precludes human sovereignty.) Put differently, Judaism is committed to a theocracy, to a polity wherein God reigns. (2) A Jewish commonwealth cannot therefore countenance a separation of the religious and the political, for they are all part of the one law of God for ordering his polity, in terms of justice and in terms of worship. (3) By implication, Jews would not make for good citizens in a polity that would strive to separate the religious and the political.

Is Locke's account of Jewish political commitment correct? This question was first confronted in the eighteenth century by Moses Mendelssohn, who advocated the civil emancipation of Jews and the attainment of equal citizenship. Mendelssohn was mostly concerned with Locke's third point, because it implied that Jews were committed precisely to the kind of pre-modern ecclesiastical politics that would bar them from achieving citizenship. In his *Jerusalem*,[3] Mendelssohn argued that the Torah was God's positive law addressed solely to the people of Israel. It is therefore inapplicable to a Gentile polity. Moreover, exile precisely means a suspension of the Torah as a political program. The maxim 'the law of the kingdom is law' guides Jewish exilic existence.

Mendelssohn's strategy of argumentation allayed the fears informing Locke's critique and proved the Jews of Europe eligible for the Lockean doctrine of toleration. Mendelssohn thus was able to formulate the basic adage of Jewish Diasporic existence in early modernity: be a Jew at home and a citizen in public. This formula of Jewish politics was essentially liberal.

Our concern here, however, is with the character of a Jewish state. Is it capable of promoting the toleration Jews so dearly valued when it was extended to them at the advent of modernity? Can it generate a civic space inclusive of all Jewish denominations, and of Jews and non-Jews of secular and religious commitments?

Answering these questions demands challenging Locke's understanding of Judaism. Locke, I will argue, was only partially correct. Although he correctly heard the voice of a certain strand in the Bible, it is not the only one, and it is certainly not the only strand existing in the rabbinic tradition. Yet, in order to correctly frame the argument, a qualification must be made. Our interpretations of rabbinic sources ought to respect the fundamental cultural and historical divides: neither the biblical prophets nor the rabbis were proto-liberals. The rise of modern republicanism necessitated new conceptions of politics and religion which were considered heretical in the eyes of the previously hegemonic Catholic Church. Pre-modern conceptions of Judaism are no different in this respect. Such conceptions view the advent of modernity as a crisis of authority and religiosity. My purpose is not to render such conceptions modern but to argue that there are sufficient resources available in the Jewish tradition for thinking differently about politics and religion.

Secularizing the Political

Locke's first point was that Judaism is committed to a theocracy, to a polity wherein God reigns. But what does this actually mean? What does this reign imply? If we turn to the Bible itself, one can argue that the Lockean reading is highly selective. The Torah raises a theocratic conception in the Book of Exodus but also provides a thoroughgoing critique of its political viability. The Book of Numbers is arguably a critique of the ideal-type of theocracy, the reign of Moses. The book painstakingly follows Moses' slow demise, and ultimate failure, as a political leader through numerous rebellions against his authority and his inability to address them adequately (one of the lowest points of which is the zealous taking of the law into private hands by Phinehas [Num. 25.1–15]). This is not to detract from Moses' foundational achievement of creating a people, but rather to say that the task of mediator between God and the people was an impossible one that doomed him to failure.

The inner biblical critique of theocracy continues in the Book of Judges that identifies God's reign with human anarchy: 'In those days there was no king in Israel, each man did what was right in his own eyes.' This verse is repeated (with slight variations) three times at the end of the book (18.1, 19.1, 21.25), stressing that idolatry, spilling of blood and incest – the cardinal sins of Judaism – are attendant on this anarchy. This critique leads finally to a new worldly conception of politics in its monarchic version, ultimately sanctioned by God.

The Bible, then, not only raises the ideal of divine reign but also arguably critiques its implications with regard to the political institutions of human life. Its thorough exposition includes a forthright critique of the attempts to translate divine reign politically in human affairs. The attempt to implement direct divine rule proves to have a destructive effect on human life: it either corrodes leadership (as in the case of Moses) or is corrosive of fundamental values thus leading to anarchy (as in the case of the Judges).

In rabbinic Judaism, the kingdom of heaven (*malkhut shamayim*) is neither a political institution nor (as the Christian Bible would have it) a historical event. It is an ever-present and non-spatial normative domain one enters in the daily recitation of the *shema* and the acceptance of the yoke of commandments.[4] Politically speaking, the Mishnah endorses the worldliness of politics as the assumed rule, declaring, 'the king neither judges [in the Sanhedrin] nor is subject to judgment' (Sanhedrin 2.3).[5] The king is placed outside the domain of divine law. Ultimately, 'there is none above him but the Lord his God' (Mishnah Horayot 3.3) – God himself, but in fact not even his law.

Locke's second point – that Judaism cannot countenance a distinction between the religious and the civil domains – was long ago contested by leading mediaeval rabbinic authorities. These authorities were acutely aware of the inadequacy of halakhic norms for guiding society. In a famous *responsum* endorsing the extra-halakhic penal codes of mediaeval Jewish communities, the thirteenth-century scholar and communal leader, Rabbi Solomon ibn Adret (Rashba) writes the following:

> For if you were to restrict everything to the laws stipulated in the Torah and punish only in accordance with the Torah's penal [code] in cases of assault and the like, the world would be destroyed, because we would require two witnesses and [prior] warning. The Rabbis have already said that 'Jerusalem was destroyed only because they restricted their judgments to Torah law' (BT Bava Metzia 30b).[6]

Halakhic criminal procedure places impossibly tight restrictions on conviction. Criminals must be forewarned by the witnesses of the penalty incurred for such felonious action, and testimony must be given by two competent witnesses who saw the crime together. Such restrictions, argues Adret, are sure to lead to the destruction of society because they make conviction impossible.

It is important to stress that these restrictions are not arbitrary but were so construed by the rabbis in order to make capital conviction impossible. The inadequacy of halakhic criminal procedure is ultimately rooted in a critique of capital punishment.[7] Adret, however, is clearly aware of the inadequacy of halakhah as a tool for social order and prescribes civil politics as the means for ensuring social order. Civil politics guided by concern for social order will better achieve its goal than the social law of religious halakhah. The pre-modern medieval Jewish community was a *kahal kadosh*, a holy community, devoted to a religious way of life predicated on divine law. Yet the Lockean notion of the one complete divine law including both civil and religious statutes never became the actual norm of Jewish communal life. In fact, it was the reasoned restriction of the application of divine law that ensured the political stability of the community.

Israeli society, of course, is a unique kind of Jewish society. Even if a messianic Jewish society were to be governed by a Lockean version of a complete Jewish law, the State of Israel is not constituted as such a society but is rather qualitatively different. Rabbi Isaac Halevi Herzog, the first chief rabbi of the State of Israel, correctly argued:

> The very founding of the State [of Israel] is a kind of partnership.
> It is as if Gentiles, let us say even heathens ... agree to allow us to

create a joint government in which we have a recognized pre-eminence and the state will bear our name.[8]

According to Herzog, the State of Israel is constituted upon a joint covenant of Jews and non-Jews together to create a political society whose public space is predominantly Jewish. Such a political entity is not the agent assumed by the Torah for executing its political commandments and vision. These commandments, argues Herzog:

> are not addressed to particular individuals but to the governing body, [that is] to a Jewish government, whatever its formal [regime], that is sufficiently empowered to discharge them. These commandments were originally addressed to the Jewish people conquering the land, who became sovereign over it independently of the [other] nations. These are the Torah's background assumptions with regard to these commandments, as is self-evident. In the absence of this background, and given the realistic circumstances whereby this state is given ... these commandments do not apply.[9]

According to this argument, the State of Israel is not charged with the implementation of the Torah's vision of a political society but it is, however, obliged not to openly legislate against Torah law. Such a stipulation goes well with the fundamental assumptions of freedom of religion in a democratic and liberal republic wherein the polity will not legislate to actively desecrate the actions prohibited by a religion.

Synagogue and State

The above critique of theocratic conceptions of Jewish law and politics and of their applicability to the State of Israel is not meant to deny the power of the theocratic impulse in the Jewish tradition. Theocratic impulses become destructive when they are conceived of as a foundation for a revolutionary politics, erroneously assuming the ability to provide an alternative institutional arrangement for human life. This occurs when the theocratic impulse is joined with the messianic yearning to overcome the constraints of human finitude and the partial character of human life, such as the unarticulated *haredi* ideal of a Torah state or the religious Zionist vision of politics as an instrument of divine history. The challenge of Jewish politics is to openly address this impulse and to tame it so it may serve as a source for constructive social criticism. Jewish politics must be worldly in character while always seeking to negotiate the place of the holy in human life. The great biblical prophets may serve as a model for us as well; they did not aspire to exercise power, but rather to serve as its conscience.

The task of constitution-making is to create guidelines for justly negotiating power. The best way for the State of Israel to promote the conscientious control of power is by encouraging Jewish religious pluralism and by strenuously affirming the value of freedom of religion. Rather than using value-neutral slogans like 'Separation of Religion and State', civic education should espouse the value-laden discourse of freedom of religion. Furthermore, espousing freedom of religion does not necessarily entail a total separation of state and synagogue. We can best formulate the guidelines of an Israeli model by reconsidering the ones enumerated earlier.

The French model of a secularly committed state would not work in Israel – because of the specific Israeli need to negotiate the holy – in that it takes a blatantly anti-religious posture towards civic space. In the case of Israel, state commitment to secularism as an ideology is as detrimental as one-sided religious commitments to the flourishing of its citizens. On the contrary, the state should equally promote the building of synagogues of different denominations and also support the building of mosques. Rather than devalue public space, the democratic debate must allow for citizens to endow their public space with their traditional values. Indeed, as custodian of the Holy Land, the State of Israel has the unique responsibility of fostering variegated religious commitments. This is a uniquely universal responsibility.

The American model is too strict in that it prohibits the state from funding the flourishing of religion in its society or its citizens' ability to democratically determine the character of public space. The democratic value of creating an agreed-upon public space should carry a greater weight than the liberal directives advocating state neutrality. The democratic debate in Israel should allow the differences in society to surface in the parliamentary deliberation as to the Jewish cultural and religious character of public space.

There are, however, important preconditions that ought to determine the validity of endowing the public space religious character. First, such enactments may not undermine the democratic character of the state. The state lacks the legitimacy to determine what is religiously obligatory for a person; it can only determine what will be civically binding; therefore its legislation, too, which owes its very authority to the *demos*, cannot be one that undermines the state's democratic character.

Religious legislation seems necessarily to imply an infringement upon freedom from religion. A further restriction must therefore be added which touches upon the content of legislative acts with regard to religion, namely, a legislative act cannot be justified in purely religious terms. Saying eating pork is forbidden by the Torah is neither a necessary, nor a sufficient condition for civic legislation. One must argue in civic and cultural terms. The idea behind this restriction is that any religiously inclined enactment must create a broader non-religious coalition to back it and lend it civic authority.

Finally, religious legislation cannot contradict the state's responsibility as custodian of the Holy Land to ensure the flourishing of all forms of religiosity. The British model we saw above is close to Israel's in its recognition of a state clergy. It is important to stress that with regard to religions other than Judaism, the State of Israel has adopted the *millet* system of the Ottoman Empire and the British Mandate to recognize the respective autonomy of non-Jewish religious groups. But in the case of Judaism itself, the adoption of a state clergy violates the need for religious pluralism by lending state recognition to one of several major options of Jewish life, thus ensuring an Orthodox monopoly on marriage and divorce procedures.

The model emerging for Israel is that of a polity ideologically committed in neither secular nor religious terms. It should therefore not have a state clergy, or at any rate no single-state clergy. The state should actively help to fund the whole variety of religious forms of life as a means of encouraging individual freedom of religion and freedom of religious association.

Conclusion: Would a Written Constitution make a Difference?

Since the assassination of Prime Minister Rabin, much effort has been invested in furthering a written constitution for Israel by a diversely motivated group of promoters who hope that a written document with broad civic support will contribute to healing the deep rifts in Israeli society. Yet there are many specific and conflicting agendas in Israeli constitutional politics. Among the Jewish citizens advocating a constitution, Democrats hope that agreed-upon procedures for political life will mitigate conflict, Liberals hope that a constitution will provide the values necessary to constrain political debate and action, and trump the initiatives of politically unreliable parliamentarians. The religious parties hope a written constitution will help enshrine state commitment to Orthodox values, or at least sanction the remnants of the religious–secular status quo of the early years of the state. Arab citizens would be satisfied if the state would live up to the values of freedom and equality it committed itself to in the Declaration of Independence of 1948. The more radical voices would like to strengthen an attenuation of the specifically Jewish commitments of the state. These latter interests highlight the biggest conundrum of Israeli constitution-making: easing the Jewish–Arab tensions necessitates a broadening of the civil character of political society, while the internal Jewish rifts require a deepening of a Jewish common denominator.

It should be noted that there already exists a weighty body of constitutional ruling by the Israeli Supreme Court, and in that sense the Israeli system is closer to its parent British system, which does not have a written constitution. Still, there is no doubt that an agreed-upon constitution would contribute to an easing of divisions in Israeli society. Yet, if my preceding analysis is correct, the real problems in Israel are not a function of the lack of a written constitution but of a lack of political will to implement what is already possible. Changing the electoral system, ceasing the funding of anti-civic educational systems, and ending the exemption of *haredi* and Arab citizens from civil service are all possible without a written constitution and would not be promoted by its enactment. Even the Law of Rabbinic Jurisdiction (1953), that stipulates that only rabbinic courts will enact marriage and divorce of Jews in Israel, does not need a constitution to be circumvented. It would be sufficient for the state to recognize the civil marriage and civil divorce of citizens who choose such procedures.

The constitutional debate in Israel overemphasizes the role of a written document at the price of recognizing the lack of political will to implement what is already possible. If this is indeed correct, the alienation of ordinary citizens from the political system in Israel will only grow to the extent that they will realize that a constitution cannot deliver what the citizens hope for. The danger to the democratic character of Israeli society lies not only in the political ineptitude of the Israeli parliament but also in the alienation of citizens from participating actively in civic life. The role of the social critic in Israel today is much like that of the great prophets of old, to educate and call attention to those values most citizens already know and regard as their own in order to help generate the political will for their proper implementation.

Notes

1 J. Locke (ed. M. Montuori), *A Letter Concerning Toleration* (The Hague, Martinus Nijhoff, 1963), p. 73.
2 *Ibid.*
3 M. Mendelssohn, *Jerusalem, or On Religious Power and Judaism* (Hanover NH, 1983).
4 See Mishnah Berakhot 2.2.
5 M. Walzer, M. Lorberbaum, N. Zohar and Y. Lorberbaum (eds), *The Jewish Political Tradition, Volume One: Authority* (New Haven, Yale University Press, 2000), p. 136.
6 Rashba, *Responsa* 3.393, in Walzer *et al.*, *The Jewish Political Tradition: Authority*, pp. 402–3.

7 See A. Kirschenbaum, 'The Role of Punishment in Jewish Criminal Law: A Chapter in Rabbinic Penological Thought', *The Jewish Law Annual* 9 (1991), 123–44; and M. Lorberbaum, *Politics and the Limits of Law* (Stanford, University of Stanford Press, 2001).

8 M. Walzer, M. Lorberbaum, N. Zohar and Y. Lorberbaum (eds), *The Jewish Political Tradition, Volume Two: Membership* (New Haven, Yale University Press, 2003), p. 530.

9 Walzer *et al.*, *The Jewish Political Tradition: Membership*, p. 529–30.

FOURTEEN

War and Peace

Noam Zohar

Peace and War

The most important biblical message about war is the radical notion that war
is not a permanent feature of human existence – it shall one day disappear
from the face of the earth. True, God sends the Israelites to make battle and
conquer the Promised Land, and even before that, in the Song on the Sea,
he is himself glorified as 'the LORD, the Warrior, LORD is His name!' (Exod.
15.3). Human history and Jewish history have included numerous wars, and
the Jewish tradition has certainly mandated warfare. Yet above this painful
reality stands Isaiah's compelling prophetic vision:

> In the days to come, the Mount of the LORD's House shall stand
> firm above the mountains and tower above the hills; and all the
> nations shall gaze on it with joy. And the many peoples shall go
> and say: 'Come, let us go up to the Mount of the LORD, to the
> House of the God of Jacob; that he may instruct us in his ways,
> and that we may walk in his paths.' For instruction shall come
> forth from Zion, the word of the LORD from Jerusalem. Thus he
> will judge among the nations and arbitrate for the many peoples,
> and they shall beat their swords into ploughshares and their spears
> into pruning hooks: Nation shall not take up sword against
> nation; they shall never again know war. (Isa. 2.2–4)

The two parts of the last verse are crucially connected. This is not a vision of
the 'end of history', in which nations shall no longer have any contrasting
interests or deep conflicts that might lead to severe confrontations. Rather,
war will be transcended because the nations will have a forum, respected by
all, for resolving their differences. Like citizens in a well-ordered society, the
various peoples will eschew violence as a mode of dealing with conflicting
claims or interests.

Isaiah did not coin the phrase 'international law', but his vision depicts
what amounts to almost the same thing: a central institution for conflict
resolution. God's role as effective arbitrator rests here not upon his might,
but upon the universal reverence for his instruction. Missing are the details:
How will complaints be lodged and processed? How will God's instruction
actually be known – will particular agents speak for him? And what of
mechanisms for enforcement?

There is, of course, little sense in complaining about the lack of such detail in the prophet's lofty poetry. This is where we should turn to the talmudic assertion that 'a sage is superior to a prophet.' According to one interpretation, this means that in order to move beyond the articulation of prophetic ideals towards their realization in practice we must employ the traditional Jewish mode of normative discourse, known as halakhah.

Halakhic teachings on these matters have been extremely meagre, and therefore one of our first actions should be a call for creative and rigorous halakhic thinking that constructively engages the experience of the United Nations and particularly that of such international tribunals as The Hague or the World Trade Organization. To be sure, these institutions all have shortcomings. Nevertheless, Isaiah's prophecy urges us not to use those failures as ammunition to demolish the ideal, but rather to work toward its more perfect fulfilment. If instead we abandon this task and turn without reserve to waging our current battles, we would be turning our back on the Jewish faith in world redemption, *tikkun olam*.

The breathtaking vision of a lasting world peace appears, within the biblical corpus, only in the period of the classical prophets (the eighth century BCE). In the Torah itself – the five books of Moses – there is no direct indication that war will be eradicated. Rather, the people of Israel are told that we will suffer attacks and defeat as punishment for our sins. Conversely, the reward for keeping God's commandments will be victory, security and peace (see Lev. 26). Still, Isaiah's prophecy is rooted in the first chapters of the Bible (Gen. 1–11), in the story of humankind's beginnings. The seemingly permanent division of humanity into many peoples who cannot communicate effectively was preceded by common ancestry. Here are two of the lessons that the Mishnah draws from this:

> Therefore Adam was created alone, to teach you (1) that whoever destroys a single life is deemed by Scripture as if he had destroyed a whole world; and whoever saves a single life is deemed by Scripture as if he had saved a whole world; and (2) for the sake of peace among people, so that one person should not say to another: 'My ancestor was greater than your ancestor!'[1]

Thus according to the rabbis, Genesis teaches both the great value of each human life and the rejection of racism – indeed, of any rhetoric of chauvinistic supremacy. This can be seen as the backdrop for Isaiah's vision; once humanity regains this original perspective, conflicts will be experienced not as between 'us' and 'them', but as intra-communal disputes, to be resolved in a civilized manner. And the ideal of peace was never relegated to the margins of Jewish consciousness; in crafting the *siddur*, a prayer for peace was placed as the prominent, concluding link in the most central liturgical units, from the *amidah* to the *kaddish*.[2]

All of this has the effect of placing wars – even those mandated by the Torah – under a moral cloud (to use Michael Walzer's phrase). In our as yet unredeemed world, certain wars must be fought; but justifying the resort to force is in principle problematic, and the loss of life a terrible tragedy.

Some people are led by this to a cynical stance: 'War is hell,' they say, and hence it can be initiated without compunction in the service of 'national interest', and conducted without inhibition, a 'total war' of unbridled fierceness. Such utter lawlessness (which in modern times has gained bogus respectability under the caption of 'Realism') is diametrically opposed to the very foundation of Judaism: the belief in a divine Sovereign whose instruction – Torah – addresses every facet of human endeavour. Rather, we must study God's teachings, investing our best skills of interpretation and reasoning in order to honestly apply these teachings to the complex reality facing us. This project of study and reasoning, of interpretation and application – known as the 'Oral Torah' – is the defining feature of traditional Judaism.[3] At its heart is a commitment to discern and describe normative differences, distinguishing the pure from the impure, the permitted (or required) from the prohibited. Accordingly, I shall proceed to discuss first (in section 2) the issue of the warrant for going to war and then (in section 3) the issue of behaviour within warfare.

What Justifies Doing Battle?

This cardinal question must be addressed on two distinct (though not unrelated) levels. First, there is the question of basic warrant: (1) On what basis can warfare be justified? Second, there is the question of concrete grounds: (2) In what circumstances is it permissible – or perhaps, requisite – that we engage in warfare?

(1) Justifying War: Three Kinds of Argument

World peace – as in Isaiah's vision – reflects fundamental Jewish values, first and foremost among them the immeasurable value of each human life. Hence any argument for justifying war must overcome a strong presumption against allowing it altogether. I will focus here on three such arguments: Commandment, Convention, and Lesser Evil.

Commandment: The category of *mitzvah* (commandment) is central to the Judaic tradition. In colloquial usage, *mitzvah* means simply a good or righteous act; but its proper meaning points not only to the quality of the deed but also to the divine source declaring it valuable or mandatory. The *mitzvot* are traditionally divided into negative and positive commandments, and it is God who commands: 'Do not do this!'; 'Do that!' For some Jewish writers – starting at least from Judah Halevi – the sacred value of the commandments draws primarily from their divine origin and authority, above and beyond whatever sense or function they may have in terms of human reason. From here it is possible to go one (crucial) step further and assert that when we receive a command from God we ought to follow it, regardless of our own assessment of the good or evil of the deed in question. This position is known as 'Divine Command Morality' – the doctrine that morality is determined or constituted by divine command, which supersedes any considerations of (fallible) human judgment.

Under the doctrine of Divine Command Morality, it may not matter that going to war seems morally troubling or even outright wrong – as long as it is commanded by God. The Mishnah and Talmud speak of a war that is a *mitzvah* – a 'commanded' or obligatory war. Following talmudic discussions, Maimonides' first example of such a war is 'the war against the seven nations', that is, the war which God ordered Israel to wage in order to conquer the Promised Land from the Canaanites.[4] According to this doctrine, the knowledge that God has commanded this war of conquest was fully sufficient to justify it.

A crucial question here is, of course: how can we know that God in fact commands us to wage any particular war? Regarding the 'war of the seven nations' the answer may seem straightforward: it is explicitly enjoined in Scripture! But this is too simple. In traditional Judaism, perusing the (apparently) plain meaning of Scripture does not conclusively define God's commandments. For alongside the 'Written Torah' stands the 'Oral Torah', whose authoritative midrashic interpretations often depart strikingly from the text's plain meaning.

Suppose, however, that a decree to wage a particular war is pronounced as God's word by some recognized authority under the proper traditional procedures. Is this in itself sufficient for its justification? Some contemporary adherents of various religions – including Judaism – evidently believe so. Yet traditional Jewish teachers and authors have rarely subscribed to the doctrine of Divine Command Morality. Indeed, we must totally reject as blasphemous any suggestion of a divine breach of moral boundaries, just as Maimonides rejected as idolatrous any suggestion of divine corporeality – even if grounded in hallowed texts and revered authorities. God's word may teach us that some things are worth fighting for, or demand exertion and even sacrifice, but the goal and the means must finally be justified on their own merits.

Convention: One of the central concepts in Michael Walzer's classic book *Just and Unjust Wars*[5] is the 'war convention' – a set of basic norms governing the conduct of war. The term 'convention' suggests a long-standing practical agreement that is binding simply because everyone accepts it. But it is very hard to grant that the vital moral norms – such as non-combatant immunity – are wholly dependent on convention, as though people could just as well reject them. As we shall see when we focus on these norms below, they do carry their own moral and religious force, informing and guiding accepted norms. Yet in our present context, the best-developed contemporary rabbinic justification for warfare in general is offered in terms of a universal convention, based on worldwide tacit consent.

Rabbi Shaul Yisre'eli cogently poses the fundamental problem of warfare: Why did the Torah not prohibit it outright?

> Why ever did the Torah leave war itself – which violates the prohibition on murder – to be permitted amongst the nations, and allowed it to Israel as well? ... The answer must depend on an extension of the idea [that legitimates political authority]. Just as a monarch's powers derive from the consent of the subjects (though not individual consent by each one, but merely by the majority) – so is the practice of the various kings and kingdoms considered to have been consented to by all humanity; if an individual nation does not agree, it is overridden by the majority. Clearly there is universal agreement that war is one means of deciding inter-national conflicts. It is only in our times that an effort is underway to achieve recognition of war as illegal, but the generation is not yet ripe and the nations are not ready to enter into such a mutual commitment. Therefore, it must be considered the nations' agreement that war is a legitimate option, as long as the battling nations observe international customs with regard to war ...[6]

The author goes on to contest the widespread premise that, according to Jewish tradition, a person has no ownership of his self, and concludes that in fact persons do have such ownership. It is by virtue of this self-ownership that people in general grant legitimacy to political authority through their tacit consent. Similarly, humankind has authorized warfare as a conventional means of resolving international disputes. Ideally, war should indeed be abolished, but in actual history it is legitimated by universal consent.

Rabbi Yisre'eli's analysis is instructive, and his argument clearly has some merit. Surely it would be strange for a person to enlist in an army and go forth to war, and at the same time to revile the opposing soldiers as murderers. Insofar as they all know what they are getting into, their mutual understanding of their actions as 'warfare' – and tacit acceptance of the implications – do have moral import. At least with respect to the killing of soldiers, this import sets war apart from plain mass murder.

Still, like any wholesale appeal to accepted practice, this argument is very conservative and excessively permissive. The mere fact that things are done a certain way does not render them right. Specifically, conscripts in modern armies are often unwilling participants, and nations are often dragged into wars against their will. Most emphatically, the argument from convention (as stated) lumps together all kinds of war, from the purely defensive to the blatantly aggressive.

It might be argued that in terms of traditional Jewish discourse, Yisre'eli is right in seeking a broad justification that can encompass all kinds of wars, since halakhah recognizes not only obligatory wars but even a category of 'optional war' (*milhemet reshut*). And admittedly, it is possible to point to formal grounds for construing this category broadly – for example, Maimonides' definition: 'The king of Israel [may initiate an] optional war, which is a war that he fights to expand Israel's realm and to increase his power and prestige'.[7]

Maimonides goes on to stipulate that this kind of war cannot be initiated by the king without authorization from the Sanhedrin – the High Court of seventy-one. Some commentators see the court's role here as consenting (or refusing) on behalf of the people; in any event, surely the Sanhedrin must scrutinize the moral dimensions of the proposed campaign. And regardless of what might be justified technically, by an appeal to conventions of international relations, some kinds of wars must certainly be judged prohibited. (The question of what we should make of 'optional war' is addressed below in the second part of this section, devoted to the circumstances that justify war.)

Lesser Evil: In a sense this is the weakest account, conceding that we have no satisfactory way of justifying war and all its horrors. It simply asserts that sometimes avoiding war is even worse than fighting. One thinks of World War II and the years preceding it: at first, the terrible shadow of World War I instilled a sense of 'peace at any price' – until the price became ever clearer and unbearable.

As I see it, the weakness of the 'lesser evil' justification is also tied to its strength, as it explicitly acknowledges the tragedy of war. Yes, it would be even worse not to fight; but there is nothing – whether divine command, or convention, or anything else – that suffices to tell us that making war is wholly noble or blameless. This recognition is reflected in the Rabbinic explanation of the two verbs used by the Torah to describe Jacob's trepidation before his confrontation with Esau (Gen. 32.8):

'Then Jacob was greatly afraid and was distressed' – R. Judah b.

> R. Ilai said: Are not fear and distress identical? The meaning
> however is that he was afraid lest he should be slain, and was
> distressed lest he should slay [others].[8]

At this juncture of the biblical narrative on the origins of Israel, Jacob is
returning from his sojourn in Aram. In contrast to his lonely journey to
Aram more than twenty years before, Jacob is now head of a large
household. His angry brother Esau is approaching with four hundred men,
and Jacob is concerned not only for his own safety but for that of his wives
and children. According to the Midrash, he is prepared to fight, and would
evidently be justified in defending himself and his family by force. Yet his
concern, or distress, extends to the killing he might do in order to prevail.

On this view, pacifists are partly right: fighting a war is never without
guilt or remorse; yet it is sometimes better to fight. The notion that we
ought to do something, and nevertheless thereby incur guilt, may seem
paradoxical; yet the notion is not foreign to either the Western or the Jewish
traditions. In contemporary political philosophy, it is known as the problem
of 'Dirty Hands' (after Sartre's play by the same name). At the very least, this
view highlights the requirement that – to justify war as the 'lesser evil' – all
alternatives must be truly terrible, and going to war truly a last resort. When
it is indeed so, the conventions of international practice can serve perhaps to
ameliorate the sense of guilt, and divine commandment might add urgency
to the commitment to do what is necessary. But the deciding factor must be
the actual determination that, given the circumstances, war is the least
horrible path.

This leads us to the second part of our discussion in this section,
namely, exploring the circumstances that might justify waging war.

(2) The Circumstances that Call for Fighting: Beyond Self-Defence?

In contemporary just-war theory, it is commonly assumed that war is
allowed only for the purpose of self-defence. In the Middle Ages, this was
understood mainly as protecting a given political unit from conquest –
which was often conceived in almost personal terms: the reigning sovereign
defending himself against an invading neighbour. One could equally speak
of defending the nation, but this virtually never amounted to actually saving
the lives of the people or even of any great number of them. In modern
times, however, vulnerable populations have all too often become the
victims of genocide, and thus 'national self-defence' may take on a chillingly
literal meaning (though in more than one case, the perpetrators have not
been conquering armies but rather local neighbours or governments). Still,
for legitimate self-defence it is not required that the threat be one of physical

annihilation: national defence consists in protecting national sovereignty and freedom.

Aggression is Inexcusable: If a defensive war is the paradigm of a justified war, by the same token the paradigm of an *impermissible* war is one of aggression. Going out to conquer the land of other people – aiming to either displace or subjugate them – is simply evil.

It is sometimes suggested that such conquest might be at least excusable when the instigators have no land of their own – the excuse (if not justification) derived from their sheer desperation. After all, as we Jews know all too well from recent experience, a land-less people are exceedingly vulnerable, and their battle for a homeland is plausibly conceived as a battle for survival. America could not have been born, one could argue, without displacing the Native American peoples; just as the ancient Israelites, tow in the Promised Land, had to dispossess the seven Cananite nations.

In the face of such claims from necessity, it is crucial to note that the Bible clearly does not accept any such justification. The divine commandment to dispossess the Canaanites and Amorites is described as due punishment for these peoples' barbaric crimes and 'abominations' (Lev. 18; Deut. 12.29–31; Deut. 18.9–12). Most importantly, Israel's desperate condition in itself is not sufficient to allow taking the land. Thus when God promises the land to Abraham, he foretells of the sojourn in Egypt:

> Know well that your offspring shall be strangers in a land not theirs, and they shall be enslaved and oppressed four hundred years ... And they shall return here in the fourth generation, *for the iniquity of the Amorites is not yet complete.* (Gen. 15.13, 16)

God knew that, living in 'a land not theirs', his people could not ultimately count on the protection of a 'good Pharaoh', and fully expected them to be 'enslaved and oppressed'. God also evidently knew that, eventually, the guilt of the Amorites would accumulate to such a degree that dispossessing them would be justified. Today, guided by the traditions of the Oral Torah, we may well criticize the underlying notion of collective punishment. But the fundamental lesson here is that sheer desperation – like sheer might – does not create right. As long as the original people were living on their land, not righteously but also not with 'complete iniquity', an Israelite invasion would have been nothing but illicit aggression.

Accordingly, the aggressive wars of conquest conducted by the ancient Chaldean empire (Babylonia) are strongly deplored in the prophetic tradition. A century and a half after Isaiah, the prophet Habakkuk spoke of:

> ...the Chaldeans,
> That fierce, impetuous nation,

Who cross the earth's wide spaces
To seize homes not their own.
They are terrible, dreadful;
They make their own laws and rules.
Their horses are swifter than leopards,
Fleeter than wolves of the steppe.
Their steeds gallop – their steeds
Come flying from afar.
Like vultures rushing toward food,
They all come, bent on rapine.
The thrust of their van is forward,
And they amass captives like sand.

You [=God] whose eyes are too pure to look upon evil,
Who cannot countenance wrongdoing,
Why do you countenance treachery,
And stand by idle
While the one in the wrong devours
The one in the right? (Hab. 1.6-9, 13)

Habakkuk's haunting poetry not only portrays the evils of aggression and empire-building, but goes beyond that to lay the complaint at God's door – bringing to the international arena the same question posed by Job as an individual: Why does God allow all this to take place? It is sadly not redundant to point to one kind of response that would be horribly inappropriate – namely, a Jewish hope for turning the tables. After all, this harsh critique of Chaldean aggression comes from a member of one of the downtrodden, conquered nations. Hence a cynic might ask: Would Habakkuk be complaining if he were a Chaldean? Surely, canonizing Habakkuk's words as an integral part of the Bible means that we could them among 'the words of prophets, spoken the trust' – not as mere partisan railings. Aggressive war is terribly wrong, whether we are its victims or – God forbid – its perpetrators. Any other position amounts to chausinism, with its characteristics idologies or racism or nationalistic supremacy.

Pre-emption: We have postulated a simple contrast: aggression is always evil, and defence against it is always permissible, perhaps even a duty. But whereas many instances of warfare fall easily under one or another of these two headings, many others do not – at least in the eyes of those who are involved. A famous example is that of the 1967 Six Day War: French President Charles de Gaulle, previously a close ally of Israel, accused it of aggression, for its 'firing the first shot'. Many Israelis believed, however, that this was a war of self-defence – not only because Egypt had blockaded the southern port of Eilat, but also because it amassed forces near Israel's border and announced its intentions of invading. From the Israeli perspective, Egypt was the aggressor, and Israel's firing the first shot was justified self-defence.

Extending 'self-defence' to include pre-emption seems quite plausible. If I see you aiming your gun at me, surely I do not have to wait for you to shoot before I may defend myself! In Talmudic terms, the mandate for such individual self-defence is known as the 'law regarding a pursuer' (*din rodef*), and in the same context the following dictum is cited: 'If someone is coming to kill you, arise and kill him first!'[9] The problem is, of course, that it is very difficult to translate the situation just described into its international analogue. What counts as one country 'aiming its gun' at another? Unlike the civil society within a nation, international society is chaotic, fraught with danger and without effective institutions for resolving conflicts. Most nations arm themselves and often hold their forces at a significant level of readiness, yet this in itself (akin to an individual having a gun in his hand) does not prove aggressive intent. It is also true that many nations are controlled by persons or groups with records of violence and cruelty, both domestic and international; but this too does not tell us about concrete, imminent threats. Nor is following stated intentions of much help: tough talk may well be merely talk, while belligerent plans might be masked behind veils of deception.

If we really know that an enemy attack constitutes a clear and present danger, a pre-emptive move may be justified. But we must be extremely alert to the great potential for abuse inherent in this licence. Even in a democracy, we must retain a healthy scepticism toward the government's assertions. Advisors and intelligence chiefs often pretend that they know more than they know, and leaders often suppress information that does not fit a combative political agenda. It is thus morally inexcusable to simply trust claims of certainty or near-certainty regarding 'the enemy's evil plans'. And allowing pre-emptive strikes against any and all potential threats is a recipe for international chaos, an endless Hobbesian war of all against all – turning our back forever on Isaiah's vision of world peace. Instead, even while – in the still-unredeemed world – we must sometimes wage wars of self-defence, the only responsible course is to maintain a highly restrictive policy with respect to pre-emptive war.

Intervention: The mandate to fight against aggression actually extends beyond self-defence; as in the individual sphere, there is also a warrant – perhaps even a duty – to fight in the defence of others. In international law, these 'others' have traditionally been only other states, whose sovereignty was violated by an aggressor. More recently, however, the focus has shifted to include the protection of individuals – or rather, most often, minority groups – whose own government is blatantly failing to protect them, or is even itself attacking them.

Military action undertaken to defend such vulnerable populations is called 'humanitarian intervention'. In emphasizing the plight of the victims, this caption is somewhat misleading: what justifies going to war, with its concomitant horrors, is not this plight in itself – as though they had been hit by some natural disaster – but also the crimes ('against humanity') being perpetrated.

Looking once again to the conception of world peace in Isaiah's vision, we note that it is constituted through God's administering global justice. In the messianic future, this will evidently be achieved through spiritual force alone; in present times, international justice requires physical enforcement. Ideally, this should be done under the auspices of a recognized international authority, such as the UN in the case of the First Gulf War. Even then, however, the actual military units were provided by particular nations who willingly undertook this common burden. In the absence of a world government with an effective policing force, the duty to intervene falls generally upon the people of the world; what is needed is that some should act – and sometimes, some decide to do so.

Humanitarian intervention is thus an 'imperfect duty' – something that definitely ought to be done, yet for each particular agent is optional. I believe this is the best way to provide a morally acceptable account of the Talmudic category of 'optional war'.[10]

It is worth adding that, even short of waging war, there are other means of enforcing international norms. In certain situations, an embargo or economic sanctions might be effective. In terms of Jewish law, it is prohibited to furnish evildoers with the means for committing their deeds, and this is applied specifically to selling weapons to barbaric nations (as well as to individual criminals).[11]

Summary: In the title of this section, we asked: 'What justifies doing battle?' In exploring the answer, we have looked at biblical and rabbinic sources and considered historical convention; yet the main justification lies in preventing an evil greater even than that of warfare. This includes not only preventing massacre (whether or not it involves invasion), but also protecting a nation's freedom and sovereignty. Thus in addition to the core case of defending against actual aggression, war may be justified (whether obligatory or 'optional') as a pre-emptive strike or as humanitarian intervention.

There is an important disparity between these two latter causes. Whereas humanitarian intervention has been evoked (and acted upon) too rarely, 'pre-emption' has been evoked too often – whether as a front for sheer aggression, or in sincere but misguided initiatives against greatly overrated threats. In all such pursuits, it is also crucial to bear in mind our responsibility to promote the prophetic vision of world peace. In the absence of the absolute urgency produced by an enemy attack, the considerations in favour of military action must always be weighed in the broader context of the fledgling society of nations. Some military actions can promote world order (and thereby, ultimately, world peace) by signalling a commitment to enforce international norms. Others tend, on the contrary, to produce a sense of insecurity and fear, undermining whatever tenuous trust may have been built among nations. Such long-term effects depend not only upon the merits of the cause for initiating war, but also upon whether it is perceived as a go-it-alone power play or as an expression of mutual commitment among nations to enforce certain basic norms.

The Conduct of War: Non-Combatant Immunity

We now turn, finally, to the question of norms regarding behaviour within warfare. Individual officers and soldiers are not in a position to decide whether their nation goes to war, and may sometimes have to make do with an educated guess that their fighting is justified. Nevertheless, they bear personal responsibility for their conduct in battle; and whatever the pressures and exigencies they face, they must still remember that even in war not everything is permitted.

Conduct in war is a complex matter, involving more than one knotty moral issue. The most important norm, however, is that soldiers may only attack enemy soldiers, and may never make civilians the object of their lethal power. This central tenet of the so-called 'war ethic' is known as the principle of non-combatant immunity.

I shall not try here to justify this principle, nor to address the subtle problems pertaining to the precise definition of 'non-combatant'. Suffice it to say that this principle is the foundation for the moral condemnation of terrorism. If they are not hypocrites, those who revile terrorists must in their own actions respect non-combatant immunity. Political or military objectives cannot justify violating this immunity, whether by clandestine organizations or by national armies.

In the contemporary international scene, some brutal governments and numerous terrorist groups reject the principle of non-combatant immunity, either outright or by rationalizing 'exceptions' that vacate it of significance. Most governments and nations, however, do subscribe to this basic principle, and non-combatant immunity is also inscribed in international law.

This absolute immunity applies, however, only to instances where civilians are attacked intentionally. Hardly any modern battle could be fought if all risk of unintended harm to civilians – as an unavoidable side effect of legitimate military operations – had to be avoided absolutely. Such harm, known as 'collateral damage', is sometimes permissible. The major moral challenge for Israel, the United States and numerous other countries involves our attitude toward unintended civilian casualties.

In traditional just-war theory, permission to knowingly bring about such casualties is grounded in the doctrine of 'double effect', wherein the main emphasis is upon intention. If you sincerely do not desire the bad side effect, it does not count as part of your moral choice in acting. Critics claim that this is no more than 'mental gymnastics' – pretending not to intend something while knowingly acting to bring it about. Against this, Michael Walzer has emphasized that in order to be morally credible, disinterest in the bad result must be reflected in more than a mental attitude. Crucially, one must make genuine efforts to reduce the risk to enemy non-combatants. These efforts include seeking alternative ways of achieving the same military objective, including ways that involve greater risk to the soldiers. In the longer run, they include planning for the fighting to take place far from civilian population, as well as producing ever more 'smart' weapons.

Sadly, many 'tough-minded' people reject the need for such efforts. Such callous disregard for human life invites critiques like that of David Roden, who reminds us in his essay 'Terrorism Without Intention',[12] that people are held responsible (both morally and legally) for the grave harm that they cause through reckless or negligent behaviour. If individuals or corporations cause deadly harm through callous disregard for human life, we would never accept a claim that 'I did not intend that outcome' – unless it was accompanied by proof that proper care had been taken to avoid it.

Moving from domestic society to the broader context of warfare, with all its attendant horrors, does not alter this judgment. We must always remember the rabbis' teaching about the deep concern voiced by our patriarch Jacob. Thinking that he was about to enter a battle to defend his family, he was not only 'afraid lest he should be slain', but also 'distressed lest he should slay [others]'.

Everyone professes a commitment to peace – even the worst dictators and most cruel aggressors. If our commitment to Isaiah's vision of world peace is to be more than lip service, we must be guided in practice by the deep recognition that all warfare is conducted under a cloud. This implies first of all that we engage in warfare only when the alternatives are truly even more horrendous, and that in fighting we take the utmost care to protect non-combatants, remembering that all humans are created in the divine image.

Notes

1 Mishnah Sanhedrin 4.5.
2 See for example also the classical homily 'Great is Peace' in Sifre Numbers 42.
3 See E. Berkovits, *Not in Heaven: The Nature and Function of Halakhah* (New York, KTAV, 1983); and D. Hartman, *A Living Covenant: The Innovative Spirit in Traditional Judaism* (New York, Free Press, 1985).
4 See *Mishneh Torah* Book 14: Judges, Laws of Kings 5.1.
5 M. Walzer, *Just and Unjust Wars* (New York, Viking, 1978).
6 S. Yisre'eli, 'The Kibbiya Incident in Halakhic Light', *Ha-Torah veha-Medinah*, 5–6 (1954), 71–113.
7 Maimonides, *Laws of Kings* 5.1.
8 Genesis Rabbah 76.2, 702.
9 Mishnah Sanhedrin 8.6–7; BT Sanhedrin 73a, 72a.
10 See N. Zohar, 'Can a War be Morally Optional?', *Journal of Political Philosophy* 4/3 (1996) 229–41.
11 See N. Zohar, 'Boycott, Crime and Sin: Ethical and Talmudic Responses to Injustice Abroad', *Ethics and International Affairs* 7 (1993), 39–53.
12 D. Roden, 'Terrorism without Intention', *Ethics* 114 (2004), 752–71.

FIFTEEN

Human Rights and Membership Rights
in the Jewish Tradition

Moshe Halbertal

Protecting the rights enjoyed by human beings simply by reason of their
humanity has been a central endeavour of the modern political and moral
consciousness. Every person is entitled, as a person, to protection of life,
liberty and property – as long as he accords the same rights to others. These
rights are distinct from the 'membership rights' accorded to individuals by
virtue of being members of a particular community. The right to stand for
public office and the right to vote, for example, are not extended to all
persons by reason of their humanity; they are limited to citizens, members of
a particular political community. We thus distinguish between human rights
and membership rights, and a society that fails to recognize the human rights
of non-members is clearly a perverse and discriminatory society. The rights
to life, to dignity, to economic opportunity and to liberty, among others, are
granted to us not because we are members of a particular religious or ethnic
group but because we are human beings. Turning them into membership
rights confined to a particular group constitutes a form of discrimination that
runs counter to our basic intuitions regarding human equality; and
maintaining a broad array of rights and obligations enjoyed by and owed
to others simply because of their humanity represents an important element
of basic humanism.

Within the Jewish tradition, the domain of human rights unrelated to
membership in a particular group is grounded in the Creation narrative and
in the duties owed to others because they are created in the image of God.
The human being who figures in the Creation story – and with regard to
whom we are instructed that 'Whoever sheds man's blood, by man shall his
blood be shed; for in the image of God made he man' (Gen. 9.6) – does not
belong to any specific ethnic, racial, or religious group. Our absolute duties
toward that human being – whom each and every one of us resembles –
predate his becoming a particular family, tribe or religion and have bound us
since before the emergence of any political or ethnic community. The deep
roots in the Creation story of this concept of inherent human worth is
expressed in the Jewish tradition through the admonitory formula,
mandated by the Mishnah in Tractate Sanhedrin, which is to be used in
interrogating accusatory witnesses in capital cases. At the very moment

when the sovereign may be about to take a human life, the halakhah emphasizes that life's absolute worth:

> Accordingly, one man alone was created, to teach you that one who destroys a single soul is considered by Scripture to have destroyed an entire world; and one who sustains a single soul is considered by Scripture to have sustained the entire world. And [the creation of but one man was] for the sake of peace among [God's] creations, so that no man may say to his fellow, 'my father was greater than your father' and to demonstrate the greatness of the Holy One, Blessed-be-He, for if a human being mints several coins from a single mould they all resemble one another, yet the King, the King of kings, the Holy One, Blessed-be-He, mints every human being on the mould of primal Adam, yet none resembles his fellow. Accordingly, each person is obligated to say 'on my account the world was created'.[1]

Through its account of the creation of a single human being, this Mishnah, redacted toward the end of the second century, offers one of the earliest and clearest formulations we have of the idea of the individual. It describes three components of the idea of the individual human being *per se*. First, a single human life has absolute value. God created only one man in order to emphasize that he is as important as the entire world and his value does not lend itself to quantitative measurement. Second, human beings are fundamentally equal. Any future claim to racial superiority is ruled out in advance by a Creation story in which all humanity is traced back to one human couple. Finally, human beings are as varied as they are numerous; the descendants of the one created man differ from one another quite clearly. The Mishnaic development of the Creation story crystallizes the idea of humanity by establishing the infinite value of individuals, their equality and their diversity.

But the duties owed to human beings *per se* by reason of having been created in God's image do not exhaust the picture. Along with those duties, the Torah uses membership terminology in formulating moral obligations. The prohibition on taking excess profit (or otherwise deceiving in various ways) is worded as 'You shall not wrong one another [or: 'one's fellow'] (Lev. 25.17). The obligation to pay monetary damages similarly relates not to man in the abstract but to one's neighbour: 'If a man's ox injures his neighbour's ox' (Exod. 21.35). And the obligation to return lost property is described in the Bible in terms of 'anything lost by your brother' (Deut. 22.3). These verses, which speak of one's 'fellow' (*amit*), 'neighbour' (*rei'a*) or 'brother' (*ah*), might be taken simply to reflect the reality that situations of the sort they consider arise most often between persons living in proximity to one another; in that event, the use of membership terminology would not be meant to limit the duty to persons within the group. Nevertheless, the Midrash, Mishnah, and halakhah contain opinions that read these membership terms as exclusive. For example, in view of the biblical term 'his neighbour', the Mishnah determines that no liability attaches when a Jew's ox injures a Gentile's, even though a Gentile whose ox injures a Jew's ox must pay full damages.[2] Similar discrimination can be found in connection with the prohibition of excess profit and the obligation to return lost property. These laws contravene our basic intuition regarding equality among people with respect to fundamental rights.

The very use of membership language and the distinction between neighbours and others with regard to fundamental duties, give rise to profound moral unease; for when all is said and done, these duties should be owed to the other simply because he or she is human. But even if we read the terms at issue – 'neighbour', 'brother' and 'fellow' – as limiting terms, it remains necessary to define the membership group within which the obligations are owed. Who is a 'brother', a 'neighbour' or a 'fellow'? If brotherhood and fellowship are defined with reference to ethnic association, so that the scope of the prohibition on profiteering is defined by ties of blood, the resulting discrimination seems to be unequivocally racist. And while we can accept the justifiable preferences generated by ties of blood and family – one is properly obligated to invest more in one's own children than in others' – that is a far cry from discrimination regarding tort liability.

Alternatively, one might define the membership group, as the Talmud itself does, on the basis not of ethnicity but of way of life. The neighbour, the brother, the fellow are those who accept the yoke of the Torah and its commandments. In that case, the distinction is not between Jews and non-Jews but between those who observe the Torah's commandments and those who do not, even if they are members of the Jewish ethnic group. That sort of distinction seems less problematic than one based on ethnicity, but it is still unsettling. Why should a person's rights be dependent on adherence to a particular way of life? The rights should be granted without regard to ethnicity, and they should similarly be granted without regard to any particular way of life.

It may also be possible to broaden the affinity group by drawing the line not between Jew and non-Jew or between one who observes the commandments and one who does not, but between monotheist and pagan. The 'neighbour' is one who renounces idolatry, a group that encompasses Muslims and Christians. The sources lend themselves to such a reading because, among other things, the Mishnah and the halakhic Midrashim, dating from the first and second centuries, do not know of any non-Jewish community that is not pagan. But even this expansion of the membership group beyond the bounds of ethnic identity and of adherence to a particular way of life does not resolve the problem. As important as the distinction between monotheism and paganism may be, it does not seem to warrant, as a matter of morality, discrimination in the allocation of rights and duties.

One must not underestimate, of course, the profound importance of socialization into a particular community, through which a person establishes his or her identity and instils meaning into his or her life through adoption of the community's culture. A life of universal cosmopolitanism, lived without a particular identity, is an impoverished life – if it is possible at all. But turning a particular affinity into a basis for granting privileges with regard to rights and duties seems to cross the fine line that divides particularism from exclusivism. The halakhic voices that call for this sort of discrimination developed at a time when the Jewish community was a persecuted, afflicted minority within the empire of the Roman 'other', which dominated and oppressed it. When such voices enter the authoritative canon, however, they afford legitimacy to discrimination even when the balance of power is reversed. One occasionally hears such voices in the religious discourse of the extreme right in the State of Israel, offered as justification for discriminating against non-Jews. Adopting the rhetoric of the weak in a position of strength is a serious distortion, an offensive tradition that Judaism and Zionism must combat with renewed force. What internal resources can be brought to bear in confronting this question?

One might want to attribute our discomfort with membership language to our adoption of the moral concepts of modern humanism. It seems, however, that the discomfort is intrinsic to the tradition itself, which is multi-vocal on the question. The following story, recounted in the Jerusalem Talmud, sharply criticizes the use of membership language as a basis for discriminating with regard to rights:

> Simeon ben Shetah dealt in flax. His students said to him: let us ease your burden; we will buy you a donkey and you will not have to labour as hard. They went and bought him a donkey from a desert nomad, and a pearl was suspended on it. They came before him and said: Rabbi, henceforth you will not have to labour much. He said to them: Why? They said: We bought you a donkey from a desert nomad and a pearl was suspended from it. He said: Did its owner know about it? They said: No. He said to them: Return it. They said: ... even one who forbids deriving benefit from property stolen from a Gentile [acknowledges] the universal opinion that a Gentile's lost property may be used. He said to them: What do you think? Is Simeon ben Shetah a

barbarian? Simeon ben Shetah wants him to say, 'Blessed is the
God of the Jews.'³

Simeon ben Shetah regards it as barbaric to distinguish between Jew and
Gentile with regard to returning lost property, even if the distinction is
grounded in one text or another. His students importune him to rely on the
distinction to turn a profit, but he replies sharply and directly: he does not
wish to become a barbarian. Distinguishing between Jew and non-Jew on
the basis of membership language is thus subjected to criticism from within
the tradition itself, a criticism powerfully and clearly voiced by Simeon ben
Shetah. Relying not only on the direct moral qualms that appear in the
argument against barbarism but also on other voices within the tradition, the
critique sees this sort of distinction as entailing actual desecration of God's
name.

The appeal to broader values as a basis for this internal critique can be
found as well in other sources that deal with the Jew's attitude to the non-
Jew. The principle of 'ways of peace' (*darkhei shalom*), for example, is used to
establish a common expanse of rights and duties for Jews and Gentiles:

> In a city that contains Jews and Gentiles, the communal officials
> collect [charitable funds] from Jews and Gentiles for the sake of
> the ways of peace. Gentile poor are supported along with Jewish
> poor for the sake of the ways of peace; Gentile dead are buried
> and mourned for the sake of the ways of peace; Gentile mourners
> are comforted for the sake of the ways of peace.⁴

The 'ways of peace' as a meta-halakhic principle thus require not only the
granting of basic rights but the elimination of all distinctions between
'friend' and 'other' with respect to all communal welfare and relief
institutions – charity, burial, and comforting of mourners.

At the conclusion of his *Laws of Slaves*, Maimonides resorts to a value-
based meta-halakhic concept to mount an internal critique of a formal
halakhic distinction. On the face of it, the halakhah permits working a
Canaanite slave with rigour, something forbidden with respect to a Hebrew
slave. Maimonides, however, writes as follows:

> It is permitted to work a heathen [i.e. Canaanite] slave with
> rigour. Though such is the rule, it is the quality of piety and the
> way of wisdom that a man be merciful and pursue justice and not
> make his yoke heavy upon the slave or distress him, but give him
> to eat and to drink of all foods and drinks ... Nor should he heap
> upon the slave oral abuse and anger, but should rather speak to
> him softly and listen to his claims. So it is also explained in the
> good paths of Job, in which he prided himself: 'If I did despise the

cause of my manservant, or of my maidservant, when they
contended with me ... Did not he that made me in the womb
make him? And did not one fashion us in the womb?' (Job 31.13,
15). Cruelty and effrontery are not frequent except with heathen
who worship idols. The children of our father Abraham,
however, i.e. the Israelites, upon whom the Holy One,
Blessed-be-He, bestowed the favour of the Law and laid upon
them statutes and judgments, are merciful people who have mercy
upon all. Thus also it is declared by the attributes of the Holy
One, Blessed-be-He, which we are enjoined to imitate: 'And his
mercies are over all His works.'[5]

After acknowledging the formal enforceability of discrimination between
the Canaanite and the Hebrew slave, Maimonides goes on to reject it as a
matter of practice, portraying such discrimination as contrary to Judaism's
fundamental stance. Subjugation of a Canaanite slave is at odds with the
common origin of all humanity and runs counter to the ways of God,
Creator of the universe, who does not distinguish among people and
extends his mercies to all. Amplifying a mode of thinking already found in
Talmudic sources, Maimonides here counters the formal authorization to
discriminate with an elaborate statement of critical meta-values that rest on
the fundamental Jewish religious ethos.

But the halakhic sources offer something more than this appeal to
broader values for a sharp internal critique of membership rhetoric. Beyond
that appeal, we can find sources that present a distinctive and profound
reinterpretation of the concept of the 'other' and draw the membership
group's boundary only at the point needed to protect morality and halakhah.
The position, articulated by Rabbi Menahem ha-Me'iri in the second half of
the thirteenth century, may be a ground-breaking step in the history of
tolerance within the West as a whole. The Me'iri determined that wherever
distinctions appear to be drawn between Israel and the other nations with
regard to rights and obligations, the distinctions pertain only to the ancient
nations that existed without religion, that is, without any system of moral
discipline: 'Here, too, one must assess, as we have already discussed, what
kind of Gentile is under consideration. What I mean is that of idolaters it is
said that they were not disciplined through the ways of religion; on the
contrary, every sin and everything repulsive is fit in their eyes.'[6] The Me'iri
formulates a comprehensive rule related to the obligation to return a
Gentile's lost property and the prohibition of theft: 'Thus, all people who
are of the nations that are disciplined through the ways of religion and
worship the divinity in any way, even if their faith is far from ours, are
excluded from this principle [of the inequality of Gentiles]; rather, they are

like full-fledged Jews with respect to these matters, even with respect to lost property and error (*ta'ut*) and all the other matters, with no distinction whatsoever.'[7] In the Me'iri's view, the halakhic dividing line is drawn not between Jews and Gentiles on the basis of ethnicity or of a particular shared way of life; it is drawn between nations bound by law and those not so bound – between barbarism and civilization. The Me'iri systematically deploys this principle with respect to compensation for property damage:

> If the ox of a Jew gores the ox of a Gentile, [the Jew] is exempt
> from [the damages that would have to be paid pursuant to the law
> applicable when one's ox gores the ox of] one's fellow ... But
> according to what the *gemara* says, this pertains specifically to
> nations not disciplined through the ways of religion and proper
> conduct ... Accordingly, all those who adhere to the seven
> [Noahidic] commandments are treated in our [courts] as we are
> treated in theirs, and we do not accord ourselves favourable
> treatment. And it therefore goes without saying that the same
> thing applies to nations disciplined through the ways of religion
> and proper conduct.[8]

The distinctions that are drawn with regard to moral rights and obligations are justified solely on the basis of whether the 'other' accepts corresponding rights and obligations; they cannot be justified on ethnic or way-of-life grounds. Particularly important is the Me'iri's equal treatment of Jew and Gentile with respect to the obligations to return lost property and assist in adjusting a beast of burden's load, the prohibition on excess profit, the payment of compensation for property damage, and the penalty for homicide. In all of these areas, discriminatory treatment had been justified by reference to Scripture's use of narrow, familial terminology – 'your neighbour', 'your brother', 'your fellow'. The Me'iri includes the entire moral community within the circle of affinity and brotherhood:

> Anyone disciplined by religious practices is within [the protection
> of the ban on] excessive profit; but idolaters are not within the
> scope of brotherhood for purposes of being included within the
> law against excessive profit in a commercial transaction. The
> rabbis established the principle as 'Do not wrong one another (*lo
> tonu ish et amito* (Lev. 25.17) – one who is with ('*im*) you in Torah
> and commandments you shall not wrong.'[9]

According to the Me'iri, those who are bound by the ways of religion are encompassed within the expression 'your fellow', interpreted in the Talmud to mean 'your fellow in Torah and commandments'.[10]

The Me'iri classifies all people possessed of religion as Israel's partners in Torah and commandments and brings them into the circle of brotherhood with respect to legal standing. By taking this remarkable step, he does away with the juridical distinction between Jew and Gentile and replaces it with a distinction between persons having religion and those lacking it. For these purposes, religion encompasses the fundamental layer of beliefs that underlies the existence of an ordered community – something shared by all believers in a divine Creator who exercises oversight and holds people to account. The Me'iri's religious tolerance stems from his recognition of the religious realm common to Jews, Christians and Muslims, and from the fact that the value of this shared religious realm is grounded in its necessary contribution to the establishment of a properly ordered society.

Establishing a moral stratum shared by all religiously bound communities requires a mindset quite different from one that distinguishes between true religion and false religion – a distinction that lies at the heart of intolerant attitudes. One must be able to set aside distinctions between true and false religions and forge a generic concept of religion encompassing all the specific religions, including Judaism, free of any inquiry into truth or falsehood. The Me'iri establishes the following rule: wherever a membership-based distinction is drawn between 'brother' and 'other' with respect to basic rights and obligations, the only pertinent component of the distinction is between lawful and lawless societies. He consistently translates the distinction between 'brother' and 'other' into these terms, thereby constructing the category of the moral community – the relevant fraternity.

Judah Halevi's *Book of the Kuzari*[11] recounts the efforts of a Jewish sage to persuade the Kuzari king of the truth and correctness of Judaism. In a particularly interesting passage, the king suggests to the sage that if power relationships between Jews and Gentiles had been other than they were, Jews might have treated gentiles as the Gentiles have treated them: '... that might indeed be so had your suffering been something you had chosen. It was, however, something imposed on you; and when you have the opportunity you, too, will kill your enemies.'[12]

This issue, raised clearly – even caustically – in the twelfth century, has today become an existential question bearing on the very future of Judaism and its standing as a religion. The Jewish tradition, as we have seen, offers a variety of attitudes toward the non-Jew. It encompasses a basic recognition of humanity's intrinsic status as a being created in God's image, and it includes sharp internal criticisms of the voices within it that emphasize membership. It includes as well a halakhic definition that brings all human beings who live in accord with the moral law within a common juridical fraternity. At a time when the Jewish people have attained political sovereignty and find non-Jewish citizens and residents within their domain, the fate and character of the State of Israel will depend in no small part on which voice within the Jewish tradition emerges as the dominant one. In this area, as in so many others, the way in which the tradition is interpreted cannot be dissociated from the values and moral sensibilities of the interpreter, who transforms the tradition from written text to living practice.

Notes

1 Mishnah Sanhedrin 4.5.
2 Mishnah Bava Qamma 4.3.
3 JT Bava Metzia 2.5 (8c).
4 Tosefta Gittin 3.13-14.
5 Maimonides, *Mishneh Torah, Hilkhot Avadim 9.8*, translated from I. Twersky (ed.), *A Maimonides Reader* (New York, Behrman House, 1972).
6 BT Avodah Zarah p. 59.
7 BT Baba Qamma p. 330.
8 *Ibid.*, p. 122.
9 BT Bava Mezia p. 219.
10 BT Bava Mezia 59a.
11 J. Ha-Levi (trans. N. D. Korobkin), *The Book of the Kuzari* (Northvale, Jason Aronson, 1988).
12 *Ibid.*, I.114.

Bibliography

Talmudic/Rabbinic Literature – Standard Editions used

Tannaitic Sources

Mishnah
Baba Qamma
Eruvin
Hagigah
Kiddushin
Sanhedrin

Tosefta
Gittin
Hagigah
Sanhedrin
Shekalim
Sotah

Midrash

Mekhilta deRabi Yishmael

Sifra

Sifre Deuteronomy

Sifre Numbers

Midrash Rabbah
Genesis Rabbah
Deuteronomy Rabbah
Bamidbar Rabbah
Leviticus Rabbah

Midrash Tanhuma
Genesis

Bamidbar Rabbah Vilna

Pesikta Rabba

Seder Eliyahu Zutta

Talmud

*Jerusalem Talmud (*Yerushalmi*)*
Baba Metzia
Hagigah
Horayot
Pesahim
Sanhedrin

Babylonian Talmud (BT)
Avodah Zara
Bava Metzia
Berakhot
Eduyot
Ketubot
Kiddushin
Menahot
Sanhedrin
Shabbat
Yadayim
Yevamot

Other Primary Sources

R. Asher ben Yehiel (Rosh), *Responsa*.

Berlin, N. T. Y. (1984), *Chumash Ha'ameq Davar* (Jerusalem, El Hamekoroth).

Feinstein, M. (1974), *Responsa Igrot Moshe* (New York, Rabbi M. Feinstein).

Ha-Levi, J. (1988, trans. N. D. Korobkin), *The Book of the Kuzari* (Northvale, Jason Aronson).

Heyyot, Z. H. (1958), *Collected Writings of Mahariz Heyyot* (Jerusalem, Divrei Hakhamim).

Hirsch, S. R. (1989, ed. I. Levy), *The Pentateuch with the Translation and Commentary of Rabbi S. R. Hirsch* (New York, Judaica Press).

Hume, D. (1980), *Dialogues Concerning Natural Religion* (Indianapolis, Hackett Publishing Company).

Lieberman, S. (1964, ed., trans. M. Fisch), *Midrash Devarim Rabbah* (Jerusalem, Wahrmann).

Locke, J. (1963, ed. M. Montuori), *A Letter concerning Toleration* (The Hague, Martinus Nijhoff).

Maimonides (1985), *Mishneh Torah* (Jerusalem, Machon Mishnat HaRambam).

—, *Mishneh Torah*, Hilkhot Avadim 9.8 in I. Twersky (ed.), *A Maimonidies Reader* (New York, Behrman House, 1972).

—, 'Introduction to Perek Helek', in M. Kneller, *Dogma in Medieval Thought* (Oxford, Oxford University Press, 1986).

—, *Shemonah Perakim* (Eight Chapters) J. Gorfinkle (trans.), The Eight Chapters of Maimonides on Ethics (New York, 1912; repr. New York, AMS, 1966).

Me'iri, M. (1965, ed. S. Dyckman), *Beit Ha'behira* (Jerusalem, Yad HaRav Herzog).

Mendelssohn, M. (1983, trans. A. Arkush, ed. A. Altmann), *Jerusalem, or On Religious Power and Judaism* (Hanover NH).

Nahmanides (1973, ed. C. B. Chavell), *Commentary on the Torah* (New York, Shiloh Publishing House).

R. Sherira Gaon (ed. B. M. Levin), *Responsa. Otsar HaGeonim* (Jerusalem, Mossad Harav Kook).

Secondary Sources

Adler, R. (2002), 'Feminist Judaism: Past and Future', *Crosscurrents*, 51, 4.

– (1998), *Engendering Judaism: An Inclusive Theology and Ethics* (Boston, Beacon Press).

Berkovitz, E. (1983), *Not in Heaven: The Nature and Function of Halakhah* (New York, KTAV).

Boyarin, D. (1993), *Carnal Israel: Reading Sex in Talmudic Culture* (Berkeley, University of California Press).

Central Conference of American Rabbis (CCAR): The Pittsburgh Platform, 1885.

Cohen, T. 'Listen to her Voice', in T. Cohen (ed.), *Ma'ayan Report: The Jewish Women's Project* (New York, 2005).

Dubowski, S. S. (2003, Director) *Trembling before God* (DVD; New Yorker studio).

Freehof, B. (1941), 'A Code of Ceremonial and Ritual Practice', *CCAR Yearbook*, 51 289–97.

Greenberg, S. (2005), *Wrestling with God and Men: Homosexuality in the Jewish Tradition* (Wisconsin, University of Wisconsin Press).

Ha-am, Ahad., 'Torah from Zion', in M. Walzer, M. Loberbaum, N. Zohar and A. Ackerman (2003), *The Jewish Political Tradition, Volume Two: Membership* (New Haven, Yale University Press), pp. 409–10.

HaLevi, H. D. (1989), *Yearbook of Israel's Chief Rabbinate*, (Shana b'Shana), pp. 185–6.

Hartman, D. (1985), *A Living Covenant: The Innovative Spirit in Traditional Judaism* (New York, Free Press).

Heshel, A. J. (1978), *God in Search of Man : A Philosophy of Judaism* (London, Octagon Books).

Kirschenbaum, A. (1991), 'The Role of Punishment in Jewish Criminal Law: A Chapter in Rabbinic Penological Thought', *The Jewish Law Annual*, 9, 123–44.

Lorberbaum, M. (2001), *Politics and the Limits of the Law* (Stanford, University of Stanford Press).

Plaskow, J. (1990), *Standing Again at Sinai: Judasim from a Feminist Perspective* (San Franscisco, Harper & Row).

Rapoport, C. (2004), *Judaism and Homosexuality: An Authentic Orthodox View* (London, Vallentine Mitchell).

Rodin, D. (2004), 'Terrorism Without Intention', *Ethics*, 114, 752–71.

Ross, T. (2004), *Expanding the Palace of Torah: Orthodoxy and Feminism* (Lebanon, NH, University Press of New England).

Sagi, A. and Statman, D. (1995), *Religion and Morality* (Amsterdam/Atalanta, Rodopi).

Soloveitchik, J. B. (1964), 'Confrontation', *Tradition*, 6/2, 5–29.

Walzer, M. (1978), *Just and Unjust War* (New York, Viking).

Walzer, M., Lorberbaum, M., Zohar, N. and Lorberbaum, Y., (2000, eds), *The Jewish Political Tradition, Volume One: Authority*, (New Haven, Yale University Press).

– (2003), *The Jewish Political Tradition, Volume Two: Membership*, (New Haven, Yale University Press).

Washofsky, M., (2004) 'Against Method: On *Halakhah* and Interpretive Communities', in J. Walter (ed.), *Beyond the Letter of the Law: Essays on Diversity in the Halakhah* (Pittsburgh, Rodef Shalom Press), pp. 17–77.

Yisre'eli, S. (1954), 'The Kibbiya Incident in Halakhic Light', *Ha-Torah veha-Medinah*, 5–6, 71–113.

Zohar, N. (1993), 'Boycott, Crime and Sin: Ethical and Talmudic Responses to Injustice Abroad', *Ethics and International Affairs*, 7, 39–53.

– (1996), 'Can a War be Morally Optional', *Journal of Political Philosophy* 4/3, 229–41.